OXFORD WORLD'S CLASSICS

YORK MYSTERY PLAYS

THE YORK MYSTERY PLAYS are the oldest and best-preserved of the four great cycles of biblical drama that have survived from late-medieval England. Composed by a number of dramatists, and frequently revised throughout their long career, they came into being in the late fourteenth century, and for the next two hundred years were normally performed annually on the feast of Corpus Christi, until they were suppressed by the agencies of militant Protestantism. The cycle consists of some fifty short plays written in robust northern dialect verse, about half of which are presented here in modern spelling. Each play was part of a chronological sequence drawn from the Old and New Testaments and their apocryphal accretions, and all were subtly related to one another and to the great epic theme of the cycle as a whole, the Fall and Redemption of humanity. Each of these individual plays was financed and brought forth by one of the craft-guilds (or 'mysteries') of the city in a vast processional production lasting from dawn until after midnight. Modern revivals by the National Theatre, by university drama departments, and by the people of York itself, continue to reveal their remarkable theatrical power to move, amuse and instruct.

RICHARD BEADLE is a University Lecturer in English and a Fellow of St John's College, University of Cambridge. He edited the complete old-spelling text of the cycle upon which this selection is based, *The York Plays* (London, 1982), and is the general editor of *The Cambridge Companion to Medieval English Theatre* (Cambridge, 1994).

PAMELA M. KING is head of the Department of English at St Martin's University College, Lancaster, and is the author of a number of articles on medieval English and Scottish literature, especially the drama.

OXFORD WORLD'S CLASSICS

For over 100 years Oxford World's Classics have brought readers closer to the world's great literature. Now with over 700 titles—from the 4,000-year-old myths of Mesopotamia to the twentieth century's greatest novels—the series makes available lesser-known as well as celebrated writing.

The pocket-sized hardbacks of the early years contained introductions by Virginia Woolf, T. S. Eliot, Graham Greene, and other literary figures which enriched the experience of reading. Today the series is recognized for its fine scholarship and reliability in texts that span world literature, drama and poetry, religion, philosophy and politics. Each edition includes perceptive commentary and essential background information to meet the changing needs of readers.

OXFORD WORLD'S CLASSICS

York Mystery Plays
A Selection in Modern Spelling

Edited by
RICHARD BEADLE
and
PAMELA M. KING

OXFORD
UNIVERSITY PRESS

OXFORD

UNIVERSITY PRESS

Great Clarendon Street, Oxford OX2 6DP

Oxford University Press is a department of the University of Oxford.
It furthers the University's objective of excellence in research, scholarship,
and education by publishing worldwide in

Oxford New York

Athens Auckland Bangkok Bogotá Buenos Aires Calcutta
Cape Town Chennai Dar es Salaam Delhi Florence Hong Kong Istanbul
Karachi Kuala Lumpur Madrid Melbourne Mexico City Mumbai
Nairobi Paris São Paulo Singapore Taipei Tokyo Toronto Warsaw

with associated companies in Berlin Ibadan

Oxford is a registered trade mark of Oxford University Press
in the UK and in certain other countries

Published in the United States
by Oxford University Press Inc., New York

© Richard Beadle and Pamela M. King 1984

The moral rights of the author have been asserted

Database right Oxford University Press (maker)

First published by the Clarendon Press 1984
First published with amendments as a World's Classics paperback 1995
Reissued as an Oxford World's Classics paperback 1999

British Library Cataloguing in Publication Data

Data available

Library of Congress Cataloging in Publication Data

Data available

ISBN 0–19–283710–9

3 5 7 9 10 8 6 4

Printed in Great Britain by
Clays Ltd, St Ives plc

PREFACE

THIS volume contains twenty-two of the forty-seven extant pageants which go to make up the York Cycle of Mystery Plays. They have been selected on the grounds of their literary and dramatic merit, and also with a view to giving some idea of the scope and nature of the oldest and best-preserved of the English Corpus Christi cycles. The selection is designed with both the general reader and the student of medieval literature and early drama in mind, and it is also hoped that, although we have deliberately not attempted to include the apparatus of a performance script, the imaginative director will find here texts that will repay production in a variety of modern theatrical settings.

As well as illustrating something of the range of style and dramatic technique at the disposal of the medieval playwright, the selection is also intended to emphasize how the shape of the cycle was governed by subject-matter of profound and enduring spiritual significance, both to its contemporary audience and in later literary and artistic tradition. We have therefore included the plays on the Creation, the Fall of Man, the Incarnation, Passion, and Resurrection of Christ, and the Last Judgement. Within this abridgement of the cycle we have also included three further Old Testament plays, but we have expanded the selection principally by including plays associated with either the Nativity or the Crucifixion, thus creating two smaller cycles within the greater framework. The Passion sequence includes six of the eight plays often attributed to the York Realist, the first great poetic dramatist to have written in English, and this is the first time that the bulk of his work has been made available in an authentic text outside scholarly editions of the cycle.

The modernized texts presented here are derived from the critical edition of the original manuscript in *The York Plays* (London: Edward Arnold, 1982), York Medieval Texts, second series, edited by Richard Beadle. The publishers and editors are grateful to Messrs Arnold for permission to use this text as the basis of the present selection. Each play is preceded by a brief Headnote drawing attention to such matters as sources, dramaturgy, versification, and staging, and also indicating some critical and interpretative approaches. The texts are accompanied by running glossaries and longer explanations of difficult lines and phrases at the foot of the page. The General Introduction deals with the origins and history of the cycle, including the circumstances of the early performances, drawing on documentary records in the civic archives at York. Attention is also paid to a number of modern productions. References to books and articles cited by the names of their authors will be found identified in the Select Bibliography, which is also intended to serve as a guide to further reading.

We would like to thank Mr R. Costley, who drew the map in the introduction. The edition is affectionately dedicated to Professor Derek Pearsall, co-Director of the Centre for Medieval Studies, University of York, by two grateful former students.

R. B.   P. M. K.

PREFACE TO THE WORLD'S CLASSICS EDITION

SINCE the publication of the Clarendon Press edition of these plays in 1984, the York cycle has continued to hold a central place in the study and performance of medieval English drama. As well as the now traditional production every third year or so as part of the York Festival, a number of the plays achieved their finest modern professional realization in the context of the National Theatre's promenade production *The Mysteries* (1977–85), subsequently filmed for Channel Four Television, and available on videotape. Equally important revivals of a different kind also took place in York in 1988 and 1992, where, under the auspices of a number of university English and drama departments, parts of the cycle were played—for the first time since the suppression of the plays in the late sixteenth century—on reconstructions of the pageant wagons, moved from station to station along sections of the original processional route through the city. These and other aspects of the plays have recently been reviewed in *The Cambridge Companion to Medieval English Theatre*, edited by Richard Beadle (Cambridge, 1994), which includes a chapter and an up-to-date bibliographical section devoted to York and its early drama. Aspects of the social, economic and ideological background are studied in *Contexts for Early English Drama*, edited by Marianne G. Briscoe and John C. Coldewey (Bloomington and Indianapolis, 1989), and a variety of recent critical approaches are brought together in *Medieval English Drama: A Casebook*, edited by Peter Happé (London, 1984).

R.B.   P.M.K.

CONTENTS

ABBREVIATIONS

GENERAL INTRODUCTION

THE York Cycle of Mystery Plays is one of the great literary and theatrical monuments of the later Middle Ages in England, though to describe the cycle as solely a medieval phenomenon is in some ways misleading. Though it came into being in the later fourteenth century, when Chaucer's *Canterbury Tales* and Langland's *Piers Plowman* were being composed, it enjoyed a generally continuous run of annual performances until the late 1560s, and Shakespeare's lifetime. The cycle was an immense undertaking for the city, both financially and in terms of the manpower required to mount it: the text as it has come down to us calls for over 300 speaking parts alone. Its spiritual purpose was the glorification of God, and its didactic intention to instruct the unlettered in the historical basis of their faith, but there is no doubt that the cycle was also intended to reflect the wealth and prestige of the city, particularly the economic pride and self-confidence of the merchants and master-craftsmen who financed the performances annually. The cycle seems to have come into being with the great flowering of York's prosperity in the second half of the fourteenth century, after the Black Death of 1349, when the city stood second only to London in national importance and wealth. Its decline after the middle of the sixteenth century parallels the economic decline of York itself during that period, whilst the rapid rise and spread of the extremer forms of Protestantism began to render the plays a doctrinally suspect relic of the old faith.

York's is the oldest and best preserved of the surviving English cycles. One similar in scope and nature has come down to us from Chester, and there are also comparable collections of plays in the 'Towneley' and 'N-Town' manuscripts. The Towneley manuscript contains plays connected with Wakefield, together with several pieces partially or wholly borrowed from York, which may well represent the Wakefield cycle. The 'N-Town' plays, judging by their dialect, originated in East Anglia, but are not known to have been connected with any particular town or with craft-guilds, as the northern cycles were. The antiquarian misnomer by which they were long known (*Ludus Coventriae*) is not now used, but fragments of the genuine Coventry cycle have survived, as have single plays from the lost cycles of Norwich and Newcastle. Many other towns and cities in the British Isles are known to have once had play-cycles, but now only fleeting

documentary references to them remain, buried in old civic muniments. Such cycles in their own day were often known—at least in
the north—by the generic title 'Corpus Christi plays'. Such was the
case at York, where the surviving medieval muniments of the city
tend to refer to the entire cycle in the singular: Corpus Christi play.
It is a pity that this authentic expression has been replaced by the late
antiquarian invention 'mystery plays'. 'Corpus Christi' preserves
reference to the festival day on which the cycle was performed
annually, and 'play' embodies the recognition that the cycle was
intended to be seen as a coherent and unified work of art, a spiritual
statement of a communal belief in God's relationship to man. The
cycles at York and elsewhere were evidently the work of several
dramatists from the start, and they were undoubtedly revised by
others over the years but, as we shall see, the artistic and spiritual
object of the whole and the subtle interrelatedness of the parts
remain. An appropriate comparison to the cycles in this respect might
be the Gothic cathedrals of northern Europe, such as York Minster,
built and decorated in a succession of styles by generations of craftsmen but unified by a single spiritual aim.

   Corpus Christi day was a movable feast, the first Thursday after
Trinity Sunday, which might fall on any date between 23 May and
24 June. It became widely observed in England in the second decade
of the fourteenth century, and was proclaimed in York in 1325.
Theologically speaking, the feast of Corpus Christi celebrated the
Real Presence of the Body of Christ in the Host at Mass. Arguments
have been put forward in an attempt to link the content and structure
of the cycles with the spiritual significance of the feast, but none is
particularly convincing. The link between the feast and the cycle may
equally have been a practical matter. When Corpus Christi was insti-
tuted it became in effect the Church's midsummer festival, coinciding
with the obvious and traditional period for outdoor celebrations and
observances of any kind, whether religious or secular or, of course,
pre-Christian. It is interesting to note that one of the official require-
ments of Corpus Christi was an outdoor procession in which the laity
and clergy followed a vessel carrying the Sacred Host around the
streets of the town. As is explained in detail below, the York cycle
was presented in the form of a procession, and the pageant-wagons
on which the individual plays were performed at first followed the
liturgical procession along a traditional ceremonial route through the
city. No documentary evidence, however, has survived to show precisely why it was decided to stage the cycle processionally, or how the
performance came to be attached to Corpus Christi. Perhaps the at-

traction of a great summer festival, which included an outdoor symbolic procession, was sufficient to stimulate the imagination of dramatists who had already brooded upon an established cycle of interrelated biblical and apocryphal subjects, common in medieval art and narrative long before the Corpus Christi cycles came into being.

The York cycle and its congeners were dramas of the Fall and Redemption of man, cast as a historical narrative, drawing on the Bible and its apocryphal accretions for the subject-matter. The medieval audiences of the plays felt themselves to be deeply implicated in this presentation of sacred history. The essential episodes were the Creation of the world and of man, man's deception by the Devil, resulting in the Fall and the expulsion from Paradise, and his Redemption through the Incarnation, Passion, and Resurrection of Christ. In addition, all the extant cycles proceeded beyond Christ's work of Redemption on earth and also treated an event of the future: Christ's second coming at the Last Judgement. One of the principal effects of the cycle as a whole in performance was to place the audience in a position of God-like omniscience as regards the continuing history and nature of their spiritual predicament on earth. Out of this arose a need for them to examine their consciences and to decide where their allegiance lay in the conflict between good and evil for possession of the souls of the human race—the need for such a decision being finally borne in upon them personally and urgently by the stark choice presented in the Last Judgement play. All the other biblical and legendary events dramatized in the cycles were in one way or another expansions or elaborations of these moments of central importance in the spiritual history of mankind. For example, the Creation and Fall were extended by dramatizing a series of Old Testament events sufficient to show the predicament of fallen man and his need for redemption, and to prefigure the coming of the Redeemer and his earthly existence. One of the chief organizing principles underlying the construction of the cycles was typology, whereby the persons and incidents of the Old Testament plays were held to foreshadow things to come later in the sequence. For instance, Noah and Moses were included as 'types' of Christ, with the Flood adumbrating the Last Judgement and the salvation of the righteous, whilst the Exodus looked forward to the Harrowing of Hell. This principle was also extended to the wicked characters of the drama, such as Pharaoh and the two Herods, whose words and actions were made to reflect those of the Devil in his various appearances in the story. The contemporary vogue for Gospel harmonies and contemplative treatments of the life of Christ led the playwrights to emphasize the events surrounding the Nativity and the Passion, at the expense of his ministry on earth. At York, the dramatization of the Passion came to occupy about half the cycle, and was much revised over the years.

At the earliest stage in the history of the York cycle a decision must have been taken to divide the long sequence of events stretching from the Creation to the Last Judgement into manageable units for the purposes of processional performance. Each of these units became a separate play, or, as it was then often known, 'pageant', and each was assigned to a particular craft-guild of the city. The craft-guilds therefore became responsible for furnishing the pageant-wagon on which the play was to be performed, and for finding suitable actors, properties, costumes, and so forth. It is also possible that the guilds commissioned scripts for their plays locally, but the names of the playwrights have not survived. Those sufficiently learned in sacred history are likely to have been clerics, such as parish priests, guild chaplains, and chantry priests, or perhaps members of the monastic or mendicant orders, who were strongly present in York. The result of this dividing-up of the long narrative was the following sequence of pageants, which for the most part reflects the cycle as it was constituted in the third quarter of the fifteenth century, about half-way through its two-hunded-year existence. The plays marked with an asterisk are those included in the present selection. Those with an obelisk against them are no longer extant, but are known through documentary references in the civic archives at York.

*	The Barkers	*The Fall of the Angels*
	The Plasterers	*The Creation*
	The Cardmakers	*The Creation of Adam and Eve*
	The Fullers	*Adam and Eve in Eden*
*	The Coopers	*The Fall of Man*
	The Armourers	*The Expulsion*
	The Glovers	*Cain and Abel*
*	The Shipwrights	*The Building of the Ark*
*	The Fishers and Mariners	*The Flood*
	The Parchmentmakers and Bookbinders	*Abraham and Isaac*
*	The Hosiers	*Moses and Pharaoh*
	The Spicers	*The Annunication and Visitation*
*	The Pewterers and Founders	*Joseph's Trouble about Mary*

* The Tilethatchers	*The Nativity*
The Chandlers	*The Shepherds*
* The Masons; The Goldsmiths	*Herod* and *The Magi*
St Leonard's Hospital	*The Purification*
* The Marshals	*The Flight into Egypt*
* The Girdlers and Nailers	*The Slaughter of the Innocents*
The Spurriers and Lorimers	*Christ and the Doctors*
The Barbers	*The Baptism*
* The Smiths	*The Temptation*
† The Vintners	*The Marriage at Cana*
The Curriers	*The Transfiguration*
† The Ironmongers	*Jesus in the House of Simon the Leper*
The Cappers	*The Woman taken in Adultery/ The Raising of Lazarus*
* The Skinners	*The Entry into Jerusalem*
* The Cutlers	*The Conspiracy*
The Bakers	*The Last Supper*
The Cordwainers	*The Agony in the Garden and the Betrayal*
* The Bowers and Fletchers	*Christ before Annas and Caiaphas*
* The Tapiters and Couchers	*Christ before Pilate (1): The Dream of Pilate's Wife*
* The Litsters	*Christ before Herod*
The Cooks and Waterleaders	*The Remorse of Judas*
* The Tilemakers	*Christ before Pilate (2): The Judgement*
The Shearmen	*The Road to Calvary*
* The Pinners	*The Crucifixion*
* The Butchers	*The Death of Christ*
* The Saddlers	*The Harrowing of Hell*
* The Carpenters	*The Resurrection*
The Winedrawers	*Christ's Appearance to Mary Magdalene*
The Woolpackers and Woolbrokers	*The Supper at Emmaus*
The Scriveners	*The Incredulity of Thomas*

The Tailors	*The Ascension*
The Potters	*Pentecost*
The Drapers	*The Death of the Virgin*
† The Linenweavers	*The Funeral of the Virgin*
The Woollenweavers	*The Assumption of the Virgin*
The Hostelers	*The Coronation of the Virgin*
* The Mercers	*The Last Judgement*

The manuscript containing the text of the cycle is a large volume, measuring about 11 inches by 8 inches, consisting of 268 parchment leaves, bound in oak boards covered with leather. It is nearly all in the handwriting of a single unidentified scribe, who probably executed the work at some time between 1463 and 1477. Known as the 'Register' of the Corpus Christi play, this manuscript constituted the city's official record of the content of the cycle, and was the property of the corporation. In the sixteenth century there are records of the fact that it was used by a city official to check what the actors were actually saying in the course of the annual performance. Many pages have later annotations deriving from this activity, showing where plays had been revised, or had even been completely rewritten since the compilation of the manuscript. Contrary to a widely held belief, these sixteenth-century annotations in the manuscript were not the work of reforming ecclesiastical censors, though we do know from other sources that the plays near the end of the cycle on the later life of the Virgin Mary were suppressed in 1548. During the eighteenth and nineteenth centuries the Register passed through the hands of several antiquarians and collectors, before coming to its final resting-place in the British Museum in 1899.

The Register was compiled from copies of the individual plays held by the craft-guilds for the purposes of rehearsal and performance. A sixteenth-century example of one of these prompt-copies, or 'originals' as they were known, has survived (the Scriveners' *Incredulity of Thomas*) but the rest are lost. For something of the history of the cycle prior to the compilation of the Register one must turn to documentary materials in the civic archives at York. Among them is the volume known as the 'A/Y Memorandum Book', which contains records of many of the most important decisions of the governing body of the city in the Middle Ages, the ordinances and constitutions of numerous craft-guilds, and an interesting document called the 'Ordo Paginarum', 'The Order of the Pageants'. This consists of a list of the guilds, similar to the one given above, with a note of the content of their respective plays. It was compiled by the Town Clerk in 1415, and was probably used to check the ordering and content of the cycle in the period before the Register was compiled. The 'Ordo Paginarum', though itself much altered and revised, reveals that the cycle had by 1415 assumed the shape and scope it was to have for the rest of its career. Comparison with the text in the Register reveals that a number of plays were revised during the fifteenth century, and that some were reassigned to other guilds. The Passion section, in particular, was extensively reworked by an outstandingly able dramatist, known as the York Realist (see the Headnote to the *Conspiracy*). However, the general aspect and scope of the cycle remained the same, as it was to do until its decline and eventual abandonment in the latter half of the sixteenth century.

The origins and progress of the cycle up to 1415 are much more difficult to trace because of the paucity of documentary evidence, but a reference in a document dated 1376, referring to the storage of three Corpus Christi pageant-wagons, is sometimes taken to imply that the entire cycle was already in existence at that date. A more certain construction may be placed on a petition, dated 1399, sent by the commons of the city to its governing body, pointing out that the Corpus Christi play was a great financial burden on the craft-guilds, and that it was tending to overrun its allotted day of performance. This petition also sets out for the first time the processional route through the city taken by the pageant-wagons, and the 'stations' where they stopped to perform before the audiences which had gathered.

The craft-guilds of medieval York were the principal units of social and economic organization in medieval English towns in general, being made up of master-craftsmen in the various trades and callings, who had gained the franchise of the city either through satisfactory apprenticeship or inheritance. As well as establishing standards of workmanship, administering the system of apprenticeship, and laying down the lines of demarcation between trades, the guilds also had important social characteristics and functions. The members of a guild, their families, and apprentices lived their lives partially in common, often occupying the same area of the city, as some of the surviving streetnames of York show (Spurriergate, Tanner Row). They tended to worship together at the same church, and dined together on the feast of their patron saint or other liturgical occasion. A number had their own halls; those of the Merchant Adventurers and Merchant Tailors are still to be seen in York. The craft-guilds were occasionally referred to as 'mysteries', and from the association of the crafts with the pageants of the Corpus Christi play arose the modern expression 'mystery plays'. 'Mystery' should not, therefore, be understood to connote anything as to the content of the cycle. The expenses of the annual performance of each play in the cycle were defrayed by a levy on the guild to which that play was assigned. Little is known as to precisely how the guilds came to have responsibility for their particular plays, owing to lack of evidence from the earliest period of the cycle's history. The appropriateness of some of the assignments to the occupations of the guilds is obvious: the Shipwrights' *Building of the Ark*, the Vintners' *Marriage at Cana* (where Christ turned the water into wine), the Bakers' *Last Supper*. These 'appropriate' assignments probably had much to do with the idea of the sanctity of a craft's daily labour, its part in the divine eternal scheme of things and the history of man's salvation, rather than the crude modern notion that the guilds used the plays to 'advertise' their products.

The performance of the cycle as a whole was organized and regulated by the governing body of the city, which was elected by and from the members of the craft-guilds. It appears that the ecclesiastical authorities had no part in it at this official level, though the parish clergy and members of religious orders were undoubtedly involved in helping to bring forth individual pageants, sometimes as 'directors'. The events leading up to the annual performance were set in motion early in Lent, when the civic authorities met and sent out formal instruction to each participating guild to bring forth its play on Corpus Christi day, three months or so hence. The guilds then held meetings to make detailed arrangements for their own productions. These were at first principally financial. Each guild elected officers known as 'pageant-masters', in effect the producers of the play, whose first task it was to collect the money paid by the craftsmen towards their play, their 'pageant silver'. As well as collecting annually from their members, the guilds also operated a system of fines for poor workmanship and various technical infringements of guild regulations, the proceeds of which also went towards the play. The pageant-masters laid out their money in a variety of ways. The storage and maintenance of the pageant-wagon and the purchase or refurbishment of properties and costumes were the main material expenses. In addition, a 'director' (though no such word then existed) and suitable actors had to be found, and their refreshments provided at rehearsal and on the day of performance. Evidence surviving in the records of the Mercers' and Bakers' guilds suggests that money was given to an individual, sometimes a cleric, who had responsibility for directing their play. It was evidently his task to hire, rehearse, and pay the actors, which suggests a degree of 'professionalism' in the presentation of the cycle. Finally, the pageant-masters gave a dinner shortly after Corpus Christi, at which the officers of the guild reviewed their financial position.

Before entering into greater detail about arrangements for the day of performance, it is necessary to enlarge upon what has already been said about the processional presentation of the plays. Each of the plays which make up the cycle was staged on a wagon. The wagons are thought to have processed in the appropriate order around the city, taking a traditionally established route, and halting at a series of 'stations' at which audiences had assembled, a performance of each play being given at each station. The number of stations along the route was usually twelve, and (though scholars differ about this) it appears that each pageant could have been given twelve times in the course of Corpus Christi day. The performance is known to have begun at 4.30 a.m., when the first pageant proceeded to the first station, and modern calculations suggest that it would not have been until after midnight when the last play ended at the twelfth station. It is not known how York arrived at this remarkable mode of presentation for its cycle, but in an age with little or no concept of a purpose-built theatre, processional production was an ingenious solution to the problem of how to show a large urban audience a cycle of plays running to over 14,000 lines.

Corpus Christi day was of course a public holiday and a day of popular festivity as well as a liturgical feast. Final arrangements for the presentation of the plays included the assignment of stations at which performances were to be given. At these stations along the processional route banners bearing the city's coat of arms were set up and a scaffold for the accommodation of the audience was built. Stations were let by the city to the highest bidder, who was then presumably in a position to charge the audience for seating and refreshments during the long performance. Many of the audience, however, must have stood in the street to see the plays, and have wandered from station to station in the course of the day.

The route along which the stations were distributed never varied, though the positions of some of the stations could change slightly from year to year. Those familiar with the topography of York will see from the accompanying map that the streets along which the pageant-wagons passed remain to this day. The pageant-masters, actors, and others concerned with mounting the performance marshalled the pageant-wagons initially on an open space in the south-west angle of the city wall known as Pageant Green (or Toft Green). From there they moved into and along Micklegate, over Ouse Bridge, and then

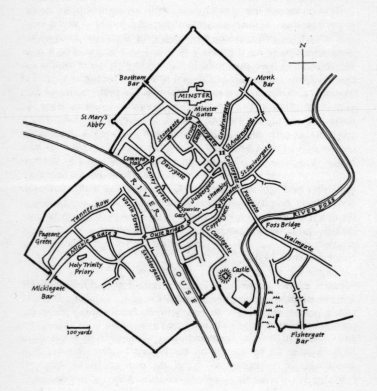

N

Bootham
Bar

Monk
Bar

St Mary's
Abbey

MINSTER

Minster
Gates
10

Stonegate

Croft

Petergate

Low Petergate

Goodramgate

St Andrewgate

Common
Hall

Davygate

Coney Street

R I V E R

Jubbergate

Shambles

Pavement

St Saviourgate

Colliergate

Fossgate

Tanner Row

North Street

Spurrier
Gate

12

Coppergate

River Foss

Foss Bridge

Pageant
Green

Micklegate

Ouse Bridge

Castlegate

Skeldergate

Walmgate

Holy Trinity
Priory

O U S E

Castle

Micklegate
Bar

Fishergate
Bar

100 yards

via Coney Street and Stonegate, past the Minster Gates, then through Low Petergate and Colliergate to the Pavement. It appears that the stations were on the right-hand side of this route, with the audiences facing them on the left. The positions of some of the stations never varied. No. 1 was at the gates of the Priory of the Holy Trinity not far from Micklegate Bar. It was here that a civic official sat with the manuscript Register and checked the first performance of each play annually. The eighth station was close to the Guildhall, and here members of the city's governing body saw the plays free. No. 10, at Minster Gates, was favoured by the cathedral clergy, and the last station, on the Pavement, brought the plays to the commercial centre of the city, the site of markets, fairs, proclamations, and executions. Given the great length of the cycle and the number of times each play was performed, the swift and unhindered passage of the pageant-wagons from station to station was of the utmost importance. The civic authorities had the power to fine any guild whose play hindered the presentation of an orderly sequence. At the end of the Wool-packers' and Woolbrokers' play of the *Supper at Emmaus* one of the characters actually says to the audience that they must now hasten to the next station:

> Here may we not mell more at this tide,
> For process of plays that presses in plight.

('That is all we can say at this time, because of the procession of pageants which is queuing up [behind us]').

To have established broadly how the cycle was designed for presentation is not to visualize what it would have looked like. It is clear, both from guild records and from internal evidence in the plays, that a pageant-wagon was neither simply a stage on wheels, nor a commercial vehicle, like the modern pageant 'float', converted for the day. The wagons used in the production of the York cycle were custom-built for each guild, to suit its play, and, what is more, were man-handled around the route, not drawn by animals. At that point, however, it becomes more difficult to be specific. York is not short of material in its civic records relating to pageant-wagons, but since everyone evidently knew what such vehicles looked like, they are never described from first principles. What comes down to the modern investigator, by and large, is a collection of cryptic accounts using unfamiliar or ambiguous terminology.

There are some references to the Bakers' pageant-wagon in the records, which supply clues to its construction, but the picture would still be highly speculative, were it not for the survival of some important materials relating to the Mercers' *Last Judgement* wagon over a period of years. The first of these is an indenture of 1433 which provides the nearest thing to a description of a wagon we are likely to find. It includes an inventory of parts for what the Mercers later call their 'great pageant'. It is a 'pageant with four wheels', but clearly not a flat cart, for it has a complicated superstructure including a 'heaven of iron'. It also appears to have incorporated integral winching gear by means of which God descended from, and ascended to, the said heaven. When the 'hell-mouth', also described as part of the structure, is added, a picture of a complicated multi-level structure begins to emerge. This is in keeping with a later account from Norwich in which the Grocers' pageant-wagon is defined as, 'a house of wainscot . . . on a cart with four wheels'.

Apart from the mechanical details concerning the transportation of God from one level to another, other items in the Mercers' indenture also give an indication of how the pageant-wagon was decorated. The mention of a backcloth, or 'coster', of red damask instantly demonstrates that the performance area had a back and a front, ruling out the possibility that the audience was grouped around the vehicle on all sides. Other cloths are also listed which would have concealed the wheels and the unsightly underside of the vehicle once it was *in situ* at a station. God had his own special backdrop, also a 'brandreth of iron', possibly like a modern fire-basket, with four ropes at the corners, in which he came and went from heaven. Heaven itself was arrayed with red and blue clouds, gold stars, sunbeams, and a wooden rainbow. In addition there was a series of model angels, nine of which were operated mechanically by a 'long small cord', which caused them to 'run about in the heaven', as the final stage direction in the play indicates.

Even with all the above information available in what is indeed an exceptional case, there has still been room for interpretation to have produced at least three careful and scholarly reconstructions which diverge in certain major respects. Crucially, none of the dimensions of the various parts is mentioned. It is also clear from further documents associated with the guild that the Mercers, in times of particular affluence, were given to improving their equipage. In 1463 the guild added what appears to have been a completely separate entity, a 'new pageant that was made for the souls to rise out of'. About this 'pageant' there is much less information; it is not even clear that it had wheels, although this is probable, as the guild had had some small wheels made in the recent past. What is more, in 1501, the Mercers scrapped the 'great pageant' of the 1433 indenture and commissioned one built 'new substantially in everything thereunto belonging'. It is not until 1526 that there is anything approaching a description of the new vehicle, and then an inventory simply lists hell-door, windows, angels, an iron seat, several pulleys, and a cloud. Reconstruction on the basis of this meagre information is not really practicable.

What then is to be learned from the history of the Mercers' pageant-wagon over a period of nearly a hundred years? Perhaps most significantly it brings home the fact that a pageant-wagon was a very specific construction, intended solely for the production of a single episode in the cycle. In a sense, therefore, the Mercers' indenture tells us only about the manner in which the *Last Judgement* was staged. It may serve as a rough guide to what the other guilds' wagons were like, but it is important here to remember that the Mercers were an extremely wealthy guild throughout the period in question; wagons belonging to less affluent bodies may not have been so elaborate. Also there are plays in the cycle to which an enclosed playing space would not have been appropriate, for example *The Crucifixion*, which could well have been performed on a flat cart.

The Mercers' records contribute to a growing sense of the cycle as an essentially fluid event. In the same way that plays changed hands and were reworked, so too the visual aspect of the cycle must have changed over the years. As a guild's fortune increased it might have its play elaborated and rewritten, or have its pageant-wagon modified or replaced. One decision could lead to another, but the evidence for each change taking place survives, if it survives at all, in a variety of different sources. Similarly, declining fortunes would perhaps lead to guilds being unable to maintain their wagons and their plays at all, which in turn might lead to amalgamations with other small guilds, or transference of the play to different ownership.

The pageant-wagon itself was an item of considerable value and prestige. From the point of view of the quality of workmanship involved, the records of the Mercers' 1501 wagon, about which there is less detail, impart one important piece of information: for the construction of the wagon the Mercers engaged a famous carver, Thomas Drawswerd. Fortunately an example of Drawswerd's work survives in the beautiful rood screen in the church of St Mary Magdalen, Newark, Nottinghamshire. A cursory examination of the quality of carving involved serves to dispel any residual connection between the pageant-wagon and the farm cart, although the chassis and wheels were, in all probability, derived from the latter. It has indeed been suggested that the superstructure of the wagon was demountable for storage purposes, since storage of a multi-level vehicle, perhaps as much as 20 feet

(6 metres) high, would pose considerable problems. Many guilds had their own 'pageant-houses' or garages for their wagons. Many of these were close to Pageant Green (from where the cycle set out), often on land rented on an annual basis from the city authority. There is some evidence also of guilds sub-letting pageant-houses to one another.

Although it is possible to tell from the records that the pageant-houses were large and stoutly constructed buildings, the actual dimensions of the York pageant-wagon cannot be ascertained with any degree of accuracy. The length and breadth must, however, have been limited, if a vehicle made of heavy materials was to be man-handled around the narrower corners in the city. Even allowing for a generous estimate of surface area, the playing space afforded was very limited, making it difficult to visualize the staging of multi-location plays, such as the Hosiers' *Moses and Pharaoh*. The Mercers' records make it clear that auxiliary 'pageants' might be used, and the Masons' and Goldsmiths' composite play shows two wagons being used in tandem, but in the absence of further evidence these must be treated as exceptions. No true picture of the staging of a play can be reached without due consideration of the evidence in the plays themselves for the use of the whole space available, not only on the pageant-wagon but also in the street around. It is in this respect that wagon performance diverges markedly from performance on the proscenium stage.

The York cycle's stage directions are few and far between, particularly when it comes to indicating movement from place to place, or the relative locations of different 'scenes' within the play. It is apparent in most of the longer plays that all of the action could not possibly have been accommodated on the deck of the wagon itself. In one of the surviving plays from the Coventry cycle there is the direction, 'Here Herod rages in the pageant and in the street also'. This has been eagerly seized upon as evidence that the arrangement suggested by the texts of many cycle plays was indeed correct. In twelfth- and thirteenth-century liturgical drama the action was divided between that which took place processionally, moving through the church, and that which was located in a symbolic area, such as around the Easter Sepulchre, an altar designed for the ritual representation of the Resurrection. It is possible to see the individual play within the cycle in the same way, except that the area on the pageant-wagon serves for all the specific playing spaces (*loci*) and the street as the area in which unlocalized action took place (*platea*). Hence, in *The Conspiracy*, the *locus* is Pilate's court, the wagon being decorated to represent that, which means that the dialogue between Judas and the Porter would be conducted outside the court, in the street. Similarly in *Joseph's Trouble*, the wagon is evidently Mary's house, and all of Joseph's long complaint, in which he solicits the sympathy of men in the audience, would have been delivered at their level. Obviously, there are still unexplained problems of staging when a play appears to involve more than one *locus*, but in broad terms the division of the action between street and wagon is the important one, particularly when the relationship between audience and players at a given moment is considered.

If the physical presentation of the York cycle can be reconstructed only in part, the manner in which it was acted is a matter of much greater speculation. As far as contemporary records are concerned, the necessary qualifications were cryptically described, but were apparently quite basic. After the 1415 'Ordo Paginarum' in the 'A/Y Memorandum Book' appears the Proclamation of the plays, which was made on the vigil of Corpus Christi, and also when the banners were set up in the designated positions for the stations, about a week before Corpus Christi. This specifies the manner in which the plays should be conducted, with an allusion to the players which simply requires that they be 'well arrayed and openly speaking'. An ordinance of 1476 shows that there was some means of auditioning the players: four of the 'most cunning [skilful], discreet and able players' were called before the mayor to examine the plays, and to dispense with the services of any player found to be wanting in 'cunning, voice or person'. These records merely confirm that the greatest offence a player can commit in an outdoor performance is to be inaudible.

In whatever way we choose to interpret this material, however, it is clear that, given a performance in which the same character was played by many different actors consecutively, there was no opportunity for anything like method acting. Indeed, a greater unity would best have been achieved by the use of a formal, demonstrative style, matching spoken word to gesture. This style was particularly appropriate to outdoor performance, which was often restricted to the confined area of the pageant-wagon, but had to be clearly understood by an audience crowding in the street. The demonstrative style was also appropriate to a drama which sought to convey eternal truths on a mythic scale. It is possible that medieval acting style in this respect owed something to the techniques advocated by the ancient rhetoricians. Echoes of Cicero's *De oratore* have been heard in the dramatist's instructions to the actors in the twelfth-century Anglo-Norman play the *Mystère d'Adam*, which exhort the players to 'speak coherently', and to 'make gestures agreeing with the thing they are speaking of'. When one considers the metrical intricacy of some of the York plays, it seems unlikely that naturalistic acting had a large part in their presentation.

There is one group of characters about which more can be said, as chance allusions to their manner of presentation have survived, namely Herod, Pilate, and—by extension—the other major figures of evil in the cycle. Chaucer's Miller in the General Prologue to the *Canterbury Tales* has a mouth like a furnace, and cries in 'Pilate's voice', whilst in the Paston Letters of the fifteenth century, the Duke of Suffolk, when in a rage, is compared to a play-Herod. Everyone is familiar with Hamlet's injunction to his players to avoid the style of over-acting that 'out-Herods Herod'. It is easy to imagine the alliterative lines of the trial plays in the York Passion sequence assisting some actors to an exaggeratedly bombastic performance.

Not all the characters in the York cycle lend themselves to stylized means of presentation, however. It seems most likely that a mixed style was employed, in keeping with the mixed physical levels of playing, introducing at certain points a more naturalistic aspect to the performance where it was desirable to achieve proximity to the audience, bringing sacred history to them as something immediate which encompassed them. It is, for instance, difficult to conceive of a demonstrative rendering of the dialogue between Judas and the Porter, alluded to above, or in the scenes of disarray amongst the soldiers in *The Resurrection*, when they discover that Christ has escaped. The plays are liberally peppered with ordinary people and there was didactic capital to be made out of presenting them as such.

In this context it is necessary to consider how the plays were costumed. Clearly, in an age which had no sophisticated perspective on chronology, there was little attempt at historical costume, the cut of clothes being whatever was contemporary, with exotic touches added to denote race or rank. Much of the evidence we have for costume is construed from surviving inventories and contemporary pictures and stained glass. Most Jews, for instance, would have worn the strange pointed hats which mark them out in contemporary iconography; the Magi, dressed by the Goldsmiths, would have appeared as royalty should, as would Herod, although he may have had something about his person to associate him with the infidel. Biblical soldiers, peasants, and tradesmen must have looked very much like fifteenth-century Yorkshiremen of the same rank, and, as is clearly the case with the Shipwrights' Noah, carried the genuine tools of their trade.

Difficulties arise in clothing those whose rank is beyond anything present in any society: the extremes of good and evil, particularly the inhabitants of heaven and hell. The main way of dealing with these characters was to conceal the players behind masks. For evidence of this we return again to the Mercers' indenture of 1433 which contains an extensive list of 'visors' or 'faces', including six devils' faces, visors and wigs for evil souls and good souls, visors and diadems for the Apostles, and a gilded visor for God. It seems that masking was relatively common in the cycle plays, from full heads to faces made up in some unnatural manner, often by gilding. Long wigs and beards were also called for to make the fashionably clean-shaven fifteenth-century man, with his pudding-basin haircut, look like a patriarch or an apostle. From the strictly practical point of view, men who had to play the part of women, which was commonly if not absolutely the rule, certainly needed wigs, if not masks as well. The use of the full-face mask, or even, in the case of devils, the whole head, is most interesting because of the effect it must have created in performance, of completely depersonalizing the wearer, dissociating the actor from normal society, and, because of the limited expression it allowed, imparting a degree of inscrutability appropriate particularly to the Godhead. Thus, the audience was called upon to identify with certain characters, such as Joseph and the shepherds, while at the same time, by means of demonstrative acting style and facial masks, it was distanced from God, Satan, and the angels. The emotional impact of much of the action was thus achieved by bringing into close proximity the natural with the supernatural, an effect nowhere more concentrated than in the events surrounding the Nativity. Increasingly, the performance of a cycle of mystery plays emerges not as the theatre of total illusion, but of selected illusory effects to a didactic end.

To bring together all the details of production methods is to discover a theatre in which audience and performers are related in a way that is entirely different from that of the theatre of the recent past. The proximity of players and audience meant that although the latter could not influence the course of events, they were none the less implicated to bear witness. Despite the apparently fragmented nature of the cycle, the message which bore down upon that audience was strongly unified iconographically. Throughout the play texts, there are strong and basic images, which transcend the cycle's episodic nature: intellectually it is drawn together by means of typology, as the events of the Old Testament are clearly framed for the manner in which they anticipate the New. The images of light and darkness, for good and evil, recur constantly. Clothing too, which takes on a specific significance in the *Trial before Herod*, must have been visually arresting throughout. Costumes, props, masks, and language were designed in these plays to serve a function more specific than mere embellishment:

they were, as Meg Twycross has convincingly demonstrated on numerous occasions, semantically expressive in themselves. Illusion was not illusion so much as a figural refinement of reality: characters and events were arranged to carry a specific didactic significance as they do in the religious art of the period. In the same way that a painting or a stained-glass window has its meaning, the cycle was a series of such pictures presented kaleidoscopically as the elements formed first one picture and were then rearranged in preparation for the appearance of another picture, framed within the space on the pageant-wagon. Considered from this point of view, it is easy to understand how mystery plays came to be defended from attacks by the Lollards against their supposed idolatry, as a 'living book'.

Finally, in reconstructing the nature of the original performance of the York cycle, it is necessary to consider the role played by music, since it too had its figural reverberations. Music played a large part in the presentation of the cycle, and many of the stage directions in the manuscript are in fact cues for music. They are invariably cues for vocal music, and, where the piece is specified, it can nearly always be traced to liturgical origins. It follows that some at least of the actors must also have been competent singers. There was apparently little or no use made of instrumental music in most of the cycle, there being only one place in the present selection where it would certainly have been heard in performance: in the *Last Judgement*, when the angels blow their trumpets, a moment perhaps the more striking if instrumental music had not been employed in the preceding plays. The vocal music was often introduced to express human thanksgiving for divine mercy, especially at or near the ends of plays, such as the *Flood*, *Moses and Pharaoh*, and the *Harrowing of Hell*. The unspecified singing called for in the *Entry into Jerusalem* is likely to have consisted of appropriate pieces from the liturgy of Palm Sunday. On occasion, singing could also have a practical function, 'covering' action on stage for which there was no dialogue. Examples are the use of the Whitsun hymn 'Veni creator spiritus' to occupy the time taken by Christ to reach the pinnacle of the temple in the *Temptation*, or the presence of angelic singing to cover Christ's assumption of the judgement seat in the *Last Judgement*. In the *Resurrection*, Christ rises from the tomb and exits without speaking, while angels sing the Easter anthem 'Christus resurgens', and here the music not only covers the action but also comments on, or rather, in a different way, expresses its nature. It is often remarked that music in the drama of this period tends to be used for representational rather than for affective purposes. This is the case in the *Resurrection*, where the singing signifies Christ's reappearance in divine form, but it is music's most marked function in scenes where God appears, or where he intervenes in human affairs. The presence of music was essential to the depiction of heaven in the *Creation* and the *Last Judgement*, where it represented the harmony of the divinely ordained and divinely sustained universe.

It would be improper to conclude without mentioning some recent productions of the cycle. Like all the drama of its period, the cycle has enjoyed a revival in recent years, following nearly four hundred years of neglect in the theatre. Modern productions fall into two broad categories: the attempted reconstruction of the style of the original productions, and the adaptation, which takes selected parts of the text from one or more cycles and applies modern theatrical techniques to it.

Amongst major 'revivals' of the York cycle, the one produced as York's contribution to the Festival of Britain in 1951 must, historically, take pride of place: it was the first, and set the pattern for those of later years. The plays, as they are presented at each York Festival, take the form of a skeletal cycle, telescoped to last only three hours and performed not processionally but in the large open-air 'theatre' created in the ruins of the Benedictine abbey of St Mary's. The text is considerably simplified and adapted. With their banks of lights, huge cast of extras, and a professional celebrity playing Christ, the York Mystery Plays as they are now performed in their native city can bear little physical resemblance to their original, unless as a gorgeous spectacle and a clear manifestation of civic pride. They continue to prove immensely popular and, if anything, rather more pious than their original.

A complete contrast to the York Festival style of revival was the production called *The Passion*, created by the National Theatre Company out of the York and Towneley cycles. The original production was first performed in April 1977 and concentrated on the episodes surrounding the Passion itself. This later became Part II, and Part I, from the Creation to the Baptism, was devised and added for the Edinburgh Festival of 1980. Both parts later appeared in the Cottesloe Theatre and toured elsewhere. Despite its sombre setting in Edinburgh's Assembly Rooms, home of the General Assembly of the Church of Scotland, which was once so effective in suppressing the cycle plays in Scotland that no texts survive, this was a most exciting and innovative production, carefully treading the line between the irreverent and the sentimental. The performance used the whole arena, so that the standing audience was constantly being assailed both visually and physically. The production, spread over two evenings, dividing after the Nativity, received a considerable critical accolade. One of its more powerful moments was the Annunciation, in which a black Gabriel, in a sumptuous robe high on a fork-lift truck, picked up the beam from a spotlight in a circular mirror and directed it on Mary kneeling below, staunchly proletarian in wellington boots. As Paula Neuss concluded, in a recent survey of modern productions, it created something new and exciting for an audience no longer automatically 'united in a common belief'.

The 1970s saw two serious and scholarly attempts to reconstruct the York cycle in its processional form. The first was presented in the grounds of the University of Leeds in 1975. Individual plays were assigned to amateur groups, many of them university departments or local educational establishments, who stood in for the original guilds. The performance of the whole cycle took three days and was performed for the first time since the 1560s, on pageant-wagons at the three 'stations' on the route. The omission of two plays notwithstanding, this was a serious attempt to approximate the experience of an original performance for players and audience alike. One of the features that emerged from the Leeds performance and which was probably true also of the original cycle, was the unevenness of quality and style of the individual groups taking part. This is a feature which a performance by professional actors completely irons out. The unevenness is not necessarily distracting, since the text itself represents a fluid entity captured at one point in its development. The overall effect, given that the performance is at least competent or better, as at Leeds, is one of desirable variety. Another salient feature of the truly processional reconstruction, particularly when the stations are in earshot of one another, is the dramatic effect of incidental simultaneous performance, for example where Mary and Joseph's escape into Egypt is enacted against a background of Herod audibly raging elsewhere.

In 1977, in Toronto, an attempt was finally and most successfully made to recreate the whole cycle on custom-built wagons, on the inspiration of the production in Leeds. There they found that wagons were easier to handle than anticipated, but discovered many other aspects of wagon performance which might otherwise have gone unobserved, particularly concerning the feasibility of performing on a stage 6 feet by 10 (2 metres by 3), and on the usefulness of long opening speeches to cover the period necessary to set up the wagon at a station. In short, what came to light was that the plays were as much custom-made for the method of presentation as vice versa. The production used eleven wagons, at three stations, finding that, in this way, it was possible to recycle each one. The basic superstructure, therefore, was varied from wagon to wagon, but the groups added their own decorations—for instance a two-storey wagon with a lift was designed primarily for the *Creation*, the *Harrowing of Hell*, and the *Last Judgement*, whereas the *Crucifixion* wagon necessarily had no roof but was equipped to support the cross.

It is not our place to suggest that any one of the methods of modern production is necessarily better than another; all those mentioned enjoyed considerable success, and the city of York looks forward to many more productions of its plays, as the Festival every three or four years has now become as much a part of the civic calendar as Corpus Christi Day once was. Any production of the cycle is a most eloquent critique, be it as illumination of the effect of technical details in reconstruction, or the appreciation of an intrinsic theatrical quality which comes from a freer modern production. Indeed the success of the major adaptations and reconstructions of the York cycle testifies more than anything else to the broad power and unity of the original, transcending changing tastes in the theatre and fashions in belief.

Presentation of the Text

The plays were originally written in the Yorkshire dialect of the fourteenth and fifteenth centuries. The scribe who copied them in their surviving form had, however, already begun to introduce modifications in the direction of the south-east Midland and London dialect, which eventually made the principal contribution to the development of modern standard English. The treatment of the text in the present selection is in some ways a wholesale extension of this process. Except where particularly glaring violations of rhyme would occur, the original words are given in their modern spellings. Certain old northern verbal inflections, such as indicative and imperative plural forms ending in *s*, have been replaced by their modern equivalents. An unavoidable effect of these procedures has been the occasional disruption of rhymes. For example, in the original one meets rhyme-sequences such as *sare*:*mare*:*care* and *blaw*:*knaw*:*saw*, which in modernized form emerge as *sore*:*more*:*care* and *blow*:*know*:*saw* on the page—though of course for a modern reader with a good northern accent some of these effects naturally disappear when the lines are spoken out loud. Indeed, it is helpful to bear in mind that much of the vital force and dramatic colour of the language derives from its dialectal origins and demotic syntax, so that speaking the dialogue according to Received Pronunciation ('BBC' English) is apt to obscure some of its most distinctive qualities.

Archaic words, and modern words used in obsolete senses, are glossed at the foot of the page on their first appearance in each play, but not subsequently, unless they reappear with a different meaning or shade of meaning.

However, though the spellings of the words are now nearly all modern, the syntax must remain that of northern Middle English. Consequently, difficult or syntactically archaic phrases, lines, and groups of lines are also rendered in modern English at the foot of the page. Readers naturally vary in the amount of help they require in this respect, and we have attempted to steer a course between reasonable generosity and a weight of explanation that would encumber the text. We have not, for example, sought to render each and every inverted or syncopated expression (*him before* before him; *pass to place* go to [the] place), or every phatic phrase or rhyming tag (*both even and morn* both evening and morning, i.e. all the time). Again, it is worth considering that the plays were of course never intended for silent reading, and that many apparent awkwardnesses readily disappear when the verse is spoken. There is very little punctuation in the manuscript, and that inserted here is all editorial. It is somewhat heavier than is now customary in many scholarly editions of early texts. A plus-sign is used after a line-number in the footnotes to indicate a special feature of the text occurring between that line and the next, e.g. a missing line. Similarly, a minus-sign preceding a line-number signifies that a special feature precedes that line.

The Latin character-designations of the original are all given in English, and a few have been slightly simplified or made uniform. The original stage directions, which are nearly all in Latin, have been translated and retained in their places in the text, but no modern or editorial stage directions have been introduced. The vocabulary of scene setting, scene-division, entrance and exit is too often inappropriate to the manner of staging envisaged by the early dramatists. It is in any case difficult to insert without implying assumptions, quite possibly anachronistic, as to how the plays might have been presented. Moreover, given that very varied alternatives exist in many places as to the *mise en scène*, we have thought it best that readers and directors should attempt to reach their own conclusions on the basis of what is implicit in the dialogue, together with the factual information offered in the introduction.

SELECT BIBLIOGRAPHY

References to books and articles cited by the names of their authors elsewhere in this volume are given in full in the bibliography, which has been
enlarged by the inclusion of many other items to serve as a guide to further
reading. The sources of the plays are dealt with in a separate section at the
end.

The most up-to-date old-spelling text of the entire cycle is R. Beadle
(ed.), *The York Plays* (London, 1982). A facsimile of the manuscript has
been published by the School of English at the University of Leeds: R.
Beadle and P. Meredith, *The York Play. A Facsimile of British Library
Additional MS 35290, together with a facsimile of the Ordo Paginarum section
of the A/Y Memorandum Book* (Leeds, 1983). The documentary records of
the cycle are excellently presented in A. F. Johnston and M. Rogerson,
Records of Early English Drama: York (2 vols., Toronto, 1979).

The current standard editions of the other cycles and fragments of cycles
are:

Spector, S., *The N-Town Play*, EETS, SS 11–12 (1991).

Craig, H., *Two Coventry Corpus Christi Plays*, EETS ES LXXXVII (1957).

Davis, N., *Non-Cycle Plays and Fragments*, EETS SS 1 (1970).

Cawley, A. C., and Stevens, M., *The Towneley Plays*, EETS, SS 13–14
(1994).

Lumiansky, R. M., and Mills, D., *The Chester Mystery Cycle*, EETS, SS 3
(1974), SS 9 (1986).

Anderson, M. D., *Drama and Imagery in English Medieval Churches* (Cambridge, 1963)

Bartlett, J. N., 'The Expansion and Decline of York in the Later Middle
Ages', *Econ. H. R.*, 2nd Ser., xii (1959), pp. 17–33.

Beadle, R., 'The Shipwrights' Craft', *Aspects of Early English Drama*, ed.
Neuss, P. (Cambridge, 1983).

—— 'The York Hosiers' Play of *Moses and Pharaoh*: A Middle English
Dramatist at Work', *Poetica*, xviii (1984).

Brawer, R. A., 'The Characterization of Pilate in the York Cycle Play', *SP*,
lxix (1972), pp. 289–303.

Butterworth, P., 'The York Mercers' Pageant Vehicle, 1433–1467: Wheels,
Steering and Control', *Medieval English Theatre*, i (1979), pp. 72–81.

Cawley, A. C., 'The Sykes Manuscript of the York Scriveners' Play', *LSE*
vii–viii (1952), pp. 45–80.

Coffman, G. R., 'A Plea for the Study of the Corpus Christi Plays as
Drama', *SP*, xxvii (1929), pp. 411–24.

Craig, H., *English Religious Drama of the Middle Ages* (Oxford, 1955).

Davidson, C., 'The Realism of the York Realist and the York Passion', *Speculum*, 1 (1975), pp. 270–83.

—— 'From *Tristia* to *Gaudium*: Iconography and the York-Towneley *Harrowing of Hell*', *American Benedictine Review*, xxviii (1977), pp. 260–75.

Dorrell (Rogerson), M., 'Two Studies of the York Corpus Christi Play', *LSE*, NS, vi (1972), pp. 63–111.

Holding, P., 'Stagecraft in the York Cycle', *Theatre Notebook*, xxxiv (1980), pp. 108–25.

Homan, R. L., 'Ritual Aspects of the York Cycle', *Theatre Journal*, xxxiii (1981), pp. 303–15.

Johnston, A. F., 'The Procession and Play of Corpus Christi in York after 1426', *LSE*, NS, vii (1973–4), pp. 55–62.

—— 'The York Cycle: 1977', *UTQ*, xlviii (1978), pp. 1–9.

—— and Dorrell (Rogerson), M., 'The Doomsday Pageant of the York Mercers, 1433', *LSE*, NS, v (1971), pp. 29–34.

—— and Dorrell (Rogerson), M., 'The York Mercers and their Pageant of Doomsday 1433–1526', *LSE*, NS, vi (1972), pp. 10–35.

Justice, A. D., 'Trade Symbolism in the York Cycle', *Theatre Journal*, xxxi (1979), pp. 47–58.

Kolve, V. A., *The Play called Corpus Christi* (Stanford, 1966).

Mackinnon, E., 'Notes on the Dramatic Structure of the York Cycle', *SP*, xxviii (1931), pp. 443–9.

McNeir, W. F., 'The Corpus Christi Passion Plays as Dramatic Art', *SP*, xlviii (1951), pp. 601–28.

Meredith, P., 'The Development of the York Mercers' Pageant Waggon', *Medieval English Theatre*, i (1979), pp. 5–18.

—— 'The York Cycle and the Beginning of Vernacular Religious Drama in England', *Le Laudi Drammatiche umbre delle Origini*, Atti del V Convegno di Studio, Centro di Studi sul Teatro Medioevale e Rinascimentale di Viterbo (Viterbo, 1981), pp. 311–33.

Mill, A. J., 'The Stations of the York Corpus Christi Play', *Yorkshire Archaeological Journal*, xxxvii (1951), pp. 492–502.

Miller, E., 'Medieval York', *VCH: City of York*, pp. 25–116; see under Tillott, P. M.

Neuss, P., 'God and Embarrassment', *Themes in Drama 5: Drama and Religion*, ed. Redmond, J. (Cambridge, 1983), pp. 241–53.

Palliser, D. M., *Tudor York* (Oxford, 1979).

Parry, D., 'The York Mystery Cycle at Toronto, 1977', *Medieval English Theatre*, i (1979), pp. 9–13.

Percy, J. W., *York Memorandum Book*, Part III, Surtees Society, clxxxvi (1973).

Prosser, E., *Drama and Religion in the English Mystery Plays: A Re-evaluation* (Stanford, 1961).

Purvis, J. S. (ed.), *The York Cycle of Mystery Plays* (London, 1951).

Raine, A., *York Civic Records*, 8 vols., Yorkshire Archaeological Society Record Series, xcviii (1939), ciii (1941), cvi (1942), cviii (1945), cx (1946), cxii (1948), cxv (1950), cxix (1953).

—— *Medieval York* (London, 1955).

Reese, J. B., 'Alliterative Verse in the York Cycle', *SP*, xlviii (1951), pp. 639–68.

Robinson, J. W., 'The Art of the York Realist', *MP*, lx (1962–3), pp. 241–51.

—— 'The Late Medieval Cult of Jesus and the Mystery Plays', *PMLA*, lxxx (1965), pp. 508–15.

—— 'A Commentary on the York Play of the Birth of Jesus', *JEGP*, lxxx (1971), pp. 241–54.

Rogerson, M., 'The York Corpus Christi Play: Some Practical Details', *LSE*, NS, x (1978), pp. 97–106.

—— see also under Dorrell, M., and Johnston, A. F.

Sellers, M., *York Memorandum Book*, Parts I and II, Surtees Society, cxx (1912) and cxxv (1915).

Stevens, J., 'Music in Medieval Drama', *Proceedings of the Royal Musical Association*, lxxxiv (1958), pp. 81–95.

Tillott, P. M., *The Victoria History of the County of York: The City of York* (Oxford, 1961).

Twycross, M., ' "Places to Hear and Play": Pageant Stations at York, 1398–1572', *REED Newsletter*, 1978: 2, pp. 10–33.

—— 'Playing "The Resurrection" ', *Medieval Studies for J. A. W. Bennett Aetatis Suae LXX*, ed. P. L. Heyworth (Oxford, 1981), pp. 273–96.

Wells, H. W., 'Style in the English Mystery Plays', *JEGP*, xxxviii (1939), pp. 360–81.

Wickham, G., *The Medieval English Theatre* (London, 1974).

Woolf, R., *The English Mystery Plays* (London, 1972).

NOTES ON SOURCES

A number of the Headnotes refer to specific sources from which the dramatists were working. Bibliographical details of them are as follows:

Moses and Pharaoh

Kalèn, H., *A Middle English Metrical Paraphrase of the Old Testament* (Gothenburg, 1923).

See also R. Beadle, 'The Origins of Abraham's Preamble in the York Play of *Abraham and Isaac*', *YES*, xi (1981), pp. 178–87, and the article by Beadle on *Moses and Pharaoh* cited in the main bibliography.

Joseph's Trouble about Mary

For the *Protevangelium* and the Gospel of the Pseudo-Matthew, see C. Tischendorf, *Evangelia apocrypha* (Leipzig, 1876). The *Protevangelium* is translated in M. R. James, *The Apocryphal New Testament* (Oxford, 1953).

The Nativity

St Bridget's revelation concerning the Nativity is printed with an English translation in H. Cornell, *The Iconography of the Nativity of Christ* (Uppsala, 1924), pp. 9–13.

The Passion plays, The Harrowing of Hell, The Resurrection

Hulme, W. H., *The Middle English Harrowing of Hell and the Gospel of Nicodemus*, EETS, ES, C (1907).

See also W. A. Craigie, 'The Gospels of Nicodemus and the York Mystery Plays', *An English Miscellany Presented to Dr. Furnivall* (Oxford, 1901), pp. 52–61.

Foster, F. A., *The Northern Passion*, EETS, OS 145, 147, 183 (1913–30).

Young, K., *The Drama of the Medieval Church* (2 vols., Oxford, 1933), i, pp. 239–410 (*Visitatio Sepulchri* of the *Resurrection*).

YORK MYSTERY PLAYS

THE BARKERS

The Fall of the Angels

The Barkers' play depicts the first moments of the creation, the disobedience of Lucifer and the rebellious angels, and their fall into hell. Near the end, God resolves to create mankind to take the place in heaven of the fallen angels. The tone and language of the piece owe much to the first two chapters of Genesis, but the fall of Lucifer and the rebellious angels is an ancient apocryphal episode based on patristic expositions of several scattered biblical passages. The York dramatist adopted a restrained and symbolic treatment of the action, as compared with the more directly dramatic versions in the other cycles, where Lucifer is depicted as a usurper. Here his offence is presented as a kind of inner or intellectual pride, and instead of being cast out by God, who remains silent at the climax, the rebellious angels fall spontaneously.

The text provides for five speaking parts, but there were certainly other angels, good and rebellious. Some may have been trained singers, judging by the stage directions calling for quotations from the *Te deum*, particularly the *Sanctus*, from the liturgy of Matins. The actors were probably costumed according to the conventions governing the representation of the subject in the visual arts of the period, with God of venerable appearance, probably in a golden mask, facial hair, and wig. Angels were often shown in white and gold, with wings, in costumes of leather coated with feathers. The rebellious angels were evidently able to effect a rapid change from this aspect to the conventional black-masked diabolic costumes for their scene in hell. It is not possible to infer a great deal about the *mise en scène* from the dialogue, beyond the fact that the action takes place on at least two levels, the rebellious angels falling from one to the other. At the lower level one may infer some contraption, doubtless the hell mouth often found in illustrations of the period, belching fire and smoke.

The verse used throughout the play is an eight-line alliterative stanza, abab₄cddc₃. It is handled with some skill. God's sonorous and memorable opening gives way to an antiphonal section, where the boasts of the rebellious angels are cast as a crescendo, abruptly interrupted in mid-stanza and mid-line by their fall. Their style is echoed later in the cycle by various wicked characters such as Pharaoh, the Herods, and Pilate. The fragmentation of the stanza in lines 112–20 is aptly expressive of evil discord, a theme which runs throughout the cycle.

The Barkers, or Tanners, were concerned in the preparation of hides for manufacture into leather goods. They were evidently a numerous and prosperous trade in medieval York, and their prestige is perhaps reflected in their ownership of the first play in the cycle throughout its recorded career.

According to the Proclamation of 1415, performance of the cycle as a whole was scheduled to begin at 4.30 a.m., and in the giving of this first play at the first station the dramatist achieved a masterstroke of theatrical effect, combining the themes of creation and light with the dawning of Corpus Christi day.

GOD: *Ego sum Alpha et O: vita, via, veritas, primus et novissimus.*

> I am gracious and great, God without beginning,
> I am maker unmade, all might is in me;
> I am life, and way unto wealth-winning,
> I am foremost and first, as I bid shall it be.
> My blessing of blee shall be blending,   5
> And hielding, from harm to be hiding,
> My body in bliss ay abiding,
> Unending, without any ending.
>
> Since I am maker unmade, and most am of might,
> And ay shall be endless, and nought is but I,   10
> Unto my dignity dear shall duly be dight
> A place full of plenty, to my pleasing at ply;
> And therewith also will I have wrought
> Many diverse doings bedene,
> Which work shall meekly contain,   15
> And all shall be made even of nought.
>
> But only the worthly work of my will
> In my spirit shall inspire the might of me;
> And in the first, faithly, my thought to fulfil,
> Bainly in my blessing I bid at here be   20
> A bliss all-bielding about me,
> In the which bliss I bid at be here
> Nine orders of angels full clear,
> In lofing ay-lasting at lout me.

> *Then the angels sing 'We praise thee O God, we acknowledge thee to*
> *be the Lord.'*

−1 *Ego . . . novissimus* I am Alpha and Omega: the life, the way, the truth, the first and the last   3 *wealth-winning* attainment of bliss   5 The blessing of my countenance will be suffusing   6 *hielding* pouring forth   *hiding* protecting   7 *ay* for ever   11 *dight* created   12 *at ply* to shape   14 *bedene* immediately   15 *contain* continue   17–18 But my power shall inspire with my spirit only the worthy work of my will   19 *faithly* truly   20 *Bainly* Immediately   *at* to   21 *all-bielding* all-protecting   24 *lofing* praise   *ay-lasting* eternal   *lout* worship

Here underneath me now a nexile I neven,   25
Which isle shall be earth. Now all be at once
Earth wholly, and hell, this highest be heaven,
And that wealth shall wield shall won in these wones.
This grant I you, ministers mine,
To-whiles ye are stable in thought—   30
And also to them that are nought
Be put to my prison at pine.

Of all the mights I have made, most next after me
I make thee as master and mirror of my might;
I bield thee here bainly in bliss for to be,   35
I name thee for Lucifer, as bearer of light.
Nothing here shall thee be dering;
In this bliss shall be your bielding,
And have all wealth in your wielding,
Ay-whiles ye are buxomly bearing.   40

Then the angels sing 'Holy, holy, holy, Lord God of hosts'.

SERAPHIM: Ah, merciful maker, full mickle is thy might,
    That all this work at a word worthily has wrought.
    Ay lofed be that lovely lord of his light,
    That us thus mighty has made that now was right nought,
    In bliss for to bide in his blessing.   45
    Ay-lasting in lof let us lout him,
    At bield us thus bainly about him,
    Of mirth nevermore to have missing.

LUCIFER: All the mirth that is made is marked in me!
    The beams of my brighthood are burning so bright,   50
    And I so seemly in sight myself now I see,
    For like a lord am I left to lend in this light.
    More fairer by far than my feres,
    In me is no point that may pair;

25 *nexile* wing, offshoot (= *isle*, 26)   *neven* name   28 *And that* And [those]
who   *won* dwell   *wones* places   30 *To-whiles* As long as   31 *And
also to* And also [I promise] to   32 *at pine* to suffer   33 *mights* powers
35 *bield* establish   *bainly* obediently   37 *dering* harming   38 *bielding*
dwelling   40 *Ay-whiles* So long as   *buxomly bearing* behaving obediently
41 *mickle* great   43 *lofed* praised   *of* for   46 *lof* praise   47 *At
bield us* To flourish   48 *missing* want   49 *Lucifer* MS has '1 Angelus
Deficiens, Lucifer'   *marked* shown   50 *brighthood* radiance   52 *lend*
dwell   53 *feres* companions   54 *pair* deteriorate

I feel me featous and fair,   55
My power is passing my peers.

CHERUBIM: Lord, with a lasting lof we lof thee alone,
   Thou mightful maker that marked us and made us,
   And wrought us thus worthily to won in this wone,
   There never feeling of filth may foul us nor fade us.   60
   All bliss is here bielding about us;
   To-whiles we are stable in thought
   In the worship of him that us wrought,
   Of dere never thar us more dowte us.

2 ANGEL: Oh, what I am featous and fair and figured full fit! 65
   The form of all fairhead upon me is fest,
   All wealth in my wield is, I wot by my wit;
   The beams of my brighthead are bigged with the best.
   My showing is shimmering and shining,
   So bigly to bliss am I brought;   70
   Me needs for to noy me right nought,
   Here shall never pain me be pining.

SERAPHIM: With all the wit at we wield we worship thy will,
   Thou glorious God that is ground of all grace;
   Ay with steadfast steven let us stand still,   75
   Lord, to be fed with the food of thy fair face.
   In life that is leally ay-lasting,
   The dole, Lord, is ay daintethly dealing,
   And whoso that food may be feeling—
   To see thy fair face—is not fasting.   80

LUCIFER: Oh, certes, what I am worthily wrought with worship,
      iwis!
   For in a glorious glee my glittering it gleams;
   I am so mightily made my mirth may not miss—

55 *featous* handsome   56 *passing* surpassing   58 *mightful* mighty   *marked*
created   60 *There* Where   *feeling* perception (or perh. *filing* defilement)   *fade*
corrupt   61 *bielding* protecting   64 We need never fear harm   65 *2 Angel*
MS has '2 Angelus Deficiens'   *figured full fit* well shaped   66 *form* appearance
fairhead beauty   *fest* fixed   67 *wield* power   68 *bigged . . . best* amongst
the most beautiful   69 *showing* appearance   70 *bigly* securely   71 I
need not be in the least concerned   72 *pining* tormenting   73 *at* that   75 *steven*
voice   77 *leally* loyally   78 Thy gift [of grace], Lord, thou art for ever
bountifully bestowing   79 *feeling* tasting   81 *certes* truly   *iwis* indeed
82 *glee* radiance   83 *miss* fail

Ay shall I bide in this bliss through brightness of beams.
Me needs not of noy for to neven,   85
All wealth in my wield have I wielding;
Above yet shall I be bielding,
On height in the highest of heaven.

There shall I set myself full seemly to sight,
To receive my reverence through right of renown;   90
I shall be like unto him that is highest on height.
Oh, what I am dearworth and deft—Oh, *Deus*! All goes down!
My might and my main is all marrand—
Help, fellows! In faith, I am falland.

2 ANGEL: From heaven are we hielding on all hand,   95
To woe we are wending, I warrant.

LUCIFER: Out! Out! Harrow! Helpless, slike hot at is here;
This is a dungeon of dole that I am to dight.
Where is my kind become, so comely and clear?
Now am I loathest, alas, that ere was light.   100
My brightness is blackest and blo now,
My bale is ay beeting and burning—
That gars one go gowling and grinning.
Out! Ay welaway! I well even in woe now.

2 DEVIL: Out! Out! I go wood for woe, my wit is all went now,   105
All our food is but filth we find us beforn.
We that were bielded in bliss, in bale are we burnt now—
Out on thee, Lucifer, lurdan, our light hast thou lorn.
Thy deeds to this dole now hast dight us,
To spill us thou was our speeder,   110
For thou was our light and our leader,
The highest of heaven had thou hight us.

85–6 I need not mention harm, I enjoy all bliss at my behest   92 *dearworth . . .
deft* worthy and exalted   *Deus* God   93 *marrand* fading   94 *falland* falling   95 *hielding . . . hand* falling on every side   97 *Lucifer* MS has 'Lucifer,
Diabolus in inferno'   *Out! Harrow!* conventional fiendish cries   I am helpless,
there is such heat here   98 *dole* misery   *to dight* thrust into   99 *Where . . .
become* What has become of my nature   101 *blo* dark   102 *bale . . . beeting*
misery is endlessly kindling   103 *gars one* makes me   *gowling* wailing   *grinning*
grimacing   104 *welaway* alas   *well* boil   105 *wood* mad   *went* gone
106 *us beforn* before us   108 *lurdan* scoundrel   *lorn* lost   110 *spill* harm
speeder instigator   112 *hight* promised

LUCIFER: Welaway! Woe is me now, now is it worse than it
    was.
Unthrivingly threap ye—I said but a thought.
2 DEVIL: We! Lurdan, thou lost us.
LUCIFER: Ye lie! Out, alas!   115
I wist not this woe should be wrought.
Out on you, lurdans, ye smore me in smoke.
2 DEVIL: This woe has thou wrought us.
LUCIFER: Ye lie! Ye lie!
2 DEVIL: Thou lies, and that shall thou buy.
LUCIFER: We! Lurdans, have at you, let look!   120

CHERUBIM: Ah, Lord, lofed be thy name that us this light lent,
    Since Lucifer our leader is lighted so low,
    For his unbuxomness in bale to be burnt—
    Thy righteousness to reward on row
    Ilk work after his wrought.   125
    Through grace of thy merciful might
    The cause I see it in sight,
    Wherefor to bale he is brought.

GOD: Those fools for their fairhead in fantasies fell,
    And had moan of my might that marked them and made them. 130
    Forthy after their works were in woe shall they well,
    For some are fallen into filth that evermore shall fade them,
    And never shall have grace for to grith them.
    So passing of power them thought them,
    They would not me worship that wrought them;   135
    Forthy shall my wrath ever go with them.

    And all that me worship shall won here, iwis;
    Forthy more forth of my work, work now I will.
    Since then their might is formarred that meant all amiss,
    Even to mine own figure this bliss to fulfil,   140
    Mankind of mould will I make.

114 *Unthrivingly* Unprofitably   *threap* chide   115 *We* diabolical cry   *lost*
ruined   116 *wist* knew   117 *smore* smother   119 *buy* pay for
120 *have . . . look* let me get at you, see here   121 *lent* gave   122 *lighted*
descended   123 *unbuxomness* disobedience   124–5 [It being characteristic
of] thy righteousness duly to repay each deed according to its deserts   129 *for*
because of   130 *had moan* complained   131 *Forthy after* Therefore according
as   133 *grith* protect   138 *more forth* yet more   139 *formarred* completely
destroyed   140 *to* in   *figure* image   *fulfil* replenish   141 *mould* earth

But first will I form him before
All thing that shall him restore,
To which that his talent will take.

And in my first making, to muster my might,   145
Since earth is vain and void and murkness amell,
I bid in my blessing ye angels give light
To the earth, for it faded when the fiends fell.
In hell shall never murkness be missing,
The murkness thus name I for night;   150
The day, that call I this light—
My after-works shall they be wissing.

And now in my blessing I twin them in two,
The night even from the day, so that they meet never,
But either in a kind course their gates for to go.   155
Both the night and the day, do duly your dever,
To all I shall work be ye wissing.
This day's work is done ilka deal,
And all this work likes me right well,
And bainly I give it my blessing.   160

142 *him before* before him   143 *restore* sustain   144 *talent . . . take* inclination
will lead   145 *muster* display   146 *vain* empty   *murkness amell* in utter
darkness   152 *after-works* later creations   *wissing* guiding   153 *twin* part
155 *kind* natural   *gates* ways   156 *dever* duty   158 *ilka deal* in every
respect   159 *likes* pleases

THE COOPERS

The Fall of Man

The Coopers were manufacturers and repairers of such items as barrels, buckets, and tubs. In York the street-name Coppergate may indicate where they were concentrated in the city. Their play initiates the human drama of the cycle. It sets in motion the chain of events which, though it is answered by Christ's sacrifice in the Passion, continues to implicate the audience in the present, its consequences not being finally exhausted until the Last Judgement. The piece is cast in an eleven-line stanza rhyming abab$_4$c$_2$bc$_4$dcdc$_3$, unique in the cycle as it survives.

The play departs from the elevated style of *The Fall of the Angels*, and, in its human and psychological approach to the characters, is closer to the twelfth-century Anglo-Norman play the *Mystère d'Adam* than to the large body of theological commentary associated with the scriptural source in Genesis 3. The play opens with the return of Satan, who adds envy and anger to pride in his catalogue of sin. Curiously, his envy is directed at man not because he is God's new favourite, but because he already knows that God himself intends to take man's form. This suggests a belief that the Incarnation was not dependent on the Fall, which Rosemary Woolf points out was an unorthodox view peculiar to the Franciscans.

It is not the doctrinal element in the play which is most striking, however, so much as the playwright's handling of tonal shifts, for instance when Satan assumes the guise of the adder. The text is reticent as to how Satan went 'in a worm's likeness', there being no stage direction to indicate whether he simply assumed an ophidian manner or whether he changed costume in front of the audience as he spoke. There was a strong iconographic tradition that Satan appeared to Eve as a serpent with a woman's face. Whatever the dramatist here intended to create visually, verbally he achieves some subtly realized dialogue as the serpent proceeds to flatter, seduce, and bully Eve into eating the fruit. In a similar vein, he shortly afterwards devises the first domestic quarrel in the cycle, as Adam turns on his wife for deluding him with 'trifles'. Their wrangling, coinciding with their fall, presages the discord which is thematically associated with evil throughout the cycle. Adam is not of particularly impressive moral stature in this play: he accepts the fruit for the same selfish reasons as Eve, rather than out of love for her. Later, when God confronts him with his crime, far from presenting an example of contrition, Adam peevishly blames his wife. The play, faithful to its source in Genesis, derives its strength from balanced dramatic dialogue, rather than doctrinal niceties.

SATAN: For woe my wit is in a were
  That moves me mickle in my mind;
  The Godhead that I saw so clear,
  And perceived that he should take kind
    Of a degree   5
  That he had wrought, and I dedigned
  That angel kind should it not be;
  And we were fair and bright,
  Therefore me thought that he
    The kind of us ta'en might,   10
  And thereat dedigned me.

  The kind of man he thought to take,
  And thereat had I great envy,
  But he has made to him a make,
  And hard to her I will me hie   15
    That ready way,
  That purpose proof to put it by,
  And fand to pick from him that prey.
  My travail were well set
    Might I him so betray,   20
  His liking for to let,
  And soon I shall assay.

  In a worm's likeness will I wend
  And fand to feign a loud leasing.
  Eve, Eve.
EVE: Who is there?
SATAN: I, a friend.   25
  And for thy good is the coming
  I hither sought.
  Of all the fruit that ye see hang
  In paradise, why eat ye nought?
EVE: We may of them ilkone   30

1 My wits are in a turmoil of rage   2 *mickle* greatly   3 *that I* that [once] I
4 *take kind* assume [the] nature   5 *degree* order of beings (i.e. mankind)   6 *wrought*
created   *dedigned* was offended   7 *angel kind* of angelic nature   10 Might
have assumed our nature   11 *dedigned me* I was offended   14 *make* mate
15 *hard* quickly   *me hie* go   17–19 In order to thwart that fixed plan, and try
to steal that prey from him. My time would be well spent   21 *liking* pleasure
let end   22 *assay* make the attempt   23 *worm's* serpent's   *wend* go
24 And attempt to fabricate a flagrant lie   29 *nought* none   30 *ilkone* each
one

Take all that us good thought,
Save a tree out is ta'en,
Would do harm to nigh it aught.

SATAN: And why that tree, that would I wit,
　　　Any more than all other by?   35
EVE: For our Lord God forbids us it,
　　The fruit thereof, Adam nor I
　　To nigh it near;
　　And if we did we both should die,
　　He said, and cease our solace sere.   40
SATAN: Yah, Eve, to me take tent;
　　　Take heed and thou shalt hear
　　　What that the matter meant
　　　He moved on that manner.

To eat thereof he you defend   45
I know it well, this was his skill:
Because he would none other kenned
These great virtues that long theretill.
For will thou see,
Who eats the fruit, of good and ill   50
Shall have knowing as well as he.
EVE: Why, what-kin thing art thou
　　That tells this tale to me?
SATAN: A worm, that wotteth well how
　　　That ye may worshipped be.   55

EVE: What worship should we win thereby?
　　To eat thereof us needeth it nought,
　　We have lordship to make mastery
　　Of all thing that on earth is wrought.
SATAN: Woman, do way!   60
　　　To greater state ye may be brought
　　　And ye will do as I shall say.

31 Take all that seems good to us　　　32 *out . . . ta'en* is excepted　　　33 It
would be harmful to go anywhere near it　　　34 *wit* know　　　35 *other by* others
near by　　　38 *nigh* approach　　　40 cease [to enjoy] our various pleasures
41 *take tent* pay attention　　　43–4 What he meant by expressing himself like that
45 *defend* forbad　　　46 *skill* reason　　　47 *kenned* knew　　　48 *long theretill*
belong therein　　　49 *will thou* do you not　　　50 *ill* evil　　　52 *what-kin* what
kind of　　　54 *wotteth* knows　　　57 *us . . . nought* we have no need　　　58 *make*
exercise　　　59 *Of* Over　　　60 *do way* enough of this　　　62 *And* If

EVE: To do is us full loath
  That should our God mispay.
SATAN: Nay, certes, it is no wothe,   65
  Eat it safely ye may.

For peril right there none in lies,
But worship and a great winning,
For right as God ye shall be wise
And peer to him in all-kin thing.   70
Aye, gods shall ye be,
Of ill and good to have knowing,
For to be as wise as he.
EVE: Is this sooth that thou says?
SATAN: Yea, why trows thou not me?   75
  I would by no-kins ways
  Tell nought but truth to thee.

EVE: Then will I to thy teaching trust
  And fang this fruit unto our food.

Then she should accept the apple.

SATAN: Bite on boldly, be not abashed,   80
  And bear Adam to amend his mood
  And eke his bliss.

Then Satan goes away.

EVE: Adam, have here of fruit full good.
ADAM: Alas woman, why took thou this?
  Our Lord commanded us both   85
  To tent the tree of his.
  Thy work will make him wroth—
  Alas, thou hast done amiss.

EVE: Nay, Adam, grieve thee not at it,
  And I shall say the reason why.   90

63 We will not do anything   64 *mispay* displease   65 *certes* indeed   *wothe* danger   67 For there is not the slightest danger therein   68 *worship* honour *winning* gain   69 *right* just   70 *all-kin* every kind of   74 *sooth* true 75 *trows* believes   76 *no-kins ways* no means   79 *fang* take   81–2 And take [some] to Adam to improve his disposition and enhance his happiness   86 *tent* pay heed to

A worm has done me for to wit
We shall be as gods, thou and I,
If that we eat
Here of this tree; Adam, forthy
Let not that worship for to get.   95
For we shall be as wise
As God that is so great,
And as mickle of price;
Forthy eat of this meat.

ADAM: To eat it would I not eschew   100
 Might I me sure in thy saying.
EVE: Bite on boldly, for it is true,
 We shall be gods and know all thing.
ADAM: To win that name
 I shall it taste at thy teaching.   105

And he accepts and eats.

Alas, what have I done, for shame!
Ill counsel, woe worth thee!
Ah Eve, thou art to blame,
To this enticed thou me—
Me shames with my lichame,   110

For I am naked as methink,
EVE: Alas Adam, right so am I,
ADAM: And for sorrow sere why ne might we sink,
 For we have grieved God almighty
 That made me man—   115
Broken his bidding bitterly.
Alas that ever we it began.
This work, Eve, hast thou wrought,
And made this bad bargain.
EVE: Nay Adam, wite me nought.   120
ADAM: Do way, lief Eve, whom then?

91 *done . . . wit* informed me   94 *forthy* therefore   95 *Let not* Do not fail
98 *mickle of price* exalted   99 *meat* food   101 Might I assure myself of the
truth of what you say   105 *teaching* instigation   107 Evil adviser, a curse
on you   110–11 I am ashamed of my body, for it seems to me I am naked
113 Now for manifold sorrows, why might we not sink [into the ground]
116 *bitterly* wickedly   120 *wite* blame   *nought* not   121 *lief* dear

EVE: The worm to wite well worthy were,
    With tales untrue he me betrayed.

ADAM: Alas that I let at thy lore
    Or trowed the trifles that thou me said.   125
    So may I bid,
    For I may ban that bitter braid
    And dreary deed, that I it did.
    Our shape for dole me deaves,
    Wherewith shall they be hid?   130

EVE: Let us take there fig leaves,
    Sithen it is thus betid.

ADAM: Right as thou says so shall it be,
    For we are naked and all bare;
    Full wonder fain I would hide me   135
    From my Lord's sight, and I wist where.
    Were I ne rought!

GOD: Adam, Adam.

ADAM: Lord.

GOD: Where art thou, yare?

ADAM: I hear thee Lord and see thee nought.

GOD: Say, whereon is it long,   140
    This work why hast thou wrought?

ADAM: Lord, Eve gart me do wrong
    And to that brigue me brought

GOD: Say, Eve, why has thou gart thy make
    Eat fruit I bade thee should hang still,   145
    And commanded none of it to take?

EVE: A worm, Lord, enticed me theretill;
    So welaway,
    That ever I did that deed so dill.

GOD: Ah, wicked worm, woe worth thee ay,   150

122 The serpent surely deserves the blame   124 *let . . . lore* heeded your advice
125 *trowed . . . trifles* believed the idle tales   *said* told   126 Now may I beg
[for mercy]   127 *ban . . . braid* curse that terrible impulse   128 *dreary*
wicked   129–30 I am stunned by shock at our appearance; what can we conceal
them (our bodies) with?   131 *take* put   132 Since it has happened thus
135 *Full . . . fain* Most gladly   136 *and . . . where* if [only] I knew where
137 Would that nobody heeded me   138 *yare* quickly   140 Tell me, what
is the reason for it   142 *gart* made   143 *brigue* plight   144–45 Tell
me, Eve, why have you caused your partner to eat the fruit which I said should for ever
remain hanging   148 *welaway* alas   149 *dill* foolish   150 *woe . . . ay* a curse
on you for ever

For thou on this manner
Hast made them swilk affray:
My malison have thou here
With all the might I may.

And on thy womb then shall thou glide,   155
And be ay full of enmity
To all mankind on ilka side,
And earth it shall thy sustenance be
To eat and drink.
Adam and Eve also, ye   160
In earth then shall sweat and swink,
And travail for your food.
ADAM: Alas, when might we sink?
  We that have all world's good,
  Full derfly may us think.   165

GOD: Now, Cherubim, mine angel bright,
  To middle-earth tite go drive these two.
ANGEL: All ready, Lord, as it is right,
  Since thy will is that it be so,
  And thy liking.   170
  Adam and Eve, do you two go,
  For here may ye make no dwelling;
  Go ye forth fast to fare,
  Of sorrow may ye sing.
ADAM: Alas for sorrow and care   175
  Our hands may we wring.

151 *For* Because   *on* in   152 *swilk affray* such trouble   153 *malison*
curse   154 *might* power   155 *womb* belly   156 *ay* for ever   157 *on*
. . . *side* in every place   161 *swink* work   162 *travail* labour   165 We
may consider ourselves most wretched   167 *tite* quickly   168 *All ready*
Willingly   173 *fare* travel

THE SHIPWRIGHTS

The Building of the Ark

York is unique amongst the extant cycles in dividing the story of Noah into two episodes, the Building of the Ark, and the Flood. The prominence this gives to the Shipwrights in both the action and the spirit of their play provides one of the cycle's most striking blends of the quotidian with the eternal. God resolves to destroy his sinful creation with a flood, sparing only Noah and his family. He calls upon the astonished Noah to build a ship, and it appears that a representation of a vessel took shape before the audience's eyes in the course of the play. The action is based on events narrated in Genesis 6 and 7, and much is made in the dialogue of the construction of the Ark, especially the details of its dimensions. This is partly because of the Ark's great symbolic significance: as the vessel of salvation it was amongst the Old Testament's most important prefigurations of the Christian Church. The York dramatist, however, also developed his source material in a different way alongside the spiritual meaning of the events. An adroit blend of humour, wonder, and some technical vocabulary drawn from the medieval shipwright's craft, presents Noah as at one moment the ancient biblical patriarch, reeling comically at God's amazing and peremptory command, and then charts his transformation through grace into a skilled contemporary shipwright. At the centre of the play is a demonstration of the Shipwrights' craft which is at the same time a sanctification of it by association with God's scheme of salvation.

God's instructions (lines 72–88) and Noah's demonstrative speech which follows (89–119) embody terms suggesting that the Ark is a medieval clinker-built vessel. Clinker-building involved the laying down of a frame made up of the keel and cross-ribs of the vessel. On to this were nailed the strakes, rows of horizontal overlapping planks, making up the hull. The gaps between the strakes, the seams, were caulked with waterproof substances. Whilst Noah demonstrates some of these aspects of shipwrightry, it appears that prefabricated sections of the Ark are brought together around him, for both he and God refer to the completed vessel near the end.

Though the stanza employed throughout is a relatively unadorned alternately rhyming octave, the style of the piece is nevertheless unobtrusively literary. A thread of diction, running throughout the play, is established by the repetition of words like 'work' (noun and verb), 'wrought', 'make', and so on. It is applied first to God, the divine artificer, and then conveyed, with his power, to Noah, the biblical-medieval craftsman. The puns on 'mark(s)' (lines 64, 68) and 'craft' (150) should not be overlooked, the latter particularly as it sums up several levels of meaning in the play: the craft of the biblical Noah and the York Shipwrights, itself a mundane reflex of the divine creative power; and the craft which they have built, the Ark.

GOD: First when I wrought this world so wide,
    Wood and wind and waters wan,
    Heaven and hell was not to hide,
    With herbs and grass thus I began.
    In endless bliss to be and bide   5
    And to my likeness made I man,
    Lord and sire on ilka side
    Of all middle earth I made him then.

A woman also with him wrought I,
    All in law to lead their life,   10
    I bad them wax and multiply,
    To fulfil this world, without strife.
    Sithen have men wrought so woefully
    And sin is now reigning so rife,
    That me repents and rues forthy   15
    That ever I made either man or wife.

But since they make me to repent
    My work I wrought so well and true,
    Without cease will not assent,
    But ever is bound more bale to brew.   20
    But for their sins they shall be shent
    And fordone wholly, hide and hue;
    Of them shall no more be meant,
    But work this work I will all new.

All new I will this world be wrought   25
    And waste away that wons therein;
    A flood above them shall be brought
    To stroy middle earth, both more and min.
    But Noah alone, leave shall it nought
    Till all be sunken for their sin;   30
    He and his sons, this is my thought,
    And with their wives away shall win.

---

2 *wan* dark   3 *not to hide* plain to see   6 *And* Then   7 *sire* ruler
ilka every   11 *wax* flourish   12 *fulfil* people   13 *Sithen* Since then
14 *reigning so rife* flourishing so abundantly   15 That therefore I repent and
regret   19–20 [They are] continually disobedient, and always ready to stir up
more trouble   21 *shent* destroyed   22 *fordone* brought to ruin   *hide and
hue* in every respect   23 *meant* said   26 And those who dwell here shall
be destroyed   27 *above* over   28 *stroy* destroy   *both . . . min* entirely
29 Except for Noah, nothing will be spared   31 *thought* intention   32 *win* escape

Noah, my servant sad and clean,
For thou art stable in stead and stall,
I will thou work without ween
A work to save thyself withal.
NOAH: Oh, mercy, Lord, what may this mean?
GOD: I am thy God of great and small
Is come to tell thee of thy teen,
And what ferly shall after fall.

NOAH: Ah, Lord, I lof thee loud and still,
That unto me—wretch unworthy—
Thus with thy word, as is thy will,
Likes to appear thus properly.
GOD: Noah, as I bid thee, do fulfil:
A ship I will have wrought in hie;
All-if thou can little skill,
Take it in hand, for help shall I.

NOAH: Ah, worthy Lord, would thou take heed,
I am full old and out of quart,
That me list do no day's deed
But if great mister me gart.
GOD: Begin my work behoves thee need
And thou will pass from pains smart,
I shall thee succour and thee speed
And give thee heal in head and heart.

I see such ire among mankind
That of their works I will take wrake;
They shall be sunken for their sin,
Therefore a ship I will thou make.
Thou and thy sons shall be therein,
They shall be saved for thy sake.
Therefore go boldly and begin
Thy measures and thy marks to take.

35

40

45

50

55

60

---

33 *sad* sober   *clean* pure   34 *stead and stall* every respect   35–6 I command
that you take care to perform a piece of work whereby to save yourself   39 *teen*
trouble   40 *ferly* marvel   *fall* happen   41 *lof* give thanks to   *loud and
still* continually   44 *Likes* Is pleased   *properly* in person   46 *in hie* quickly
47 Even though you have little skill [in shipbuilding]   50 *quart* healthy condition
51–2 So that I should be disinclined to do a day's work unless great need constrained
me   53–4 You must needs begin my work if you mean to escape from severe
afflictions   55 *speed* assist   56 *heal* health   57 *ire* sinful turmoil   58 *wrake*
vengeance   64 *marks* dimensions

NOAH: Ah, Lord, thy will shall ever be wrought,   65
    As counsel gives of ilka clerk,
    But first, of ship-craft can I right nought,
    Of their making have I no mark.
GOD: Noah, I bid thee heartly, have no thought,
    I shall thee wis in all thy work,   70
    And even till it to end be wrought;
    Therefore to me take heed and hark.

    Take high trees and hew them clean,
    All by square and not of squin,
    Make of them boards and wands between,   75
    Thus thrivingly, and not over-thin.
    Look that thy seams by subtly seen
    And nailed well that they not twin;
    Thus I devise ilk deal bedene,
    Therefore do forth, and leave thy din.   80

    Three hundred cubits it shall be long,
    And fifty broad, all for thy bliss;
    The height, of thirty cubits strong,
    Look leally that thou think on this.
    Thus give I thee gradely ere I gang   85
    Thy measures, that thou do not miss.
    Look now that thou work not wrong
    Thus witterly since I thee wis.

NOAH: Ah, blissful Lord, that all may bield,
    I thank thee heartly both ever and ay;   90
    Five hundred winters I am of eld—
    Methink these years as yesterday!
    Full weak I was and all unwield,
    My weariness is went away,
    To work this work here in this field   95
    All by myself I will assay.

---

66 So every learned man advises   67 *of . . . nought* I know nothing about ship-building   68 *mark* skill   69 *heartly* earnestly   *have no thought* do not worry   70 *wis* guide   73 *clean* neatly   74 Squarely, and not on a slant   75 *and wands between* with battens to go between   76 *thrivingly* skilfully   77 *seams* gaps between planks making up hull   *subtly seen* carefully attended to   78 *twin* come apart   79 *deal* thing   *bedene* altogether   80 *do forth* get on with it   *leave thy din* say no more   84 *leally* truly   85 *gradely* carefully   *gang* go   86 *miss* err   88 *witterly* surely   89 *blissful* blessed   *bield* protect   91 *eld* age   93 *unwield* feeble   94 *went* gone   96 *assay* endeavour

To hew this board I will begin,
But first I will lay on my line;
Now bud it be all inlike thin,
So that it neither twin nor twine.   100
Thus shall I join it with a gin
And sadly set it with simmon fine:
Thus shall I work it both more and min
Through teaching of God, master mine.

. . . .

More subtly can no man sew;   105
It shall be clinked everilka deal
With nails that are both noble and new,
Thus shall I fast it fast to feal.
Take here a rivet, and there a rew,
With these the bow now work I well;   110
This work I warrant both good and true.

Full true it is, who will take tent,
But fast my force begins to fold.
A hundred winters away is went
Since I began this work, full gradely told,   115
And in such travail for to be bent
Is hard to him that is thus old.
But he that to me these messages sent,
He will be my bield, thus am I bold.

GOD: Noah, this work is near an end,   120
And wrought right as I warned thee.
But yet in manner it must be mend,
Therefore this lesson learn at me:
For diverse beasts therein must lend,
And fowls also in their degree,   125

98 *line* measuring line   99 *bud* must   *inlike* equally   100 *twine* warp
101 *gin* tool   102 And carefully secure it with good cement (*sc.* substance used
for caulking seams)   103 *both . . . min* in every respect   104+ Line missing
in MS   105 *subtly* skilfully   *sew* join seams   106 *clinked* clenched   *everilka
deal* in each and every part   107 *noble* fine   108 Thus shall I fasten it
tightly, to cover [it] (i.e. the hull)   109 *Take* Put   *rew* rove, burr   112 *tent*
note   113 *force* strength   *fold* ebb   115 *full . . . told* most carefully
enumerated   116 *bent* exerting oneself   119 *bield* support   *bold* bold
[to assert]   121 *warned* instructed   122 *manner* a certain respect   *mend*
improved   123 *at* from   124 *lend* dwell   125 *degree* appropriate place

And for that they shall not sam blend
Diverse stages must there be.

And when that it is ordained so
With diverse stalls and stages sere,
Of ilka kind thou shall take two,   130
Both male and female fare in fere.
Thy wife, thy sons, with thee shall go,
And their three wives, without were;
These eight bodies, without mo,
Shall thus be saved on this manner.   135

Therefore to my bidding be bain,
Till all be harboured, haste thee fast;
After the seventh day shall it rain
Till forty days be fully past.
Take with thee gear such as may gain   140
To man and beast, their lives to last.
I shall thee succour for certain
Till all thy care away be cast.

NOAH: Ah, Lord, that ilka miss may mend,
I lof thy lore both loud and still,   145
I thank thee both with heart and hend
That me will help from angers ill.
About this work now bus me wend,
With beasts and fowls my ship to fill.
He that to me this craft has kenned,   150
He wis us with his worthy will.

126 *for* so   *sam blend* mingle together   127 *stages* compartments   128 *ordained* arranged   129 *sere* various   131 *fare in fere* going together   133 *were* doubt 134 *mo* more   136 *bain* obedient   137 *harboured* lodged   140 *gear* provisions   *gain* be useful   141 *last* sustain   143 *care . . . cast* tribulations are over   144 *miss* fault   145 I praise your counsel ceaselessly   146 *hend* hands   147 *angers ill* severe troubles   148 *bus . . . wend* must I go   150 *kenned* taught

THE FISHERS AND MARINERS

The Flood

The Flood prefigures the second and final destruction of the world at the Last Judgement, an event to which Noah himself alludes near the end of the play (lines 299 ff.). He was, according to Genesis 6:9, the sole righteous man who 'walked with God', and in the play he and his sons and daughters-in-law are presented as models of godly rectitude and obedience. Much of the dramatic tension and life of the piece is generated by the contrast between Noah's formidable wife and the rest of the family. The tradition of her disobedience was rooted in Eastern legend, which told that, as had been the case with Eve, her violation of the natural order was due to the temptations of Satan, who sought once again to thwart God's plan through the agency of a woman. The York dramatist was clearly aware of both the figural and the comic potential of her role in the action. The celebrated scene of her domestic fisticuffs with Noah and the others is quickly followed by her complete quiescence upon entering the Ark, the entire episode being figurally interpreted as the reluctance of the hardened sinner to enter the Church until the moment of death. Her muted contributions in the latter half of the play, first a brief lamentation for her lost friends, then a qualm lest the universal destruction of fire is about to follow immediately, are touchingly set off against the unwavering zeal of Noah.

The play is written in a comparatively elaborate fourteen-line stanza, $ababababab_4cdcccd_3$, which lends itself well to the choric resignation, prayer, and thanksgiving of Noah's family as they move through suffering to salvation. Yet by means of dividing a number of lines between speakers and by using contrasting diction, the form is also shown to be sufficiently flexible to present some lively demotic exchanges between Noah's wife and the rest of the family. No stage directions exist to show how flood, animals, raven, dove, and rainbow were managed in performance. Some clues may be gathered from the versions in the Chester cycle and the Towneley manuscript, which are more explicit in this area. Clear indications of movement and positioning of characters are, however, embedded in the dialogue. For instance, in the passage after line 75, Noah is on the Ark/pageant-wagon, whilst his wife is in the street below, and their positioning in relation to each other offers implicit correction to the inverted hierarchy which she is at pains to maintain. The sole stage direction in the play, that near the end the family should all sing, signals the final restoration of harmony at all levels.

The appropriateness of the *Flood* to the Fishers and Mariners need not be laboured. Fish was a very significant element in the medieval diet, partly because meat was quite frequently forbidden owing to religious observances, and was in any case difficult to keep. York had large fishmarkets and numerous fishermen. The Mariners' or Shipmen's trade was chiefly distributive; they handled the river traffic between Hull, York, and the upper reaches of the Ouse.

NOAH: That Lord that lives ay-lasting life,
    I lof thee ever with heart and hand,
    That me would rule by reason rife,
    Six hundred years to live in land.
    Three seemly sons and a worthy wife   5
    I have ever at my steven to stand;
    But now my cares are keen as knife,
    Because I ken what is comand.
    There comes to ilk country,
    Yea, cares both keen and cold.   10
    For God has warned me
    This world wasted shall be,
    And certes the sooth I see,
    As forefathers have told.

    My father Lamech who, likes to neven,   15
    Here in this world thus long gan lend,
    Seven hundred years, seventy and seven,
    In such a space his time he spend.
    He prayed to God with stable steven
    That he to him a son should send,   20
    And at the last there came from heaven
    Such hetting that him mickle amend,
    And made him grub and grave
    As ordained fast before,
    For he a son should have,   25
    As he gan after crave;
    And as God vouchsave
    In world then was I born.

1 *ay-lasting* everlasting   2 *lof* praise   3–4 Who, according to abundant reason, ordains that I should live on earth for six hundred years   6 I have perpetually at my command   7 *keen* sharp   8 *ken* know   *comand* to come 9 *ilk* every   13 And I perceive the truth indeed   15 *likes . . . neven* it is suitable to mention   16 *thus . . . lend* lived this long   18 *spend* spent 19 *stable steven* steady voice   22 Words of promise that were greatly to improve his lot   23 *grub* dig   *grave* delve   24 *fast* firmly   *before* beforehand 26 What he longed for   27 *vouchsave* condescended

When I was born Noah named he me,
And said these words with mickle win: 30
'Lo', he said, 'this ilk is he
That shall be comfort to mankind.'
Sirs, by this well wit may ye,
My father knew both more and min
By certain signs he could well see,   35
That all this world should sink for sin;
How God should vengeance take,
As now is seen certain,
And end of mankind make,
That sin would not forsake;   40
And how that it should slake,
And a world wax again.

I would God it wasted were,
So that I should not tent theretill.
My seemly sons and daughters dear,   45
Take ye intent unto my skill.
1 SON: Father, we are all ready here,
   Your bidding bainly to fulfil.
NOAH: Go call your mother, and come near,
   And speed us fast that we not spill.   50
1 SON: Father, we shall not fine
   Till your bidding be done.
NOAH: All that lives under line
   Shall, son, sooner pass to pine.
1 SON: Where are ye, mother mine?   55
   Come to my father soon.

WIFE: What says thou, son?
1 SON: Mother, certain
   My father thinks to flit full far.
   He bids you hasten with all your main
   Unto him, that nothing you mar.   60

---

30 *mickle win* great joy   31 *ilk* same   33 Sirs, by this you may well understand   34 *min* less   41 *slake* end   42 *wax* grow   44 So that I
would not have to attend to it   46 Pay attention to my purpose   48 *bainly*
readily   49 *near* back   50 Let us hurry up so that we are not destroyed
51 *fine* pause   53 *lives under line* lives   54 *sooner* in a short time   *pine*
torment   56 *soon* at once   58 *flit . . . far* remove far away   59 *main*
strength   60 so that nothing harms you *or* so that you do not spoil anything

WIFE: Yah, good son, hie thee fast again
    And tell him I will come no nar.
1 SON: Dame, I would do your bidding fain,
    But you bus wend, else be it war.
WIFE: War? That would I wit.   65
    We bourd all wrong, I ween.
1 SON: Mother, I say you yet,
    My father is bound to flit.
WIFE: Now certes, I shall not sit
    Ere I see what he mean.   70

1 SON: Father, I have done now as ye command,
    My mother comes to you this day.
NOAH: She is welcome, I well warrand;
    This world shall soon be wasted away.
WIFE: Where art thou Noah?
NOAH: Lo, here at hand.   75
    Come hither fast, dame, I thee pray.
WIFE: Trows thou that I will leave the hard land
    And turn up here on tor deray?
    Nay, Noah, I am not boun
    To fond now over these fells.   80
    Do bairns, go we and truss to town.
NOAH: Nay, certes, soothly then mun ye drown.
WIFE: In faith, thou were as good come down
    And go do somewhat else.

NOAH: Dame, forty days are near-hand past   85
    And gone since it began to rain,
    On life shall no man longer last
    But we alone, is not to lain.
WIFE: Now, Noah, in faith thou fons full fast,
    This fare will I no longer frayne;   90

61 *hie . . . again* go quickly back again   62 *nar* nearer   63 *fain* gladly
64 But you ought to go or else things will be worse   65–6 Worse? I should like
to see that. I believe we are barking up the wrong tree   68 *is . . . flit* is sure to be
on the move   69–70 Now, indeed, I shall not rest until I find out what he
means (by this)   73 *warrand* affirm   77–8 Do you believe that I will leave
dry land and get up here in such complete confusion?   79 *boun* prepared   80 To
set out now over these hills   81 *Do* come on   *bairns* children   *truss* depart
82 *certes* indeed   *soothly* truly   *mun* must   83–4 In faith, you might as well
come down and do something worthwhile   85 *near-hand* nearly   88 *is . . .*
lain it is not to be concealed   89 *thou . . . fast* you are acting extremely foolishly
90 *fare* matter   *frayne* enquire into

Thou art near wood, I am aghast,
Farewell, I will go home again.
NOAH: Oh, woman, art thou wood?
Of my works thou nought wot;
All that has bone or blood 95
Shall be over flowed with the flood.
WIFE: In faith, thou were as good
To let me go my gate.

We! Out! Harrow!
NOAH:⠀⠀⠀⠀⠀⠀⠀What now, what cheer?
WIFE: I will no nar for no-kins need. 100
NOAH: Help, my sons, to hold her here,
For to her harms she takes no heed.
2 SON: Be merry mother, and mend your cheer;
This world be drowned, without dread.
WIFE: Alas, that I this lore should lere. 105
NOAH: Thou spills us all, ill might thou speed.
3 SON: Dear mother, won with us,
There shall nothing you grieve.
WIFE: Nay, needlings home me bus,
For I have tools to truss. 110
NOAH: Woman, why does thou thus?
To make us more mischief?

WIFE: Noah, thou might have let me wit.
Early and late thou went thereout,
And ay at home thou let me sit 115
To look that nowhere were well about.
NOAH: Dame, thou hold me excused of it,
It was God's will without doubt.
WIFE: What, weens thou so for to go quit?
Nay, by my troth, thou gets a clout. 120

91 *wood* mad⠀⠀⠀*I . . . aghast* I fear⠀⠀⠀⠀94 you understand nothing⠀⠀⠀⠀97–8 In faith, you may as well let me go my way⠀⠀⠀⠀99 *We! Out! Harrow!* conventional exclamation of distress⠀⠀⠀*what cheer?* what's the matter?⠀⠀⠀⠀100 *for . . . need* on any account⠀⠀⠀102 For she does not seem to care about the peril she is in⠀⠀⠀103 *mend . . . cheer* cheer up⠀⠀⠀104 *without dread* undoubtedly⠀⠀⠀105 Alas that I should learn this information⠀⠀⠀106 A curse on you, you'll be the death of us all⠀⠀⠀107 *won* stay⠀⠀⠀⠀109–10 No, I have to go home because I have utensils to gather together 111–12 Woman, why are you behaving like this? To do us more harm?⠀⠀⠀⠀113 *wit* know⠀⠀⠀⠀116 To make sure that everything was all right nowhere (i.e. wasting time)⠀⠀⠀119 What, do you believe that you will get away with that?⠀⠀⠀120 *clout* blow

NOAH: I pray thee dame, be still.
   Thus God would have it wrought.
WIFE: Thou should have wit my will,
   If I would assent theretill,
   And Noah, for that same skill,   125
   This bargain shall be bought.

   Now at first I find and feel
   Where thou hast to the forest sought,
   Thou should have told me for our sele
   When we were to such bargain brought.   130
NOAH: Now dame, thou tharf not dread a deal,
   For to account it cost thee nought.
   A hundred winters, I wot well,
   Are went since I this work had wrought.
   And when I made ending,   135
   God gave me measure fair
   Of every-ilka thing;
   He bad that I should bring
   Of beasts and fowls young,
   Of ilka kind a pair.   140

WIFE: Nowe certes, and we should scape from scathe
   And so be saved as ye say here,
   My co-mothers and my cousins both,
   Them would I went with us in fere.
NOAH: To wend in the water it were wothe,   145
   Look in and look without were.
WIFE: Alas, my life me is full loath;
   I live over-long this lore to lere.
1 DAUGHTER: Dear mother, mend your mood,
   For we shall wend you with.   150

---

123 *wit* found out   124 *theretill* to it   125 *skill* cause   126 You will pay the penalty for these goings-on   127 *at first* for the first time   *feel* perceive 128 Why you have resorted to the forest   129 *sele* well-being   130 *bargain* undertaking   131 *tharf . . . deal* you need have no fear   132 For in financial terms it cost you nothing.   134 Have passed since I began to perform this task. 136 *measure fair* clear indication   137 Of every single thing   141 if we are to escape harm   143–4 I should like both my gossips and my relatives to accompany us   145 *wend* go   *wothe* dangerous   146 Come in without more ado   147–8 Alas my life is very burdensome to me, I have lived too long to receive this news   149 MS has *I Filia*—the three young women are, of course, Noah's sons' wives.

WIFE: My friends that I from yode
    Are over flowed with flood.
2 DAUGHTER: Now thank we God all good
    That us has granted grith.

3 DAUGHTER: Mother, of this work now would ye not ween,   155
    That all should worth to waters wan.
2 SON: Father, what may this marvel mean?
    Whereto made God middle-earth and man?
1 DAUGHTER: So selcouth sight was never none seen,
    Since first that God this world began.   160
NOAH: Wend and spear your doors bedene,
    For better counsel none I can.
    This sorrow is sent for sin,
    Therefore to God we pray
    That he our bale would blin.   165
3 SON: The king of all mankind
    Out of this woe us win,
    As thou art Lord, that may.

1 SON: Yea, lord, as thou let us be born
    In this great bale, some boot us bid.   170
NOAH: My sons, see ye midday and morn
    To these cattle take good heed;
    Keep them well with hay and corn;
    And women, fang these fowls and feed,
    So that they be not lightly lorn   175
    As long as we this life shall lead.
2 SON: Father, we are full fain
    Your bidding to fulfil.
    Nine months passed are plain
    Since we were put to pain.   180
3 SON: He that is most of main
    May mend it when he will.

151 *yode* went   154 *grith* protection   155 *ween* believe   156 That all
should be covered in dark water   158 *Whereto* To what end   159 *selcouth*
remarkable   161 Go and shut your doors immediately   162 *can* know
165 That he would put an end to our trouble   169–70 as you allowed us to be
born into these troubled circumstances, give us some help   171 *see* make sure
174 look after and feed these birds   175 *lightly lorn* carelessly lost   179 *plain*
fully   180 subjected to torment

NOAH: Oh bairns, it waxes clear about,
  That may ye see there where ye sit.
1 SON: Ay, lief father, look ye thereout,   185
  If that the water wane aught yet.
NOAH: That shall I do without doubt,
  Thereby the waning may we wit.
  Ah, Lord, to thee I lof and lout,
  The cateracts I trow be knit.   190
  Behold, my sons all three,
  The clouds are waxed clear.
2 SON: Ah, Lord of mercy free,
  Ay lofed might thou be.
NOAH: I shall assay the sea,   195
  How deep that it is here.

WIFE: Loved be that Lord that gives all grace,
  That kindly thus our care would keel.
NOAH: I shall cast lead and look the space,
  How deep the water is ilka deal.   200
  Fifteen cubits of height it has
  Over ilka hill fully to feal;
  But be well comforted in this case,
  It is waning, this wot I well.
  Therefore a fowl of flight   205
  Full soon shall I forth send,
  To seek if he have sight,
  Some land upon to light;
  Then may we wit full right
  When our mourning shall mend.   210

  Of all the fowls that men may find
  The raven is wight, and wise is he.
  Thou art full crabbed and all thy kind,
  Wend forth thy course I command thee,
  And warily wit, and hither thee wind   215

---

183 *waxes* grows   185 *lief* dear   186 begins to subside yet   189 *lof* offer
praises   *lout* bow   190 I believe the flood-gates of heaven are shut   193 *free*
gracious   194 *Ay lofed* Eternally praised   195–6 I shall sound the sea [to
discover] how deep it is here   198 Who graciously relieves our troubles thus
199 I shall put down a plumb and look for a while   200 *ilka deal* everywhere
202 *feal* cover   208 Of some land to alight on   210 plight shall be amended
212 *wight* bold   213 *crabbed* perverse   214 *Wend . . . course* Go your way
215 Cautiously explore, and come back here

If thou find either land or tree.
Nine months here have we been pined,
But when God will, better must be.

1 DAUGHTER: That Lord that lends us life   220
  To lere his laws in land,
  He made both man and wife,
  He help to stint our strife.

3 DAUGHTER: Our cares are keen as knife,
  God grant us good tidand.

1 SON: Father, this fowl is forth full long;   225
  Upon some land I trow he lend,
  His food there for to find and fang—
  That makes him be a failing friend.

NOAH: Now son, and if he so forth gang,
  Since he for all our wealth gan wend,   230
  Then be he for his works wrong
  Evermore waried without end.
  And certes, for to see
  When our sorrow shall cease,
  Another fowl full free   235
  Our messenger shall be;
  Thou dove, I command thee
  Our comfort to increase.

A faithful fowl to send art thou
Of all within these wones wide;   240
Wend forth I pray thee, for our prow,
And sadly seek on ilka side
If the floods be falling now,
That thou on the earth may bield and bide.
Bring us some tokening that we may trow   245
What tidings shall of us betide.

2 DAUGHTER: Good Lord, on us thou look,
  And cease our sorrow sere,

219 *lends* gives   220 To obey all his laws   222 May he help to bring our
troubles to an end   223 *keen* sharp   224 *tidand* news   225 *forth* away
226 *lend* stays   227 To find and partake of his food there   229 if he has gone
away in this manner   230 Since he went for the good of all of us   232 *waried*
accursed   238 To improve our circumstances   240 Above all within this
whole place   241 *prow* good   242 *sadly* earnestly   244 So that you may
remain and stay on the earth   245 *tokening* sign   *trow* know   246 What
will become of us   248 *sere* diverse

Since we all sin forsook
And to thy lore us took.   250
3 DAUGHTER: A twelve-month but twelve week
Have we been hovering here.

NOAH: Now bairns, we may be blithe and glad
And lof our Lord of heavens king;
My bird has done as I him bad,   255
An olive branch I see him bring.
Blessed be thou fowl, that never was fade,
That in thy force makes no failing;
More joy in heart never ere I had,
We mun be saved, now may we sing.   260
Come hither, my sons, in hie,
Our woe away is went,
I see here certainly
The hills of Armenie.
1 SON: Lofed be that Lord forthy   265
That us our lives has lent.

Then Noah and his sons should sing.

WIFE: From wreaks now we may win
Out of this woe that we in were;
But Noah, where are now all our kin
And company we knew before?   270
NOAH: Dame, all are drowned, let be thy din,
And soon they bought their sins sore.
Good living let us begin,
So that we grieve our God no more;
He was grieved in degree   275
And greatly moved in mind
For sin, as men may see:
Dum dixit 'Penitet me'.

250 And respected your teachings   252 *hovering* waiting   257 *fade* untrustworthy   258 Who in your strength has no failing   261 *in hie* quickly
264 *Armenie* Armenia   265–6 Therefore praised be that Lord who has granted us our lives   267–8 Now may we escape from vengeances and from the tribulations that we were in   271 be quiet   272 Straight away they paid severely for their sins   275 *in degree* duly   276 *moved in mind* troubled   278 'When he said, "I repent me" ' (Genesis 6: 7 'for it repenteth me that I have made them').

Full sore forthinking was he
That ever he made mankind.   280

That makes us now to toll and truss;
But sons, he said—I wot well when—
'*Arcum ponam in nubibus*',
He set his bow clearly to ken
As tokening between him and us,   285
In knowledge to all Christian men
That from this world were fined thus,
With water would he never waste it then.
Thus has God most of might
Set his sign full clear   290
Up in the air of height;
The rainbow it is right,
As men may see in sight
In seasons of the year.

2 SON: Sir, now since God our sovereign sire   295
Has set his sign thus in certain,
Then may we wit this world's empire
Shall evermore last, is not to lain.
NOAH: Nay son, that shall we not desire,
For and we do we work in vain;   300
For it shall once be wasted with fire,
And never worth to world again.
WIFE: Ah, sir, our hearts are sore
For these saws that ye say here,
That mischief must be more.   305
NOAH: Be not afraid therefore,
Ye shall not live then
By many hundred year.

1 SON: Father, how shall this life be led
Since none are in this world but we?   310

279 He was very deeply sorry   281 That makes us now heave and haul
283 Genesis 9: 13 'I do set my bow in the clouds'.   284 *ken* make known
287–8 That when this world were thus ended, he would never again destroy it with
water   291 *of height* on high   297–8 Then may we know that this world's
domain shall last for ever, and that should not be concealed   300 For if we do, we
labour under a misapprehension   301 *once* one day   302 And never become
the world again   304 *saws* words   306 *therefore* of that   307 You
shall not live that long

NOAH: Sons, with your wives ye shall be stead,
   And multiply your seed shall ye.
   Your bairns shall ilk one other wed
   And worship God in good degree;
   Beasts and fowls shall forth be bred,   315
   And so a world begin to be.
   Now travail shall ye taste
   To win you bread and wine,
   For all this world is waste;
   These beasts must be unbraced,   320
   And wend we hence in haste,
   In God's blessing and mine.

311 *stead* settled   312 *seed* offspring   313 *ilk one other* each one one of
the others'   317 Now you will know hard work   320 *unbraced* set free

THE HOSIERS

Moses and Pharaoh

The York *Moses and Pharaoh* dramatizes the main episodes in the epic narrative of Exodus 3–14, and includes several striking and ambitious scenes: God's appearance to Moses in the Burning Bush, the Ten Plagues which afflict the Egyptians, and the passage of the Israelites across the Red Sea, followed by the drowning of Pharaoh and his host who are in pursuit. The selection and treatment of some of the characters and incidents is unusual. The Pharaoh of the play is a conflation of two biblical Pharaohs, and the persecution of the infant Moses mentioned in lines 63–72 and 89–91 is an apocryphal element introduced by the dramatist in order to present Moses as a prefiguration of Christ in the *Slaughter of the Innocents* later in the cycle. At the centre of the play is a personal confrontation between Moses and Pharaoh; Aaron, who is prominent in the biblical version of the story, is absent. The scene therefore becomes notable for the way in which it looks forward to Christ's encounter with Satan in the *Harrowing of Hell*: Pharaoh and Satan share the same insolent tone and fondness for diabolical oaths, whilst Moses and Christ both have a calm and laconic confidence in the ability of divine power to overcome evil and release those in bondage.

Many of the play's unusual features derive from the dramatist's use of a contemporary source, the *Middle English Metrical Paraphrase of the Old Testament*, a long narrative poem written in the north of England around the turn of the fourteenth century. It is in the same metre as the Hosiers' play (abababab$_4$cdcd$_3$), and embodies legendary material about Moses which the dramatist used for the play.

The cast is quite large (there are ten speaking parts), and the staging must undoubtedly have been more complex than that of most plays in cycle. Several 'scenes' are called for: Pharaoh's court, where much of the action occurs; Sinai, where God appears to Moses; Goshen, where the Jews languish in slavery; and the Red Sea. One doubts whether a pageant wagon alone would have been adequate for the presentation, and it seems likely that parts of the action took place in the street. Special effects have a prominent role. God's appearance in the Burning Bush may have involved elaborate costuming or, conceivably, fireworks. Moses' rod-serpent is still a familiar conjuring trick, employing a series of hollow cylindrical sections threaded on a cord. The Red Sea in which Pharaoh and his host were drowned may have consisted of lengths of cloth manipulated by supernumeraries.

The Hosiers' play is probably among the older ones in the cycle. A *Moses and Pharaoh* play attributed to the guild is mentioned as early as 1403. There is a sombre echo of the times in lines 345–8, where the dramatist substituted 'great pestilence' for the last of the vengeances with which God afflicted the Egyptians, the death of the first-born (Exodus 12). By 'pestilence' the audience would have understood the bubonic plague, and 'the great pestilence' was a phrase commonly applied to its most terrible visitation, the Black Death of 1348–9.

PHARAOH: O peace, I bid that no man pass,
   But keep the course that I command,
   And take good heed to him that has
   Your life all wholly in his hand.
   King Pharaoh my father was,   5
   And led the lordship of this land;
   I am his heir as eld will as,
   Ever in his stead to stir and stand.
   All Egypt is mine own
   To lead after my law,   10
   I will my might be known
   And honoured as it owe.

   Therefore as king I command peace
   To all the people of this empire,
   That no man put him forth in press   15
   But that will do as we desire.
   And of your saws I rede you cease,
   And see to me, your sovereign sire,
   That most your comfort may increase
   And at my list lose life and lire.   20
1 COUNSELLOR: My lord, if any were
   That would not work your will,
   And we wist which they were,
   Full soon we should them spill.

PHARAOH: Throughout my kingdom would I ken,   25
   And can them thank that could me tell,
   If any were so waried then
   That would aught fand our force to fell.

---

6 *lordship* nobility   7 *as . . . as* as is appropriate with my coming of age   8 To occupy his place in every respect   12 *owe* ought [to be]   15 *put . . . press* assert himself   16 *But that* Unless he   17 *saws* talking   *rede* advise 18 *see* attend   20 *list* will   *lose* destroy   *lire* limb   21–2 My lord, if there were anybody who would not obey you   23 *wist* knew   24 *spill* destroy 25 *ken* seek   27 *waried* wicked   28 That they would attempt anything which might overthrow our power

2 COUNSELLOR: My lord, there are a manner of men
That muster great masteries them amell,   30
The Jews that won here in Goshen
And are named the children of Israel.
They multiply so fast
That soothly we suppose
They are like, and they last,   35
Your lordship for to lose.

PHARAOH: Why, devil, what gauds have they begun?
Are they of might to make affrays?
1 COUNSELLOR: Those felonious folk, sir, first was found
In King Pharaoh your father's days.   40
They come of Joseph, Jacob's son,
That was a prince worthy to praise,
And sithen in rest forth are they run,
Now are they like to lose our lays.
They shall confound us clean   45
But if they sooner cease.
PHARAOH: What devil ever may it mean
That they so fast increase?

2 COUNSELLOR: How they increase full well we ken,
As our elders before us found,   50
They were told but sixty and ten
When they entered into this land.
Sithen have they sojourned here in Goshen
Four hundred year, this we warrand,
Now are they numbered of mighty men   55
Well more than three hundred thousand,
Without wife and child
And herds that keep their fee.
PHARAOH: So might we be beguiled;
But certes, that shall not be,   60

29 *manner* certain type   30 Who behave in a high-handed fashion   31 *won* dwell   34 *soothly* truly   35 *like* likely   *and . . . last* if they continue to do so   36 *lordship* power   37 *gauds* deceitful tricks   38 *of might* sufficiently powerful   39 *felonious* wicked   43 And since then they have flourished undisturbed   44 *lays* way of life   45 *confound* destroy   *clean* completely   46 Unless they quickly stop   47 *What devil* What the devil   49 *ken* know   51 *told* numbered   53 *Sithen* Since   *sojourned* lived   54 *warrand* assert   56 *Well* Many   58 *herds* herdsmen   *fee* cattle   60 *certes* indeed

For with quantise we shall them quell,
That they shall no farrer spread.
1 COUNSELLOR: Lord, we have heard our fathers tell
How clerks, that full well could rede,
Said a man should wax them amell   65
That should fordo us and our deed.
PHARAOH: Fie on them, to the devil of hell!
Swilk destiny shall we not dread.
We shall make midwives to spill them,
When our Hebrews are born,   70
All that are man-kind, to kill them;
So shall they soon be lorn.

For of the other have I none awe.
Swilk bondage shall we to them bid:
To dike and delve, bear and draw,   75
And do all swilk unhonest deed.
Thus shall the lads behold law,
As losels ever their life to lead.
2 COUNSELLOR: Certes, lord, this is a subtle saw,
So shall the folk no farrer spread.   80
PHARAOH: Yea, help to hold them down,
That we no faintise find.
1 COUNSELLOR: Lord, we shall ever be boun
In bondage them to bind.

MOSES: Great God, that all this ground began,   85
And governs ever in good degree,
That made me, Moses, unto man,
And saved me sithen out of the sea—
King Pharaoh he commanded then
So that no sons should saved be,   90
Against his will away I won—
Thus has God showed his might in me.

---

61 *quantise* cunning   *quell* suppress   62 *farrer* further   64 *rede* prophesy
65 *wax . . . amell* rise up amongst them   66 *fordo* overthrow   *deed* doings
67 *Fie* A curse   68 *Swilk* Such   69 *spill* destroy   72 *lorn* eradicated
73 *the other* (the person referred to in ll. 65–6)   *none awe* no fear   74 *to
them bid* provide for them   75 To dig and delve, fetch and carry   76 *unhonest
deed* menial tasks   77 *lads* worthless persons   *behold law* be brought to abide
by the law   78 *losels* wretches   79 *saw* speech   82 *faintise* treachery
83 *boun* ready   85 *ground* world   86 *degree* order   88 *sithen* afterwards   90 *saved be* be spared   91 *won* escaped

Now am I here to keep,
Set under Sinai side,
The bishop Jethro's sheep,   95
So better boot to bide.

Ah, mercy, God, mickle is thy might,
What man may of thy marvels mean?
I see yonder a full selcouth sight
Whereof before no sign was seen.   100
A bush I see yonder burning bright
And the leaves last ay inlike green;
If it be work of worldly wight
I will go wit without ween.

GOD: Moses, come not too near,   105
But still in that stead dwell,
And take heed to me here,
And tent what I thee tell.

I am thy Lord, without lack,
To length thy life even as me list,   110
And the same God that sometimes spake
Unto thine elders, as they wist;
Both Abraham and Isaac
And Jacob, said I, should be blist
And multiplying, them to make,   115
So that their seed should not be missed.
And now King Pharaoh
Fouls their children full fast.
If I suffer him so
Their seed should soon be passed.   120

To make thee message have I meaned
To him that them so harmed has,
To warn him with words hend

93 *keep* tend   94 On the slope of Mt Sinai   96 *boot* fortune   *bide* await
97 *mickle* great   98 *mean* speak   99 *full selcouth* most amazing   102 *last*
. . . *green* still remain green   103 *worldly wight* earthly creature   104 *go* . . .
ween without doubt go and find out   106 *stead* place   *dwell* remain   108 *tent*
pay attention to   109 *without lack* undoubtedly   110 *length* prolong   *me list*
it pleases me   111 *sometime spake* once spoke   114 *blist* blessed   115 *make*
prosper   116 *seed* offspring   *missed* allowed to die out   118 Oppresses their
descendants most cruelly   119 *suffer . . . so* permit him to continue   120 *passed*
wiped out   121 *message* messenger   *meaned* formed the intention   123 *with*
. . . *hend* in moderate terms

So that he let my people pass,
That they to wilderness may wend   125
And worship me as whilom was.
And if he longer gar them lend
His song full soon shall be 'alas'.
MOSES: Ah, Lord, since, with thy leave,
That lineage loves me nought,   130
Gladly they would me grieve
And I slike bodeword brought.

Therefore, Lord, let some other frast
That has more force them for to fear.
GOD: Moses, be not abashed   135
My bidding boldly to bear.
If they with wrong aught would thee wrast,
Out of all woths I shall thee were.
MOSES: We, Lord, they will not to me trast
For all the oaths that I may swear.   140
To neven slike note of new
To folk of wicked will,
Without token true,
They will not take tent theretill.

GOD: And if they will not understand   145
Ne take heed how I have thee sent,
Before the king cast down thy wand
And it shall seem as a serpent.
Sithen take the tail in thy hand
And hardily up thou it hent.   150
In the first state as thou it found,
So shall it turn by mine intent.
Hide thy hand in thy barm
And as a leper's it shall be like,

---

125 *wend* go   126 *whilom* formerly   127 *gar . . . lend* should cause them to
remain   130 *lineage* nation   *nought* not at all   131 *grieve* injure   132 *slike*
bodeword such a message   133 *frast* try   134 *force . . . fear* power to intimidate
them   135 *abashed* afraid   137–8 If they should maliciously attempt to
thwart you, I shall protect you from all dangers   139 *We* expr. of consternation
to me trast trust me   141 To announce such a matter peremptorily   143 *token*
true clear signs of proof   144 *take . . . theretill* believe what they are told   146 *Ne*
Nor   147 *wand* rod   149 *Sithen* Then   150 And boldly pick it up
152 *by . . . intent* according to my will   153 *barm* garment covering the bosom
154–5 And it will appear to be leprous, then afterwards completely healed

Sithen whole without harm;   155
Thy signs shall be slike.

And if he will not suffer then
My people for to pass in peace,
I shall send vengeance nine or ten
To sue him sorer, ere I cease.   160
But the Jews that won in Goshen
Shall not be marked with that mes,
As long as they my laws will ken
Their comfort shall I ever increase.
MOSES: Ah, Lord, lofed be thy will   165
That makes thy folk so free,
I shall tell them until
As thou tells unto me.

But to the king, Lord, when I come
And he ask me what is thy name,   170
And I stand still then, deaf and dumb,
How shall I be without blame?
GOD: I say this: *ego sum qui sum*,
I am he that I am the same,
And if thou might not move ne mum   175
I shall thee save from sin and shame.
MOSES: I understand this thing
With all the might in me.
GOD: Be bold in my blessing,
Thy bield ay shall I be.   180

MOSES: Ah, Lord of life, lere me my lare,
That I these tales may truly tell.
Unto my friends now will I fare,
The chosen children of Israel,
To tell them comfort of their care,   185
And of their danger that they in dwell.

---

156 *slike* such   157 *suffer* permit   159 nine or ten revenges   160 *sue him sorer* pursue him more fiercely   162 *marked* afflicted   *mes* visitation   163 *ken* recognize   165 *lofed* praised   167 *them until* to them   172 How shall I escape censure?   173 *ego . . . sum* I am that I am   175 *move ne mum* speak nor whisper   177 *thing* matter   180 *bield* protection   *ay* always   181 *lere* teach   *lare* skill   185 To bring news of relief from their suffering   186 *of* from   *in dwell* are in

God maintain you and me evermore,
And mickle mirth be you amell.

1 YOUTH: Ah, Moses, master dear,
    Our mirth is all mourning,   190
    We are hard holden here
    As carls under the king.

2 YOUTH: Moses, we may mourn and min,
    There is no man us mirths mase;
    And since we come all of a kin,   195
    Ken us some comfort in this case.

MOSES: Be of your mourning blin,
    God will defend you of your foes.
    Out of this woe he will you win
    To please him in more plainer place.   200
    I shall carp to the king,
    And fand to make you free.

3 YOUTH: God send us good tiding,
    And always with you be.

MOSES: King Pharaoh, to me take tent.   205
PHARAOH: Why, what tidings can thou tell?
MOSES: From God of heaven thus am I sent
    To fetch his folk of Israel;
    To wilderness he would they went.
PHARAOH: Yah, wend thou to the devil of hell!   210
    I make no force how thou has meant,
    For in my danger shall they dwell.
    And, faitour, for thy sake,
    They shall be put to pine.
MOSES: Then will God vengeance take   215
    On thee and on all thine.

PHARAOH: Fie on thee, lad! Out of my land!
    Weens thou with wiles to lose our lay?

---

188 *you amell* amongst you   191 *hard holden* badly treated   192 *carls* slaves
193 *min* ponder   194 There is nobody to inspire us with joy   195 *come
. . . kin* belong to the same race   196 Comfort us in this predicament   197 Do
not grieve any longer   198 *of* from   199 *win* rescue   200 To do
his will in a more unconfined place   201 *carp* speak   202 *fand* attempt
203 *tiding* news   205 *take tent* pay attention   211 I think nothing of what
you have said   212 *danger* power   213 *faitour* liar   214 *put to pine*
punished   218 Do you believe you can destroy our power with trickery?

Whence is this warlock, with his wand,
That would thus win our folk away?   220
2 COUNSELLOR: It is Moses, we well warrand,
Against all Egypt is he ay.
Your father great fault in him found,
Now will he mar you if he may.
PHARAOH: Nay, nay, that dance is done,   225
That lurdan learnt over-late.
MOSES: God bids thee grant my boon,
And let me go my gate.

PHARAOH: Bids God me? False lurdan, thou lies!
What token told he, took thou tent?   230
MOSES: Yea sir, he said thou should despise
Both me and all his commandment.
In thy presence cast, on this wise,
My wand, he bad by his assent,
And that thou should thee well avise   235
How it should turn to a serpent.
And in his holy name
Here shall I lay it down:
Lo, sir, see here the same.
PHARAOH: Ah! Dog! The devil thee drown!   240

MOSES: He said that I should take the tail,
So for to prove his power plain,
And soon, he said, it should not fail
For to turn a wand again.
Lo, sir, behold.
PHARAOH: Hap ill-hail!   245
Now certes, this is a subtle swain,
But these boys shall bide here in our bail,
For all their gauds shall nought them gain;
But worse, both morn and noon,
Shall they fare for thy sake.   250

219 *Whence . . . warlock* Where has this wizard come from   220 *win* take   221 *we
. . . warrand* we confidently assert   224 *mar* destroy   225 *dance . . . done*
affair is over   226 *lurdan* scoundrel   *over-late* too late   227 *boon* request
228 *gate* way   230 *told* showed   *tent* note   233 *on . . . wise* in this manner
234 *bad . . . assent* commanded   235 *thee . . . avise* note carefully   242 *plain*
openly   245 *Hap ill-hail* A curse (on you)   246 *subtle swain* cunning fellow
247 *boys* knaves   *bide* remain   *bail* custody, captivity   248 *nought . . . gain*
be of no advantage to them   249 *both . . . noon* all the time   250 *for thy
sake* because of you

MOSES: God send some vengeaunce soon,
And on thy work take wrake.

1 EGYPTIAN: Alas, alas, this land is lorn,
On life we may no longer lend.
2 EGYPTIAN: So great mischief is made since morn   255
There may no medicine us amend.
1 COUNSELLOR: Sir king, we ban that we were born,
Our bliss is all with bales blend.
PHARAOH: Why cry you so, lads? List you scorn?
1 EGYPTIAN: Sir king, such care was never kenned.   260
Our water, that was ordained
To men and beasts' food,
Throughout all Egypt land
Is turned to red blood.

Full ugly and full ill is it   265
That was full fair and fresh before.
PHARAOH: This is great wonder for to wit,
Of all the works that ever were.
2 EGYPTIAN: Nay, lord, there is another yet
That suddenly sues us full sore: 270
For toads and frogs we may not flit,
Their venom loses less and more.
1 EGYPTIAN: Lord, great mises, both morn and noon
Bite us full bitterly,
And we hope all be done   275
By Moses, our enemy.

1 COUNSELLOR: Lord, whilst we with this meinie move
Mun never mirth be us among.
PHARAOH: Go say we shall no longer grieve—
But they shall never the titer gang.   280

252 *wrake* retribution   253 *lorn* ruined   254 We may no longer live
255–6 *Such great misfortune has happened since this morning that there is no remedy
for it*   257 *ban* curse   258 *Our happiness has been overtaken by disasters*
259 *List . . . scorn?* Do you mock?   260 *kenned* known   262 *food* sustenance
265 *ugly* horrible   *ill* unpleasant   267 *wit* discover   268 *works* hap-
penings   270 *sues . . . sore* afflicts us severely   271 *flit* move   272 *loses
. . . more* destroys everything   273 *mises* gnats   274 *bitterly* severely
275 *hope* believe   277 *with . . . move* associate with these people   278 We
shall never lead a tolerable life   279 *grieve* be vexed   280 *never . . . gang*
no more readily escape [*Aside*]

2 EGYPTIAN: Moses, my lord has granted leave
At lead thy folk to liking land,
So that we mend of our mischief.
MOSES: I wot full well these words are wrong;
That shall full soon be seen, 285
For hardily I him heet,
And he of malice mean
More marvels mun he meet.

1 EGYPTIAN: Lord, alas, for dole we die,
We dare not look out at no door. 290
PHARAOH: What devil ails you so to cry?
2 EGYPTIAN: We fare now worse than ever we fore.
Great lops, over all this land they fly,
That with biting make mickle blore.
1 EGYPTIAN: Lord, our beasts lie dead and dry 295
As well on midden as on moor—
Both ox, horse and ass
Fall dead down suddenly.
PHARAOH: Thereof no man harm has
Half so mickle as I. 300

2 COUNSELLOR: Yes, lord, poor men have mickle woe
To see their cattle be out cast.
The Jews in Goshen fare not so,
They have all liking in to last.
PHARAOH: Go say we give them leave to go 305
To time these perils be over-past—
But ere they flit over-far us fro
We shall gar fast them four so fast.
2 EGYPTIAN: Moses, my lord gives leave
Thy men for to remewe. 310
MOSES: He mun have more mischief
But if his tales be true.

282 *At* To   *liking land* the Promised Land   283 *mend . . . mischief* recover
from our misfortune   284 *wot* know   286–8 For confidently I promise
him, if he intends malice, he must endure more amazing things   289 *dole* misery
290 *no* any   292 *fore* fared   293 *lops* flies   294 *make . . . blore* cause
great lamentation   295 *dry* shrivelled   296 Both on dungheap and moor
299–300 Nobody is half so badly afflicted by that as I am   302 *out cast* destroyed
304 They continue to lead a pleasant life   306 *To* Until [the]   *be over-past*
are over   307–8 But before they depart too far from us, we shall cause them to
be bound four times as securely [*Aside*]   310 *remewe* lead away   311 *mun*
must   312 *But if* Unless

1 EGYPTIAN: We, lord, we may not lead this life.
PHARAOH: Why, is there grievance grown again?
2 EGYPTIAN: Such powder, lord, upon us drive 315
 That where it beats it makes a blain.
1 EGYPTIAN: Like mesels makes it man and wife.
 Sithen are they hurt with hail and rain;
 Our vines in mountains may not thrive,
 So are they thrust and thunder-slain. 320
PHARAOH: How do they in Goshen,
 The Jews, can ye aught say?
2 EGYPTIAN: This care nothing they ken,
 They feel no such affray.

PHARAOH: No? Devil! And sit they so in peace 325
 And we ilk day in doubt and dread?
1 EGYPTIAN: My lord, this care will ever increase
 Till Moses have leave them to lead.
1 COUNSELLOR: Lord, were they went, then would it cease,
 So should we save us and our seed, 330
 Else be we lorn—this is no lease.
PHARAOH: Let him do forth, the devil him speed!
 For his folk shall no far
 If he go welling wood.
2 COUNSELLOR: Then will it soon be war, 335
 Yet were it better they yode.

2 EGYPTIAN: We, lord, new harm is come to hand.
PHARAOH: No! Devil! Will it no better be?
1 EGYPTIAN: Wild worms are laid over all this land,
 They leave no fruit ne flower on tree; 340
 Against that storm may nothing stand.
2 EGYPTIAN: Lord there is more mischief think me,
 And three days has it been durand,

---

314 *grievance grown* misfortune come 315 *powder* ash *drive* rains down
316 *beats* strikes *blain* boil 317 It makes everybody look like lepers
318 *Sithen* Then 320 *thrust* beaten down *thunder-slain* destroyed by 'thunder'
(*sc.* lightning) 322 *aught* say anything [about them] 323 They are
unaffected by these disasters 324 *affray* misfortune 326 *ilk* every *doubt*
fear 329 *went* gone 330 *us ... seed* ourselves and our offspring 331 *lease*
lie 332 *do forth* continue *speed* prosper 333 *far* further [go] 334 *welling*
wood raving mad 335 *war* worse 336 *yode* went 337 *is ... hand*
has appeared 339 *Wild worms* Locusts 340 *ne* nor 341 *storm* assault
342 *think me* I believe 343 *durand* persisting

So murk that none might other see.
1 EGYPTIAN: My lord, great pestilence   345
Is like full long to last.
PHARAOH: Oh, comes that in our presence?
Then is our pride all passed.

2 EGYPTIAN: My lord, this vengeance lasts long,
And mun, till Moses have his boon.   350
1 COUNSELLOR: Lord, let them wend, else work we wrong,
It may not help to hover ne hone.
PHARAOH: Go say we grant them leave to gang,
In the devil way, since it bus be done—
For so may fall we shall them fang   355
And mar them ere tomorn at noon.
1 EGYPTIAN: Moses, my lord has said
Thou shall have passage plain.
MOSES: And to pass am I paid.
My friends, be now fain,   360

For at our will now shall we wend,
In land of liking for to lend.
1 YOUTH: King Pharaoh, that felonious fiend,
Will have great care from this be kenned,
Then will he shape him us to shend   365
And soon his host after us send.
MOSES: Be not afeared, God is your friend,
From all our foes he will us fend.
Therefore come forth with me;
Have done, and dread you nought.   370
2 YOUTH: My Lord, lofed mot thou be,
That us from bail has brought.

3 YOUTH: Such friendship never before we found,
But in this fare defaults may fall.

344 So dark that people cannot see one another   345 *pestilence* plague
346 Is likely to last for a long time   351 *work we wrong* we are making a great
mistake   352 *hover ne hone* hesitate nor delay   353 *gang* go   354 *devil
way* devil's name   *bus* must   355–6 For it may be that we shall recapture
them, and destroy them before noon tomorrow [*Aside*]   358 *passage plain* free-
dom to leave   359 *pass* go   *paid* pleased   360 *fain* glad   362 *land
of liking* the Promised Land   *lend* dwell   364 Will be enraged when this becomes
known   365 *shape him* prepare himself   *shend* destroy   368 *fend* protect
370 Be silent, and have no fear   371 *mot* may   374 But misfortunes may
befall [us] on this journey

The Red Sea is right near at hand,   375
  There bus us bide till we be thrall.
MOSES: I shall make us way with my wand,
  For God has said he save us shall;
  On either side the sea shall stand,
  Till we be went, right as a wall.   380
  Therefore have ye no dread,
  But fand ay God to please.
1 YOUTH: That Lord to land us lead,
  Now wend we all at ease.

1 EGYPTIAN: King Pharaoh, these folk are gone.   385
PHARAOH: How now, is there any noise of new?
2 EGYPTIAN: The Hebrews are went ilkon.
PHARAOH: How says thou that?
1 EGYPTIAN: These tales are true.
PHARAOH: Horse-harness tite, that they be ta'en,
  This riot radly shall them rue.   390
  We shall not cease ere they be slain,
  For to the sea we shall them sue.
  Do charge our chariots swithe,
  And freckly follow me.
2 EGYPTIAN: My lord, we are full blithe   395
  At your bidding to be.

2 COUNSELLOR: Lord, to your bidding we are boun
  Our bodies boldly for to bid
  We shall not bide, but ding them down
  Till all be dead, without dread.   400
PHARAOH: Heave up your hearts ay to Mahound,
  He will be near us in our need.
  Out! Ay harrow! Devil, I drown!
1 EGYPTIAN: Alas, we die for all our deed.

376 There must we wait until we are recaptured   378 *save us shall* will preserve
us   380 *right as* just like   381 *have . . . dread* do not be afraid   382 *fand
ay* always strive   386 *noise of new* news   387 *went ilkon* all gone   389 *tite*
quickly   *ta'en* recaptured   390 They will soon repent this outrage   392 *sue*
pursue   393 *charge* load   *swithe* quickly   394 *freckly* swiftly   395 *blithe*
glad   398 *bodies* selves   *bid* offer   399 *ding* strike   400 *without dread*
without a doubt   401 *Mahound* Muhammad (*intended diabolically*)   403 *Out . . .
harrow* expressions of consternation   404 *deed* doings

1 YOUTH: Now are we won from woe, 405
  And saved out of the sea,
  Cantemus domino,
  To God a song sing we.

405 *won* escaped   407 'Let us sing unto the Lord' (Exodus 15: 1)

THE PEWTERERS AND FOUNDERS

Joseph's Trouble about Mary

The substance of *Joseph's Trouble* derives not primarily from the Gospels but from the apocryphal writings associated with them, notably the narratives known as the *Protevangelium* and the Gospel of the Pseudo-Matthew. The dramatist interpreted the legends he found there partly in terms of contemporary *mal marié* and anti-feminist literature, particularly secular adultery farces and fabliaux of the type celebrated by Chaucer in the *Miller's Tale*, where an elderly carpenter is cuckolded by his young wife. Although the comic potential of an apparently similar situation is at first exploited in the York play, the piece is nevertheless thematically linked on a doctrinal level with other episodes and characters in the cycle. Joseph's initial view of Mary looks back to aspects of the presentation of Eve and to Noah's wife, and the symbolic resonances of their disobedience, but much in the play turns on the irony that Mary is the second Eve through whose meek obedience the pattern of the Fall is to be reversed.

Joseph's serious function is that of the 'natural man', whose physical decay is an extension of his fallen condition, and with whom the audience can sympathize in his struggle to comprehend the divine mystery of the virgin birth. In his opening monologue and subsequent questioning of Mary and her maidens, he is presented by turns as pathetic, comic, and aggressive. None the less, however farcical his role becomes, the laughter is not allowed to touch Mary herself. She remains benign, aloof, and theologically exact, though this does not prevent a brief but very human reconciliation scene at the end of the play.

Apart from a few unclassifiable fragments of verse, there are two stanza-forms found in the play. Lines 79–166 are in the same eleven-line stanza as the *Fall of Man*, while most of the rest is in an equally complicated ten-line form (abab₄ccbccb₃) not found elsewhere in the cycle. Two locations for the action seem to be required: Mary's dwelling, which is likely to have occupied the pageant-wagon, and the wild place where Joseph wanders and encounters the angel. These parts of the action may have been presented in the street. The guilds who brought forth *Joseph's Trouble* had in common the fact that they were primarily makers of metal domestic utensils, such as kettles, pans, and pewter mugs and dishes.

JOSEPH: Of great mourning may I me mean,
    And walk full wearily by this way,

---

1 I may speak of great grief

For now then wend I best have been
At ease and rest by reason ay.
For I am of great eld,   5
Weak and all unwield,
As ilk man see it may;
I may neither busk ne bield
But either in frith or field;
For shame what shall I say,   10

That thus-gates now on mine old days
Have wedded a young wench to my wife,
And may not well trine over two straws?
Now Lord, how long shall I lead this life?
My bones are heavy as lead   15
And may not stand in stead,
As kenned it is full rife.
Now Lord, thou me wis and rede
Or soon me drive to dead,
Thou may best stint this strife.   20

For bitterly then may I ban
The way I in the temple went,
It was to me a bad bargain,
For ruth I may it ay repent.
For therein was ordained   25
Unwedded men should stand,
All sembled at assent,
And ilkone a dry wand
On height held in his hand,
And I ne wist what it meant.   30

Among all others one bore I;
It flourished fair, and flowers on spread,

3–4 For now it seems to me that the best [of my life] is past, and as was reasonable, always in ease and rest   5 *eld* age   6 *unwield* impotent, feeble   7 *ilk* each   8 *busk* move quickly   *bield* remain   9 *But either* Except   *frith* wood   11 *thus-gates* in this way   *on* in   13 And can not step properly over two straws   16 *in stead* in [this] place   17 *kenned* known   *rife* everywhere   18 *wis* guide   *rede* advise   19 *me drive to dead* impel me towards death   20 *stint this strife* bring an end to this trouble   21 *ban* curse   23 *bargain* undertaking   24 *ruth* sorrow   *ay* for ever   27 All assembled at an appointed time and place   28–9 And each one held a dead stick on high in his hand   30 *ne wist* did not understand

And they said to me forthy
That with a wife I should be wed.
The bargain I made there,   35
That rues me now full sore,
So am I straitly stead.
Now casts it me in care,
For well I might evermore
Anlepi life have led.   40

Her works me works my wangs to wet;
I am beguiled—how, wot I not.
My young wife is with child full great,
That makes me now sorrow unsought.
That reproof near has slain me,   45
Forthy if any man frayne me
How this thing might be wrought,
To gab if I would pain me,
The law stands hard again me:
To death I mun be brought.   50

And loath methinketh, on the other side,
My wife with any man to defame,
And whether of these two that I bide
I mun not scape without shame.
The child certes is not mine;   55
That reproof does me pine
And gars me flee from home.
My life if I should tine,
She is a clean virgin
For me, without blame.   60

But well I wot through prophecy
A maiden clean should bear a child,
But it is not she, sikerly,

---

33 *forthy* therefore   36 Now that is a great source of regret to me   37 *straitly
stead* sorely tried   40 *Anlepi* Solitary   41 Her activities cause me to wet
my cheeks   42 *wot* know   44 That now brings me unlooked-for sorrow
45 *reproof* disgrace   46 *frayne* enquire of   48 If I bothered to prevaricate
49 *again* against   50 *mun* must   51 And on the other hand, I am loath
53 And whichever of these two I endure   54 *scape . . . shame* avoid disgrace
55 *certes* certainly   56 *does me pine* torments me   57 *gars* makes   58 If
I should lose my life (i.e. I stake my life on it)   60 *For me* As far as I am
concerned   63 *sikerly* truly

Forthy I wot I am beguiled.
And why ne would some young man take her?   65
For certes I think over-go her
Into some woods wild,
Thus think I to steal from her.
God shield these wild beasts slay her,
She is so meek and mild.   70

Of my wending will I none warn,
Nevertheless it is mine intent
To ask her who got her that bairn,
Yet would I wit fain ere I went.

All hail, God be herein.   75
1 MAIDEN: Welcome, by God's dear might.
JOSEPH: Where is that young virgin
     Mary, my bird so bright?

1 MAIDEN: Certes Joseph, ye shall understand
     That she is not full far you fro,   80
     She sits at her book full fast prayand
     For you and us, and for all tho
     That aught has need.
     But for to tell her will I go
     Of your coming, without dread.   85
     Have done and rise up, dame,
     And to me take good heed—
     Joseph, he is come home.
MARY: Welcome, as God me speed.

Dreadless to me he is full dear;   90
Joseph my spouse, welcome are ye.
JOSEPH: Gramercy Mary, say what cheer,
     Tell me the sooth, how is't with thee?
     Who has been there?
     Thy womb is waxed great, think me,   95

65 *ne would* would not   66 Indeed I think I shall pass her by   69 God forbid   71 *wending* departure   74 I should still like to know that before I went   75 Greetings, God be with you here   80 That she is not very far away from you   81 *full fast prayand* very earnestly praying   82 *tho* those   83 Who have any need   85 *dread* doubt   86 Stop what you are doing and get up, lady   87 *take good heed* pay attention   90 *Dreadless* Undoubtedly   92 Thank you, Mary; tell me, how are you?   93 *sooth* truth

Thou art with bairn, alas for care.
Ah, maidens, woe worth you,
That let her lere such lore.
2 MAIDEN: Joseph, ye shall not trow
In her no feeble fare.   100

JOSEPH: Trow it not harm? Lief wench, do way!
Her sides show she is with child.
Whose is't Mary?
MARY: Sir, God's and yours.
JOSEPH: Nay, nay,
Now wot I well I am beguiled,
And reason why?   105
With me fleshly was thou never filed,
And I forsake it here forthy.
Say, maidens, how is this?
Tell me the sooth, rede I;
And but ye do, iwis,   110
The bargain shall ye aby.

2 MAIDEN: If ye threat as fast as ye can,
There is nought to say theretill,
For truly here came never no man
To wait the body with none ill   115
Of this sweet wight,
For we have dwelt ay with her still,
And was never from her day nor night.
Her keepers have we been
And she ay in our sight,   120
Come here no man between
To touch that bird so bright.

1 MAIDEN: No, here came no man in these wones
And that ever witness will we,

---

96 *bairn* child   *care* woe   97 shame on you   98 Who allowed her to
learn such conduct   99–100 Joseph, you shall not believe such poor behaviour
of her   101 Believe she is innocent? Dear girl, enough of this!   102 *sides* i.e.
body   105 And for what reason   106 You were never physically violated by me
107 *forsake* reject   108 Tell me, maidens, how this came about?   110–11 Unless
you do, indeed, you will pay the penalty for this state of affairs   112–13 However
earnestly you threaten, there is nothing to say [of relevance] to this   115–16 To
harm the body of this sweet creature with any evil deed   117 *still* all the time
121 *between* in the meantime   123 *these wones* this place

Save an angel ilka day once, 125
With bodily food her fed has he;
Other came none.
Wherefore we ne wot how it should be
But through the Holy Ghost alone.
For truly we trow this, 130
His grace with her is gone,
For she wrought never no miss,
We witness everilkone.

JOSEPH: Then see I well your meaning is
The angel has made her with child. 135
Nay, some man in angel's likeness
With somekin gaud has her beguiled,
And that trow I.
Forthy needs not such words wild
At carp to me deceivingly. 140
We, why gab ye me so
And feign swilk fantasy?
Alas, me is full woe,
For dole why ne might I die?

To me this is a careful case; 145
Reckless I rave, reft is my rede.
I dare look no man in the face,
Derfly for dole why ne were I dead;
Me loathes my life.
In temple and in other stead 150
Ilk man to hething will me drive.
Was never wight so woe,
For ruth I all to-rive;
Alas, why wrought thou so
Mary, my wedded wife? 155

---

125 *ilka* each   127 No one else came   131 His grace goes with her   132 For she never did anything amiss   133 *everilkone* each one [of us]   137 *somekin* some kind of   *gaud* deceitful trick   139 Therefore such wild suggestions are not necessary   140 *At carp* To tell   141 *We* Go on (conventional expression of derision)   *gab* lie to   142 *swilk* such   144 *dole* sorrow   145 *careful case* woeful circumstance   146 I rave to no avail, my wits are taken away   148 *Derfly* Wretchedly   149 *Me loathes* I hate   150 *stead* place   151 will hold me up for scorn   153 I am broken down completely by sorrow

MARY: To my witness great God I call,
  That in mind wrought never no miss.
JOSEPH: Whose is the child thou art withal?
MARY: Yours sir, and the king's of bliss.
JOSEPH: Yea, and how then?   160
  Nay, selcouth tidings then is this,
  Excuse them well these women can.
  But Mary, all that see thee
  May wit thy works are wan,
  Thy womb always it wrays thee   165
  That thou has met with man.

  Whose is it, as fair mote thee befall?
MARY: Sir, it is yours and God's will.
JOSEPH: Nay, I ne have nought ado withal—
  Name it no more to me, be still!   170
  Thou wot as well as I,
  That we two sam fleshly
  Wrought never swilk works with ill.
  Look thou did no folly
  Before me privily   175
  Thy fair maidenhead to spill.

  But who is the father? Tell me his name.
MARY: None but yourself.
JOSEPH: Let be, for shame.
  I did it never; thou dotest dame, by books and bells!
  Full sackless should I bear this blame after thou tells,   180
  For I wrought never in word nor deed
  Thing that should mar thy maidenhead,
  To touch me till.

157 I who never thought to do anything wrong   158 *withal* therewith, with
161 *selcouth tidings* amazing news   162 *them* themselves   164 Can perceive your behaviour is wicked   165 *wrays* betrays   166 *met* had inter-
course   167 as you hope to prosper   169 No, I have nothing to do with it
170 *Name* Mention   172–3 That we two together never did such evil things
physically   174 *Look* Be sure   175 Behind my back, secretly   176 *spill*
violate   179 you speak foolishly, woman, by book and bell (articles of exorcism)
180 According to you, I must take the blame for this even though I am innocent
182 *mar* spoil   183 As far as I was concerned

For of slike note were little need,
Yet for mine own I would it feed,   185
Might all be still;

Therefore the father tell me, Mary.
MARY: But God and you, I know right none.
JOSEPH: Ah, slike saws make me full sorry,
With great mourning to make my moan.   190
Therefore be not so bold,
That no slike tales be told,
But hold thee still as stone.
Thou art young and I am old,
Slike works if I do would,   195
These games from me are gone.

Therefore, tell me in privity,
Whose is the child thou art with now?
Certes, there shall none wit but we,
I dread the law as well as thou.   200
MARY: Now great God of his might
That all may dress and dight,
Meekly to thee I bow.
Rue on this weary wight,
That in his heart might light   205
The sooth to ken and trow.

JOSEPH: Who had thy maidenhead Mary? Has thou aught
      mind?
MARY: Forsooth, I am a maiden clean.
JOSEPH: Nay, thou speaks now against kind,
Slike thing might never no man of mean.   210
A maiden to be with child?
These works from thee are wild,
She is not born I ween.

184–6 There is no need for such difficulty as this, for I would bring it [the child] up
as my own, for the sake of peace   188 *But* Except   *right none* none at all
189 *slike saws* such words   193 *hold thee still* keep quiet   195–6 Even if I
were inclined, I am past doing such things   197 *privity* confidence   199 *none
wit* no one know   202 *dress* ordain   *dight* accomplish   204 *Rue* Have
pity   205 *light* alight   207 *aught mind* any recollection   209 *kind*
nature   210 Such a thing no man could ever assert   212 What you say is
mad   213 *ween* believe

MARY: Joseph, ye are beguiled,
    With sin was I never filed,   215
    God's sand is on me seen.

JOSEPH: God's sand? Yah, Mary, God help!
    But certes that child was never ours two.
    But woman-kind if them list help,
    Yet would they no man wist their woe.   220
MARY: Certes it is God's sand

    .   .   .   .   .

    That shall I never go fro
JOSEPH: Yah, Mary, draw thine onde,
    For further yet will I fond,
    I trow not it be so.   225

    The sooth from me if that thou lain,
    The child-bearing may thou not hide;
    But sit still here till I come again,
    Me bus an errand here beside.
MARY: Now great God he you wis,   230
    And mend you of your miss
    Of me, what so betide.
    As he is king of bliss,
    Send you some sand of this,
    In truth that ye might bide.   235

JOSEPH: Now Lord God that all thing may
    At thine own will both do and dress,
    Wis me now some ready way
    To walk here in this wilderness.
    But ere I pass this hill,   240
    Do with me what God will,
    Either more or less,
    Here bus me bide full still
    Till I have slept my fill,
    My heart so heavy it is.   245

---

215 *filed* besmirched   216 God's dispensation in me is seen   219–20 But if women want help, they would still have no man understand their problem.
221+ *Line missing in MS*   222 I shall never deny that   223 draw your breath (i.e. be quiet)   224 *fond* enquire   226 *lain* conceal   229 I have to attend to an errand near by   231 And amend your misapprehension   232 whatever happens   234 [May he] send you some proof of this   238 Inform me now of some easy way   240 *ere* before   243 Here I must rest

ANGEL: Waken, Joseph, and take better keep
　　To Mary, that is thy fellow fast.
JOSEPH: Ah, I am full weary, lief, let me sleep,
　　Forwandered and walked in this forest.
ANGEL: Rise up, and sleep no more,　　　　　　　　　250
　　Thou makest her heart full sore
　　That loves thee alther best.
JOSEPH: We, now is this a ferly fare
　　For to be caught both here and there,
　　And nowhere may have rest.　　　　　　　　　　255

　　Say, what art thou? Tell me this thing.
ANGEL: I, Gabriel, God's angel full even
　　That has taken Mary to my keeping,
　　And sent is thee to say with steven
　　In leal wedlock thou lead thee.　　　　　　　　260
　　Leave her not, I forbid thee,
　　Ne sin of her thou neven,
　　But to her fast thou speed thee
　　And of her nought thou dread thee,
　　It is God's sand of heaven.　　　　　　　　　　265

　　The child that shall be born of her,
　　It is conceived of the Holy Ghost.
　　All joy and bliss then shall be after,
　　And to all mankind now alther most.
　　Jesus his name thou call,　　　　　　　　　　270
　　For slike hap shall him fall
　　As thou shall see in haste.
　　His people save he shall
　　Of evils and angrice all,
　　That they are now embraced.　　　　　　　　　275

JOSEPH: And is this sooth, angel, thou says?
ANGEL: Yea, and this to token right:

246 pay more attention　　　　247 who is your faithful mate　　　　248 *lief* sir
249 *Forwandered* Weary with wandering　*walked* exhausted with walking　　252 *alther best* best of all　　　253 Well, now this is an extraordinary thing　　254 *caught* pursued　　　257 *full even* truth to tell　　　258 *keeping* care　　259–60 I am sent to bring you a command to keep yourself in loyal wedlock　　262 *neven* mention 264 And doubt her no longer　　　265 *sand of* message from　　　269 *alther most* most of all　　271 *hap* fortune　　*fall* befall　　272 *in haste* soon　　274 *Of* From *angrice* tribulations　　　275 In which they are now entangled　　277 Yes, and take this as a true sign

Wend forth to Mary thy wife always,
Bring her to Bethlehem this ilk night.
There shall a child born be,   280
God's son of heaven is he
And man ay most of might.
JOSEPH: Now, Lord God, full well is me
That ever that I this sight should see,
I was never ere so light.   285

For for I would have her thus refused,
And sackless blame that ay was clear;
Me bus pray her hold me excused,
As some men does with full good cheer.
Say Mary, wife, how fares thou?   290
MARY: The better, sir, for you.
Why stand ye there? Come near.
JOSEPH: My back fain would I bow
And ask forgiveness now,
Wist I thou would me hear.   295

MARY: Forgiveness sir? Let be, for shame,
Slike words should all good women lack.
JOSEPH: Yea, Mary, I am to blame
For words long-ere I to thee spake.
But gather sam now all our gear,   300
Slike poor weed as we wear,
And prick them in a pack.
To Bethlehem bus me it bear,
For little thing will women dere;
Help up now on my back.   305

278 *wife always* faithful wife   279 *ilk* very   283 I am very glad   285 *light*
light-hearted   286–8 For I would have thus condemned her, and blamed the
innocent who was always pure. I must beg her to fogive me   291 *for you* for
seeing you   293 *fain* gladly   295 If I thought you would be prepared to
hear me out   297 *lack* do without   299 *long-ere* some time ago   300–5 But
now gather together all our possessions, such poor clothes as we wear, and fasten them
in a pack. To Bethlehem I must carry it, for women are vexed by little things. Help me
up with it.

THE TILETHATCHERS

The Nativity

The moment of the Incarnation, of God becoming man, was of central importance in the mystery cycles because it marked the beginning of the movement
towards redemption by means of Christ's atonement for the sin of Adam. The
version of the event in the York cycle is conspicuous for a tranquil beauty and
lyrical simplicity of the kind often found in the most moving medieval paintings
of the Nativity. Though it is one of the shortest plays in the cycle, requiring
only a cast of two and a simple set—Joseph and Mary, the ruined stable—it
nevertheless reveals on closer examination and in performance a number of
subtle poetic and dramatic effects. The difficult episode of the birth itself is
managed on stage by means of the Virgin kneeling in prayer to God (lines
48–9), then rising and parting her cloak to reveal the child before her—
a surprising and enchanting moment for the audience, but also an important
one thematically, as the birth is seen to be serene and painless, unlike all
others since the Fall. For this and several other features the dramatist was
indebted to an influential meditative account of the Nativity, the *Revelations* of
St Bridget (*c.*1400), as J. W. Robinson has shown in an illuminating commentary on the play.

The simplicity of the seven-line stanza, abab$_4$c$_2$b$_4$c$_2$, conceals a variety of
effects. For example, though the aged Joseph's touching speech at the beginning is primarily motivated by his solicitude for Mary (and likewise his
subsequent ironical errand for a candle and firewood), it enables the dramatist
to initiate motifs and images which run throughout the play. Jesus brings
light, warmth, and the promise of redemption to the dark, cold, and ruined
postlapsarian world into which he is born. Some of the imagery recalls the
chiaroscuro effects first evoked in the *Fall of the Angels*, and adumbrates those
to come in the *Harrowing of Hell*. Links with other plays in the cycle are the
formal 'Hail' lyrics delivered by Joseph and Mary over the child, which anticipate those at the end of the *Entry into Jerusalem* and in *Herod and The Magi*;
they are later repeated in malevolent parody by the torturers in the play of
Christ's second appearance before Pilate.

In line 18 the dramatist probably intended to draw the attention of the
audience to the craft of the Tilethatchers, who roofed buildings, and who
would presumably have attended to this feature of their pageant-wagon. The
broken roof may later have had a function in the play, letting the light of the
star shine in to mingle with that radiating from the child (lines 92–8), as is
the case in some early paintings of the scene.

JOSEPH: All-wielding God in trinity,
    I pray thee, Lord, for thy great might,
    Unto thy simple servant see,
    Here in this place where we are pight,
    Ourselves alone.   5
    Lord, grant us good harbour this night
    Within this wone.

    For we have sought both up and down
    Through diverse streets in this city,
    So mickle people are come to town   10
    That we can nowhere harboured be,
    There is slike press;
    Forsooth, I can no succour see,
    But bield us with these beasts.

    And if we here all night abide   15
    We shall be stormed in this stead,
    The walls are down on ilka side,
    The roof is raved above our head,
    As have I ro;
    Say Mary, daughter, what is thy rede,   20
    How shall we do?

    For in great need now are we stead,
    As thou thyself the sooth may see,
    For here is neither cloth ne bed,
    And we are weak and all weary   25
    And fain would rest.
    Now gracious God, for thy mercy,
    Wis us the best.

MARY: God will us wis, full well wit ye;
    Therefore, Joseph, be of good cheer,   30
    For in this place born will he be

---

3 *simple* humble   *see* pay heed   4 *pight* situated   6 *harbour* shelter
7 *wone* place   10 *mickle* many   11 *harboured* lodged   12 *slike press*
such a crowd   13–14 Truly, I can see no alternative but to shelter with these
animals   16 *stormed* exposed to the elements   *stead* place   17 *ilka* each
18 *raved* torn open   19 As I hope to have peace   20 *daughter* dear wife
rede counsel   22 *stead* placed   23 *sooth* truth   24 *cloth* bedclothes   *ne* nor
26 *fain* gladly   27 *for* through   28 Show us what is best to do   29 *wis*
guide   *wit* know

That shall us save from sorrows sere,
Both even and morn.
Sir, wit ye well the time is near
He will be born.   35

JOSEPH: Then behoves us bide here still,
    Here in this same place all this night.
MARY: Yea, sir, forsooth it is God's will.
JOSEPH: Then would I fain we had some light,
    What so befall.   40
It waxes right murk unto my sight,
    And cold withal.

I will go get us light forthy,
    And fuel fand with me to bring.
MARY: All-wielding God you govern and gy,   45
    As he is sovereign of all thing
For his great might,
    And lend me grace to his lofing
That I me dight.

Now in my soul great joy have I,   50
I am all clad in comfort clear,
Now will be born of my body
Both God and man together in fere,
    Blessed mote he be.
Jesu, my son that is so dear,   55
    Now born is he.

Hail, my Lord God, hail, prince of peace,
Hail, my father, and hail my son;
Hail, sovereign segge all sins to cease,
Hail, God and man in earth to won.   60
Hail, through whose might
All this world was first begun,
    Murkness and light.

---

32 *sere* manifold   33 All the time   36 *bide* remain   38 *forsooth* truly
39 *fain* be glad that   40 Whatever happens   41-2 It seems to me to be
growing very dark, and cold, too   43 *forthy* therefore   44 *fand* try   45 *gy*
guide   48-9 And bestow grace upon me, so that I might devote myself to his
praise   51 My being is suffused with serene bliss   53 *fere* company   54 *mote*
may   59 Hail, king, who will put an end to all sins   60 *won* dwell   63 *Murk-*
ness Darkness

Son, as I am simple subject of thine,
Vouchsafe, sweet son I pray thee,   65
That I might thee take in these arms of mine
And in this poor weed to array thee.
Grant me thy bliss,
As I am thy mother chosen to be
In soothfastness.   70

JOSEPH: Ah, Lord God, what the weather is cold,
The fellest freeze that ever I feeled.
I pray God help them that are old
And namely them that are unwield,
So may I say.   75
Now, good God, thou be my bield
As thou best may.

Ah, Lord God, what light is this
That comes shining thus suddenly?
I cannot say, as have I bliss.   80
When I come home unto Mary
Then shall I speer.
Ah, hered be God, for now come I.
MARY: Ye are welcome, sir.

JOSEPH: Say Mary, daughter, what cheer with thee?   85
MARY: Right good, Joseph, as has been ay.
JOSEPH: Oh, Mary, what sweet thing is that on thy knee?
MARY: It is my son, the sooth to say,
That is so good.
JOSEPH: Well is me I bode this day   90
To see this food.

Me marvels mickle of this light
That thusgates shines in this place;
Forsooth, it is a selcouth sight.

---

65 *Vouchsafe* Grant   67 *weed* garment   *array* dress   70 *soothfastness* truth
71 *what . . . cold* how cold it is   72 The keenest frost I have ever felt   74 *namely*
particularly   *unwield* infirm   76 *bield* protection   80 *as . . . bliss* as I
hope to be saved   82 *speer* enquire   83 *hered* praised   85 *what . . .*
thee? how are you?   86 *as . . . ay* and have always been   90–1 I am glad I lived
long enough to see this child   92 I am utterly amazed by this light   93 *thusgates*
in this way   94 *selcouth* marvellous

MARY: This has he ordained of his grace, 95
　　My son so young,
　　A star to be shining a space
　　At his bearing.

For Balaam told full long before
How that a star should rise full high, 100
And of a maiden should be born
A son that shall our saving be
From cares keen.
Forsooth, it is my son so free
By whom Balaam gan mean. 105

JOSEPH: Now welcome, flower fairest of hue,
　　I shall thee mensk with main and might.
　　Hail, my maker, hail Christ Jesu,
　　Hail, royal king, root of all right,
　　Hail, saviour. 110
　　Hail, my Lord, leamer of light,
　　Hail, blessed flower.

MARY: Now, Lord that all this world shall win,
　　To thee, my son, is that I say,
　　Here is no bed to lay thee in. 115
　　Therefore, my dear son, I thee pray,
　　Since it is so,
　　Here in this crib I might thee lay
　　Between these beasts two.

And I shall hap thee, mine own dear child, 120
With such clothes as we have here.
JOSEPH: Oh, Mary, behold these beasts mild,
　　They make lofing in their manner
　　As they were men.
　　Forsooth, it seems well by their cheer 125
　　Their Lord they ken.

---

95 *of* through　　　97 *a space* for a time　　　98 *bearing* birth　　　102 *saving*
salvation　　　103 *keen* bitter　　　104 *free* gracious　　　105 To whom Balaam
referred　　　107 *mensk* worship　　　*main* strength　　　111 *leamer . . . light* radiant
one　　　113 *win* redeem　　　120 *hap* wrap　　　122 *beasts mild* tender creatures
123 *make lofing* offer praise　　　125 *cheer* demeanour　　　126 *ken* know

MARY: Their Lord they ken, that wot I well,
   They worship him with might and main;
   The weather is cold, as ye may feel,
   To hold him warm they are full fain   130
   With their warm breath,
   And onde on him, is not to lain,
   To warm him with.

   Oh, now sleeps my son, blessed mote he be,
   And lies full warm these beasts between.   135
JOSEPH: Oh, now is fulfilled, forsooth I see,
   That Habbakuk in mind gan mean
   And preached by prophecy.
   He said our saviour shall be seen
   Between beasts lie,   140

   And now I see the same in sight.
MARY: Yea, sir, forsooth the same is he.
JOSEPH: Honour and worship both day and night,
   Ay-lasting Lord, be done to thee
   Always, as is worthy;   145
   And Lord, to thy service I oblige me
   With all mine heart, wholly.

MARY: Thou merciful maker, most mighty,
   My God, my Lord, my son so free,
   Thy handmaiden forsooth am I,   150
   And to thy service I oblige me,
   With all mine heart entire.
   Thy blessing, beseech I thee,
   Thou grant us all in fere.

127 *wot* know   130 They are anxious to keep him warm   132 *onde* breathe
is . . . lain clearly   133 Thereby to warm him   137 *in . . . mean* made note
of   140 To lie between beasts   141 *in sight* clearly   146 *oblige me*
dedicate myself   154 *in fere* together

THE MASONS; THE GOLDSMITHS

Herod and The Magi

The staging of *Herod* and *The Magi* was unusual, in that it appears to have involved the pageant-wagons and actors of two guilds simultaneously at the same station. The Masons presented Herod and his court on a 'Jerusalem' pageant-wagon, whilst the Goldsmiths provided 'Bethlehem' and the Holy Family on another. The Three Kings, who were also found by the Goldsmiths, moved between the two locations in the street, probably on horseback. Separate texts were registered in the manuscript for the two guilds, including a passage in duplicate (lines 130–272), the scene involving both the Masons' and the Goldsmiths' actors, where the Three Kings come to Herod's court. The bulk of the play is in the twelve-line stanza, $ababab ab_4 cdcd_3$, also found in several other plays in this selection. The opening scene at Herod's court is in an assortment of stanzas, cast in the long alliterative line, and reminiscent in style of the 'York Realist', whose work is found in the Passion section of the cycle.

The unusual manner of staging contrasts the noisy spectacle of Herod's court with, on the one hand, the quiet faith, learning, and ceremony of the Three Kings, and, on the other, the lyrical simplicity of the Bethlehem stable. Herod, who voices his extravagant belief in his omnipotence in opening boasts marked by a traditional virtuoso vocabulary of ranting threats, is pointedly contrasted with the unaccommodated infant who is truly God and king. As they approach the stable, the Magi are greeted by a maidservant whose questions initiate an exchange clearly based on the numinous dialogue between the Angel and the Three Marys in the *Resurrection* play later in the cycle, when God and man again become distinct. The 'Hail' speeches of the Magi echo elsewhere in the cycle, in the *Nativity*, the *Entry into Jerusalem*, and (in cruel parody) in Christ's second trial before Pilate.

There was some propriety in the Goldsmiths presenting the Three Kings. The gifts of gold, frankincense, and myrrh were probably carried in the kind of richly worked caskets and vessels one sees in medieval paintings of the scene.

[THE MASONS]

HEROD: The clouds clapped in clearness that these climates
     enclose—
  Jupiter and Jove, Mars and Mercury amid—
  Raiking over my royalty on row me rejoices,
  Blundering their blasts to blow when I bid.
  Saturn my subject, that subtly is hid,   5
  Lists at my liking and lays him full low.
  The rack of the red sky full raply I rid,
  Thunders full throly by thousands I throw
  When me likes.
  Venus his voice to me owes,   10
  That princes to play in him pick.

  The prince of planets that proudly is pight
  Shall brace forth his beams that our bield blithe,
  The moon at my mint he musters his might,
  And Caesars in castles great kindness me kithe.   15
  Lords and ladies, lo, lovely me lithe,
  For I am fairer of face and fresher on fold—
  The sooth if I say shall—seven and sixty sithes
  Than glorious gules that gayer is than gold
  In price.   20
  How think ye these tales that I told?
  I am worthy, witty, and wise.

1 SOLDIER: All kings to your crown may clearly commend
  Your law and your lordship as lodestar on height;
  What traitor untrue that will not attend,   25
  Ye shall lay them full low, from leam and from light.

1–3 The clouds adorned in beauty that enclose these regions of the earth, with Jupiter and Jove, Mars and Mercury in the midst [of them], delight me as they rush forth over my kingdom   4 *Blundering* Churning about   *bid* command   6 *Lists* Takes heed   *liking* desire   7–9 Very quickly I remove the mass of clouds from the red sky, and fiercely I throw down thunderbolts in their thousands whenever it pleases me   10 *voice* duty   11 So that princes choose to play upon him   12 *The prince of planets* i.e. the sun   *pight* adorned   13 Shall radiate his beams to gladden our leisure   14 *mint* gesture   *musters* displays   15 *me kithe* manifest towards me   16 willingly attend on me   17 *on fold* on earth   18 If I tell the truth—sixty-seven times   19 *gules* red decoration (in heraldry)   21 What do you think of these things that I have said? ·   22 *witty* clever   24 *lordship* authority   *lodestar . . . height* as a guiding light on high   26 *from* out of   *leam* brightness

2 SOLDIER: What faitour, in faith, that does you offend,
    We shall set him full sore, that sot, in your sight.
HEROD: In wealth shall I wis you to wone ere I wend,
    For ye are wights full worthy, both witty and wight.   30

    But ye know well, sir knights in counsel full cunning,
    That my region so royal is ruled here by rest,
    For I wot of no wight in this world that is wonning
    That in forges any felony, with force shall be fast.
    Arrest ye tho ribalds that unruly are rounding,   35
    Be they kings or knights, in care ye them cast,
    Yea, and wield them in woe to wone, in the waning;
    What broll that is brawling his brain look ye brast,
    And ding ye him down.
1 SOLDIER: Sir, what food in faith will you feeze,   40
    That sot full soon myself shall him sieze.
2 SOLDIER: We shall not here doubt to do him disease,
    But with countenance full cruel we shall crack here his crown.

HEROD: My son that is seemly, how seems thee these saws?
    How comely these knights they carp in this case.   45
SON: Father, if they like not to listen your laws,
    As traitors untrue ye shall teach them a trace,
    For father, of unkindness ye kithe them no cause.
HEROD: Fair fall thee, my fair son, so featous of face.
    And knights, I command, who to dole draws,   50
    Those churls as chevaliers ye chastise and chase,
    And dread ye no doubt.
SON: Father, I shall fell them in fight,
    What renk that reaves you your right.

27 *faitour* impostor   28 We shall cause him great pain, that fool, in your sight
29 *wis* arrange for   *wone* dwell   *ere* before   *wend* go   30 *wights* men
wight bold   32 *by rest* peaceably   33 *wot* know   *wonning* living   34 Who
plots any crime, [and anyone who does] shall be secured by force   35 Arrest
those knaves who are muttering unlawfully   36 *care* suffering   37 Yes,
cause them to groan for woe in that evil hour   38 *broll* brat   *brast* burst   39 *ding*
hammer   40 Sir, whomsoever you wish to prosecute   41 *sot* blockhead
42 *disease* injury   44 *seemly* well mannered   how do these words seem to you
45 *carp* speak   *case* matter   46 Father if they do not care to heed your laws
47 *trace* lesson   48 you give them no reason to be unkind   49 *featous*
handsome   50 whoever falls into evil ways   51–2 Like knights you punish
and pursue those churls, and fear no scruple   54 *renk* fighting man   *reaves*
you robs you of

1 SOLDIER: With dints to death is he dight   55
   That list not your laws for to lout.

[THE GOLDSMITHS]
1 KING: Ah, Lord that lives, everlasting light,
   I lof thee ever with heart and hand,
   That me has made to see this sight
   Which my kindred was covetand.   60
   They said a star with leams bright
   Out of the east should stably stand,
   And that it should move mickle might
   Of one that should be lord in land,
   That men of sin should save.   65
   And certes I shall say,
   God grant me hap to have
   Wissing of ready way.

2 KING: All-wielding God that all has wrought,
   I worship thee as is worthy,   70
   That with thy brightness has me brought
   Out of my realm, rich Arabie.
   I shall not cease till I have sought
   What selcouth thing it shall signify,
   God grant me hap so that I might   75
   Have grace to get good company,
   And my comfort increase
   With thy star shining sheen;
   For certes, I shall not cease
   Till I wit what it mean.   80

3 KING: Lord God that all good has begun
   And all may end, both good and ill,
   That made for man both moon and sun,
   And stead yon star to stand stone still,
   Till I the cause may clearly con,   85

---

55 May he be condemned to death with blows   56 *list* should he choose   *lout*
reverence   58 *lof* praise   60 *covetand* desirous of   61 *leams* beams
62 *stably* firmly   63 *move* indicate   *mickle* [the] great   65 *of* from   66 *certes*
indeed   67 *hap* chance   68 *Wissing* Guidance   69 *All-wielding* Almighty
73 *sought* found out   74 *selcouth* remarkable   78 *sheen* brightly   79 *cease*
stop searching   80 *wit* know   82 *ill* evil   84 *stead* fixed   85 *con*
get to know

God wis me with his worthy will.
I hope I have here fellows fon
My yearning faithfully to fulfil.
Sirs, God you save and see,
And were you ever from woe.   90

1 KING: Amen, so might it be,
And save you sir, also.

3 KING: Sirs, with your will, I would you pray
To tell me some of your intent,
Whither ye wend forth in this way,   95
And from what country ye are went?

2 KING: Full gladly, sir, I shall you say.
A sudden sight was to us sent,
A royal star that rose ere day
Before us in the firmament,   100
That gart us fare from home
Some point thereof to prove.

3 KING: Certes sirs, I saw the same
That makes us thus to move;

For sirs, I have heard say certain   105
It should be sign of selcouth sere,
And further thereof I would frayne;
That makes me move in this manner.

1 KING: Sir, of fellowship are we fain,
Now shall we wend forth all in fere,   110
God grant us ere we come again
Some good hearting thereof to hear.
Sir, here is Jerusalem
To wis us as we go,
And beyond is Bethlehem,   115
There shall we seek also.

3 KING: Sirs, ye shall well understand,
For to be wise now were it need;

---

86 *wis* direct   87 *hope* believe   *fon* found   89 *see* take care of   90 *were*
defend   94 *intent* purpose   96 *went* come   101 That caused us to
journey from home   102 *point* matter   *prove* enquire into   105 *certain*
for sure   106 *selcouth sere* diverse remarkable things   107 *frayne* enquire
109 *fain* desirous   110 *wend* go   *fere* companionship   112 *hearting*
encouragement   118 *were . . . need* is it necessary

Sir Herod is king of this land
And has his laws here for to lead.   120
1 KING: Sir, since we nigh now thus nearhand,
    Unto his help us must take heed,
    For have we his will and his warrant
    Then may we wend without dread.
2 KING: To have leave of the lord,   125
    That is reason and skill.
3 KING: And thereto we all accord,
    Wend we and wit his will.

[THE MASONS AND THE GOLDSMITHS]
MESSENGER: My lord Sir Herod, king with crown!
HEROD: Peace, dastard, in the devil's despite.   130
MESSENGER: My lord, new note is near this town.
HEROD: What, false harlot, list thee flite?
    Go beat yon boy and ding him down.
2 SOLDIER: Lord, messengers should no man wite,
    It may be for your own renown.   135
HEROD: That would I hear, do tell on tite.
MESSENGER: My lord, I met at morn
    Three kings carping together
    Of a bairn that is born,
    And they hight to come hither.   140

HEROD: Three kings, forsooth?
MESSENGER: Sir, so I say,
    For I saw them myself all fere.
1 COUNSELLOR: My lord, appose him I you pray.
HEROD: Say fellow, are they far or near?
MESSENGER: My lord, they will be here this day,   145
    That wot I well, without were.
HEROD: Do rule us then in rich array,
    And ilk man make them merry cheer,

120 *lead* uphold   121 come now this close   126 *skill* good sense   127 *accord*
agree   128 *wit* discover   130 *dastard* dullard   *despite* malice   131 *note*
news   132 *harlot* wretch   *list thee flite* how dare you argue   133 *boy*
knave   134 *wite* blame   136 *tite* quickly   137 *at morn* in the morning
139 *bairn* child   140 *hight* promised   141 *forsooth* indeed   142 *fere*
together   143 *appose* interrogate   146 *without were* indisputably   147 *rule
us* dress me   *array* clothing   148 *ilk* each   *make . . . cheer* behave in a
friendly manner toward them

That no semblant be seen
But friendship fair and still,   150
Till we wit what they mean,
Whether it be good or ill.

1 KING: The Lord that lends ay-lasting light
    Which has us led out of our land,
    Keep thee, sir king and comely knight   155
    And all thy folk that we here find.
HEROD: Mahound, my god and most of might,
    That has my heal all in his hand,
    He save you sirs, seemly in sight;
    And tell us now some new tidand.   160
2 KING: Some shall we say you, sir—
    A star stood us before,
    That makes us speak and speer
    Of one that is new-born.

HEROD: New-born? That burden hold I bad;   165
    And certes, unwitty men ye were
    To leap over land to lait a lad.
    Say, when lost ye him? Aught long before?
    All wise men will ween ye mad,
    And therefore move this never more.   170
3 KING: Yes certes, such hearting have we had,
    We will not cease ere we come there.
HEROD: This were a wonder-thing.
    Say, what bairn should that be?
1 KING: Forsooth, he shall be king   175
    Of Jews and of Judé.

HEROD: King? In the devil's name, dogs, fie!
    Now see I well ye roy and rave.
    By any shimmering of the sky
    When should ye know either king or knave?   180

---

149 *semblant* appearance   153 *lends* bestows   *ay-lasting* eternal   155 *comely*
manly   157 *Mahound* Muhammad (understood diabolically)   158 *heal* well-
being   160 *tidand* news   163 *speer* enquire   165 *burden* birth   166 *unwitty*
foolish   167 *lait* look for   168 At all long ago?   169 *ween* consider
170 *move* mention   173 *wonder-thing* marvel   176 *Judé* Judea   177 *fie*
a curse [on you]   178 *roy* talk nonsense

SON: Nay, he is king and none but he,
  That shall ye ken if that ye crave,
  And he is judge of all Jewry,
  To speak or spill, to say or save.
HEROD: Swilk gauds may greatly grieve,   185
  To witness that ne'er was.
2 KING: Now lord, we ask but leave
  By your power to pass.

HEROD: Whitherward, in the devil's name?
  To lait a lad here in my land?   190
  False harlots, but ye hie you home
  Ye shall be beat and bound in band.
2 COUNSELLOR: My lord, to fell this foul defame,
  Let all these high words fall on hand,
  And speer them sadly of the same,   195
  So shall ye stably understand
  Their mind and their meaning,
  And take good tent thereto.
HEROD: I thank thee of this thing,
  And certes so shall I do.   200

  Now kings, to catch all care away,
  Since ye are come out of your kith,
  Look not ye ledge against our lay,
  Upon pain to lose both limb and lith.
  And so that ye the sooth will say,   205
  To come and go I grant you grith;
  And if your points be to my pay
  May fall myself shall wend you with.
1 KING: Sir king, we all accord,
  And say a bairn is born   210
  That shall be king and lord,
  And leech them that are lorn.

---

182 *ken* find out   *crave* seek   184 To speak up for or to ruin, to condemn or to save   185–6 Such deceitful tricks may cause grave offence, to bear witness to something which cannot be   191 *but* unless   *hie* hasten   192 *beat* beaten *band* bonds   193 *fell* put an end to   *defame* predicament   194 *high words* angry speech   *fall on hand* be put aside   195 *sadly* soberly   *the same* this matter   196 *stably* clearly   197 *mind* purpose   *meaning* intention 199 And pay good heed to that   201 to snatch trouble away   202 *kith* native land   203 *ledge against* speak against   *lay* law   204 *limb and lith* whole body (i.e. pain of death)   205 *And so* If   *sooth* truth   206 *grith* protection   207 *points* words   *pay* satisfaction   208 *May fall* It may happen 212 *leech* cure   *lorn* lost

2 KING: Sir ye tharf marvel nothing
　　Of this ilk note that thusgates news,
　　For Balaam said a star should spring　　　215
　　Of Jacob's kind, and that is Jews.
3 KING: Isaiah says a maiden young
　　Shall bear a bairn among Hebrews,
　　That of all countries shall be king
　　And govern all that on earth grows;　　　220
　　Emanuel is his name,
　　To say, 'God's son of heaven',
　　And certes this is the same
　　That we here to you neven.

1 KING: Sir, the proved prophet Hosé　　　225
　　Full truly told in town and tower,
　　A maiden of Israel, forsooth said he,
　　Shall bear one like to the lily flower.
　　He means a child conceived shall be
　　Without seed of man's succour,　　　230
　　And his mother a maiden free,
　　And he both son and saviour.
2 KING: That fathers told me before
　　Has no man might to mar.
HEROD: Alas, then am I lorn,　　　235
　　This waxes ay war and war.

1 COUNSELLOR: My lord, be ye nothing abashed,
　　This brigue to end shall well be brought,
　　Bid them go forth and friendly fraist
　　The sooth of this that they have sought,　　　240
　　And tell it you—so shall ye trust
　　Whether their tales be true or not.
　　Then shall ye wait them with a wrest
　　And make all waste that they have wrought.

HEROD: Now certes, this is well said,   245
    This matter makes me fain.
    Sir kings, I hold me paid
    Of all your purpose plain.

    Wend forth your foreward to fulfil,
    To Bethlehem is but here at hand.   250
    And speer gradely both good and ill
    Of him that should be lord in land.
    And come again then me until
    And tell me truly your tidand,
    To worship him then were my will,   255
    This shall ye stably understand.
2 KING: Certes sir, we shall you say
    The sooth of that same child,
    In all the haste we may.
2 COUNSELLOR: Farewell—ye are beguiled.   260

HEROD: Now certes this is a subtle train.
    Now shall they truly take their trace,
    And tell me of that swittering swain,
    And all their counsel in this case.
    If it be sooth, they shall be slain,   265
    No gold shall get them better grace;
    But go we till they come again
    And play us in some other place.
    This hold I good counsel,
    Yet would I no man wist;   270
    For certes, we shall not fail
    To lose them as us list.

The Herod passeth, and the three kings come again to make their
    offerings.

---

246 *fain* well-disposed   247 I consider myself content   248 *purpose plain* clear
intentions   249 *foreward* undertaking   251 *gradely* properly [of]   253 *me
until* to me   254 *tidand* news   255 It would then be my desire to worship
him   261 *train* deceit   262 *take their trace* make their way   263 *swittering*
fluttering (i.e. trivial)   *swain* boy   266 No amount of gold will win them better
favour   270 *wist* knew   272 To destroy them in whatever way should
please us

[THE GOLDSMITHS]
1 KING: Ah, sirs, for site what shall I say?
      Where is our sign? I see it not.
2 KING: No more do I. Now dare I lay   275
      In our wending some wrong is wrought.
3 KING: Unto that prince I rede we pray,
      That to us sent his sign unsought,
      That he wis us in ready way
      So friendly that we find him might.   280
1 KING: Ah, sirs, I see it stand
      Above where he is born,
      Lo, here is the house at hand,
      We have not missed this morn.

HANDMAID: Whom seek ye sirs, by ways wild,   285
      With talking, travelling to and fro?
      Here wons a woman with her child
      And her husband, here are no mo.
2 KING: We seek a bairn that all shall bield,
      His certain sign hath said us so,   290
      And his mother, a maiden mild,
      Here hope we to find them two.
HANDMAID: Come near, good sirs, and see,
      Your way to end is brought;
      Behold here sirs, hear and see   295
      The same that ye have sought.

1 KING: Lofed be that lord that lasts ay,
      That us has kid thus courteously
      To wend by many a wilsome way,
      And come to this clean company.   300
2 KING: Let us make now no more delay,
      But tite take forth our treasury
      And ordained gifts of good array,
      To worship him as is worthy.
3 KING: He is worthy to wield   305
      All worship, wealth, and win;

---

273 *site* sorrow   275 Now I would wager   276 We have gone astray
somewhere in our journey   277 *uede* advise   278 *unsought* unexpectedly
280 So that we might find him easily   284 *missed* failed   *morn* morning
287 *wons* dwells   288 *mo* others   289 *bield* defend   294 *way* journey
297 Praise be to that Lord who will endure for ever   298 *kid* shown   299 *wilsome*
difficult   300 *clean* pure   303 *ordained* intended   306 *win* felicity

And for honour and eld
Brother, ye shall begin.

1 KING: Hail, the fairest of field, folk for to find,
From the fiend and his feres faithfully us fend;   310
Hail, the best that shall be born to unbind
All the bernes that are born and in bale bend.
Hail, thou mark us thy men and make us in mind,
Since thy might is on mould misease to amend.
Hail, clean, that is come of a king's kind,   315
And shall be king of this kith, all clergy has kenned.
And since it shall worth on this wise,
Thyself have I sought soon, I say thee,
With gold that is greatest of price;
Be payed of this present I pray thee.   320

2 KING: Hail, food that thy folk fully may feed,
Hail flower fairest, that never shall fade,
Hail, son that is sent of this same seed
That shall save us of sin that our sires had.
Hail mild, for thou met to mark us to meed,   325
Of a maid makeless thy mother thou made;
In that good through grace of thy Godhead
As the gleam in the glass gladly thou glade.
And since thou shall sit to be deeming,
To hell or to heaven for to have us,   330
Incense to thy service is seeming.
Son, see to thy subjects and save us.

3 KING: Hail, bairn that is best our bales to beet,
For our boot shall thou be bound and beat;
Hail, friend faithful, we fall to thy feet,   335
Thy Father's folk from the fiend to thee fetch.

---

307 And on account of honour and age   309 Hail, fairest in the world, supporter
of people   310 *feres* allies   *fend* defend   312 *bernes* people   *in bale
bend* are bound in hell's pains   313 take note that we are your men and remember
us   314 *mould* earth   *misease* distress   315 *clean* pure one   *kind* family
316 *kith* land   *kenned* made known   317 And since it will take place in this
way   320 *Be payed of* Be pleased to accept   321 *food* pun on 'child' and
'food'   324 *of* from   *sires* forefathers   325 Hail, meek one, for you arranged
to select us for favour   326 *makeless* pure   327 *In* Into   *good* worthy
person   328 *glade* glided   329 *to . . . deeming* in judgement   331 *seeming*
fitting   333 *beet* assuage   334 *boot* help

Hail, man that is made to thy men meet,
Since thou and thy mother with mirths are met;
Hail, duke that drives death under feet,
But when thy deeds are done to die is thy debt.   340
And since thy body buried shall be,
This myrrh will I give to thy graving.
The gift is not great of degree,
Receive it, and see to our saving.

MARY: Sir kings, ye travel not in vain.   345
As ye have meant, here may ye find,
For I conceived my son certain
Without miss of man in mind,
And bore him here without pain,
Where women are wont to be pined.   350
God's angel in his greeting plain
Said he should comfort all mankind,
Therefore doubt you no deal
Here for to have your boon,
I shall witness full well   355
All that is said and done.

1 KING: For solace sere now may we sing,
All is performed that we for prayed;
But good bairn, give us thy blessing,
For fair hap is before thee laid.   360
2 KING: Wend we now to Herod the king
For of this point he will be paid,
And come himself and make offering
Unto this same, for so he said.
3 KING: I rede we rest a throw   365
For to maintain our might,
And then do as we owe,
Both unto king and knight.

---

337 *meet* equal   338 with joy are brought together   339 *drives* tramples
340 *debt* duty   342 *graving* burial   344 *saving* salvation   346 *meant*
sought   348 *miss of* sin on the part of   350 *pined* troubled   353 *no*
deal not at all   354 *boon* desire   357 *solace sere* diverse good tidings   360 *fair*
hap good fortune   362 *point* matter   *paid* pleased   365 *throw* short time
366 To conserve our strength   367 *owe* ought

ANGEL: Now courteous kings, to me take tent
    And turn betimes ere ye be teened,   370
    From God himself thus am I sent
    To warn you as your faithful friend.
    Herod the king has malice meant
    And shapes with shame you for to shend,
    And for that ye none harms should hent,   375
    By other ways God will ye wend
    Even to your own country.
    And if ye ask him boon,
    Your bield ay will he be
    For this that ye have done.   380

1 KING: Ah, Lord, I lof thee inwardly.
    Sirs, God has goodly warned us three,
    His angel here now heard have I,
    And how he said.
2 KING: Sir, so did we.
    He said Herod is our enemy,   385
    And makes him boun our bale to be
    With feigned falsehood, and forthy
    Far from his force I rede we flee.
3 KING: Sirs, fast I rede we flit,
    Ilkone to our country,   390
    He that is well of wit
    Us wis, and with you be.

369 *take tent* pay attention   370 *betimes* promptly   *teened* harmed   373 *meant* planned   374 And shamefully plans to destroy you   375 *for* so   *hent* receive   378 *boon* a favour   381 *inwardly* fervently   382 *goodly* kindly 386 *boun* ready   387 *forthy* therefore   389 *flit* go   390 *Ilkone* Each one of us   391 *well of wit* source of wisdom

THE MARSHALS

The Flight into Egypt

The short and simple episode of *The Flight into Egypt* was the responsibility of the Marshals' guild. The Marshals were farriers, dealing with all aspects of the management of horses. The play is written in a twelve-line stanza, $ababcc_4dde_2fef_3$, which does not occur elsewhere in the cycle. There are only three speaking parts: Joseph, Mary, and Gabriel; it is impossible to tell whether the Christ child would have been a real infant or not, although evidence from elsewhere suggests this as a distinct possibility. If, as was the case in the Noah plays, there was here any correlation between the guild's occupation and the matter of their play, doubtless a real donkey was used. There is little dramatic action as such in the play, as it does not deal with the flight itself or the apocryphal miracles associated with it; it is more concerned with demonstrating, in their preparations for flight, the nature of the Holy Family and its doctrinal implications.

The play opens with Joseph making his complaint to God. His words are reminiscent of the complaints of the shepherds who reflect the plight of fallen man in the world which Christ came to save. After he has received his warning and further instructions to flee from Gabriel, he, like other old men in the cycle, grumbles a little about being allotted a task which he feels he is too weak and old to fulfil. In this play, however, his grumbling is muted, as the dramatist wants to emphasize his devotional role as earthly guardian of the Virgin and her child. He assumed this role in the cycle the moment he learned the true cause of Mary's pregnancy and he maintains it throughout. He does not, of course, want to undertake a long and arduous journey, but his major anxiety is that he will die before they reach their destination; he may cut a comic figure, but it is mainly because he insists on packing all their household utensils and tools to take with them. In other words, the author clearly controls Joseph's comic possibilities, because he wishes to present a devotional picture of a conscientious and protective spouse.

Mary too has her complexities in this play. She completes the touchingly comic picture of anxious, poverty-stricken parents who have been singled out for election. Although they are willing enough, their tasks seem perpetually to be beyond their practical capabilities. Here, for instance, the playwright indicates that Mary cannot ride very well. She becomes so distressed about Herod's intentions to kill her child that she does not hear Joseph say where they must go. He is quite rough in reminding her; but then it transpires that neither of them knows in which direction Egypt lies anyway. Here Mary contributes to the humourous dimension of the play.

All that Mary says, however, about the danger her son is in, presages the later laments to which she gives voice in the *planctus* at the base of the Cross. Her protestations of their absolute innocence remind the audience of the degree to which Christ the man, like his parents, will always appear to be the innocent victim of the rest of mankind. Broader doctrinal implications are thus combined with the naturalistic domestic situation. The play ends optimistically, on a most touching line,

> I have our help here in mine arm,

as Joseph experiences literally the strength and comfort to be derived from taking Christ to his heart.

JOSEPH: Thou maker that is most of might,
 To thy mercy I make my moan;
 Lord, see unto this simple wight
 That has none help but thee alone.
 For all this world I have forsaken,   5
 And to thy service I have me taken
 With wit and will
 For to fulfil
 Thy commandment.
 Thereon mine heart is set   10
 With grace thou has me lent,
 There shall no lede me let.

 For all my trust, Lord, is in thee
 That made me man, to thy likeness.
 Thou mightful maker, have mind on me   15
 And see unto my simpleness.
 I wax as weak as any wand,
 For feeble me fails both foot and hand;
 Whatever it mean
 Methink mine eyen   20
 Heavy as lead.
 Therefore I hold it best
 A while here in this stead
 To sleep and take my rest.

---

2 *moan* complaint 3 *see unto* look after *simple wight* humble man 11 *me lent* bestowed on me 12 No man shall obstruct me in that 14 *to thy likeness* in your likeness 15 *mightful* mighty *have mind on* remember 16 And look after me in my lowly condition 17 *wax* grow *wand* shoot 18 Foot and hand both fail me for feebleness 20 *eyen* eyes 23 *stead* place

MARY: Thou lovely Lord that last shall ay,   25
My God, my Lord, my son so dear,
To thy Godhead heartily I pray
With all mine heart wholly entire.
As thou me to thy mother chose,
I beseech thee of thy grace   30
For all mankind
That has in mind
To worship thee.
Thou see thy souls to save,
Jesu my son so free,   35
This boon of thee I crave.

ANGEL: Waken Joseph, and take intent,
My saws shall cease thy sorrow sore.
Be not heavy, thy hap is hent,
Therefore I bid thee sleep no more.   40
JOSEPH: Ah, mightful Lord, whatever that meant?
So sweet a voice heard I never ere.
But what art thou with steven so shill
Thus in my sleep that speaks me till?
To me appear   45
And let me hear
What that thou was.
ANGEL: Joseph, have thou no dread,
Thou shalt wit ere I pass,
Therefore to me take heed.   50

For I am sent to thee,
Gabriel, God's angel bright,
Is come to bid thee flee
With Mary and her worthy wight.
For Herod the king gars do to dead   55
All knave-children in ilka stead,
That he may ta

---

25 *ay* for ever   27 *heartily* earnestly   30 *of* for   35 *free* gracious
36 *boon* request   37 *take intent* pay attention   38 *saws* words   *cease* end
39 *heavy* downcast   your luck has changed   40 *bid* command   41 whatever
was meant by that?   42 *ere* before   43 *steven* voice   *shill* resonant   44 *till*
to   49 You will understand before I depart   54 *worthy wight* precious child
55 *gars do to dead* is causing to be put to death   56 All boy children everywhere
57 *ta* capture

With years twa
That are of eld.
Till he be dead away   60
In Egypt shall ye bield
Till I wit thee for to say.

JOSEPH: Ay-lasting Lord, lofed mote thou be
That thy sweet sand would to me send.
But Lord, what ails the king at me,   65
For unto him I never offend?
Alas, what ails him for to spill
Small young bairns that never did ill
In word nor deed,
Unto no lede   70
By night nor day?
And since he will us shend,
Dear Lord, I thee pray,
Thou would be our friend,

For be he never so wood or wroth   75
For all his force thou may us fend.
I pray thee Lord, keep us from scathe,
Thy succour soon to us thou send;
For unto Egypt wend we will
Thy bidding bainly to fulfil,   80
As worthy is
Thou king of bliss,
Thy will be wrought.
Mary my daughter dear,
On thee is all my thought.   85
MARY: Ah, lief Joseph, what cheer?

JOSEPH: The cheer of me is done for ay.
MARY: Alas, what tidings heard have ye?

58–9 Who are within two years of age   60 *dead away* dead and gone   61 *bield*
dwell   62 Until I inform you otherwise   63 Everlasting Lord, may you be
praised   64 *sand* messenger   65 what does the king hold against me
67 what is wrong with him to make him kill   68 *bairns* children   *ill* wrong
70 *lede* man   72 And since he wants to harm us   75–6 For however mad
and angry he may be, you can defend us from all his power   77 *scathe* harm
78 *succour* help   79 *wend* go   80 *bainly* willingly   81 As is fitting
83 *wrought* done   84 *daughter* darling   86 Ah, dear Joseph, how are you?
87 My happiness is gone for ever   88 *tidings* news

JOSEPH: Now certes, full ill to thee at say,
  There is nought else but us must flee   90
  Out of our kith where we are known,
  Full wightly bus us be withdrawn
  Both thou and I.
MARY: Lief Joseph, why?
  Lain it not,   95
  To dole who has us deemed,
  Or what wrong have we wrought
  Wherefore we should be flemed?

JOSEPH: Wrought we harm? Nay, nay, all wrong,
  Wit thou well it is not so.   100
  That young page's life thou must foregang
  But if thou fast flee from his foe.
MARY: His foe? Alas, what is your rede,
  Who would my dear bairn do to dead?
  I dark, I dare,   105
  Who may my care
  Of bales blin?
  To flee I would full fain,
  For all this world to win
  Would I not see him slain.   110

JOSEPH: I warn thee, he is throly threat
  With Herod king, hard harms to have.
  With that miting if that we be met
  There is no salve that him may save.
  I warn thee well, he slays all   115
  Knave-children, great and small,
  In town and field
  Within the eld
  Of two year,
  And for thy son's sake   120

89 Now indeed, very hard to have to tell you   90 There is no alternative
91 *kith* native land   92 We must go away very swiftly   95 *lain* conceal
96 Who has condemned us to trouble   98 *flemed* driven out   100 *Wit thou
well* You know well   101 You must relinquish that young boy's life   102 *But
if* Unless   103 *rede* counsel   105 *dark* shrink back   *dare* fear   106–7 Who
may put a stop to my fear of misfortune?   108 *fain* gladly   109 For all the
world   111 *throly* angrily   *threat* threatened   112 *With* By   113 *miting*
little thing   114 *salve* remedy   118 *eld* age

He will fordo that dear,
May that traitor him take.

MARY: Lief Joseph, who told you this?
How had ye wittering of this deed?
JOSEPH: An angel bright that came from bliss   125
These tidings told, without dread,
And wakened me out of my sleep
That comely child from cares to keep,
And bad me flee
With him and thee   130
Unto Egypt.
And certes, I dread me sore
To make any small trip,
Ere time that I come there.

MARY: What ail they at my bairn   135
Such harms him for to hete?
Alas, why should I tharn
My son his life so sweet?
His heart ought to be full sore,
On such a food him to forfare   140
That never did ill,
Him for to spill,
And he ne wot why.
I were full will of wone
My son and he should die,   145
And I have but him alone.

JOSEPH: We, lief Mary, do way, let be!
I pray thee, leave off thy din,
And fand thee forth fast for to flee,
Away with him for to win,   150
That no mischief on him betide,
Nor none unhap in no-kin side

121 *fordo* kill   124 *wittering* information   126 *dread* doubt   132–4 And
indeed, I'm too frightened to undertake even the shortest journey before we get there
135 *What . . . at* What do they have against   136 *hete* threaten   137 *tharn* give
up   140 *food* child   *forfare* wreak vengeance   142 *spill* kill   143 *ne wot*
does not know   144 I would be at a loss   145 *and if*   147 *lief* beloved
do . . . be! have done, stop it!   148 Stop your clamouring   149 *fand thee*
prepare yourself   150 *win* get   151 *on him betide* happen to him   152 Nor
any misfortune anywhere

By way nor street,
That none meet
To slay him.   155
MARY: Alas Joseph, for care,
Why should I forgo him,
My dear bairn that I bare?

JOSEPH: That sweet swain if thou save
Do tite pack sam our gear,   160
And such small harness as we have.
MARY: Ah, lief Joseph, I may not bear.
JOSEPH: Bear harm? No, I trow but small.
But God it wot I must care for all,
For bed and back   165
And all the pack
That needs unto us.
It furthers to feign me;
This packald bear me bus,
Though of all I pledge and plain me.   170

But God grant grace I not forget
No tools that we should with us take.
MARY: Alas Joseph, for grievance great,
When shall my sorrow slake,
For I wot not whither to fare?   175
JOSEPH: To Egypt—told I thee long ere.
MARY: Where standeth it?
Fain would I wit.
JOSEPH: What wot I?
I wot not where it stand.   180
MARY: Joseph, I ask mercy,
Help me out of this land.

JOSEPH: Now certes Mary, I would full fain
Help thee all that I may,

157 *forgo him* give him up   158 *bare* bore   159–60 If you would save that
dear boy, quickly pack our belongings together   161 *harness* baggage   162 I
cannot carry   163 *I . . . small* I know that you cannot tolerate adversity
167–8 That we need. I must put a good face on things   169 *packald* bundle
170 Though I complain about it all   174 *slake* be ended   175 Because I
don't know where to go?   176 I told you long before this   177–8 Where
is it? I should dearly like to know   179 How should I know?   181 Joseph,
I beg your pardon

And at my power me pain   185
To win with him and thee away.
MARY: Alas, what ails that fiend
Thus wilsome ways make us to wend?
He does great sin,
From kith and kin   190
He gars us flee.
JOSEPH: Lief Mary, leave thy greet.
MARY: Joseph, full woe is me
For my dear son so sweet.

JOSEPH: I pray thee Mary, hap him warm   195
And set him soft that he not sile,
And if thou will aught ease thine arm
Give me him, let me bear him a while.
MARY: I thank you of your great good deed;
Now good Joseph to him take heed,   200
That food so free,
To him ye see
Now in this tide.
JOSEPH: Let me and him alone,
And if thou can ill ride   205
Have and hold thee fast by the mane.

MARY: Alas Joseph, for woe,
Was never wight in world so will.
JOSEPH: Do way Mary, and say not so,
For thou shall have no cause theretill.   210
For wit thou well, God is our friend,
He will be with us whereso we lend.
In all our need
He will us speed,
This wot I well.   215
I lof my Lord of all;

185 And try to the best of my ability   186 *win* go   188 To make us go by such
lonely ways   191 *gars* makes   192 *leave . . . greet* stop crying   195 *hap* wrap
196 And put him down gently so that he does not slip   197 *aught . . . arm* rest
your arm at all   202 You attend to him   203 *tide* time   204 *Let* Leave
205–6 And if you cannot ride well, hold on tightly to the mane   208 *will*
distraught   210 *theretill* for that   212 *whereso . . . lend* wherever we stay
214 *speed* assist   216 I praise my Lord above all

Such force methink I feel,
I may go where I shall.

Ere was I weak, now am I wight.
My limbs to wield ay at my will.   220
I lof my maker most of might
That such grace has grant me till.
Now shall no hathel do us harm,
I have our help here in mine arm.
He will us fend   225
Whereso we lend
From teen and tray.
Let us go with good cheer—
Farewell and have good day—
God bless us all in fere.   230
MARY: Amen, as he best may.

217 *force* strength   218 I can move as I like   219 *Ere* Previously   *wight*
strong   220 To use my limbs however I want to   223 *hathel* man   225 *fend*
defend   227 From strife and treachery   230 *in fere* together

THE GIRDLERS AND NAILERS

The Slaughter of the Innocents

The Nativity sequence reaches its climax in the episode of the *Slaughter of the Innocents*, with its powerful figural reverberations and evocative action. The York version was presented by the Girdlers and Nailers, who made a variety of small metal objects; the Girdlers, as their name suggests, studded belts, harness, dog-collars, and so forth. The play is written in an eight-line stanza, rhyming ababcaac, with three stresses to the line, a verse form not found elsewhere in the cycle.

Herod, whose court probably occupied the pageant-wagon, is surrounded by sinister counsellors and sadistic soldiery. The behaviour of the latter is at gross and ironic variance with the chivalry that is attributed to them—one of the many implicit comments in the cycles on the mores and pretensions of the English upper classes of the day. The potentate's tendency to despotic rage, already amply displayed in the Magi play, was to become a theatrical byword, whilst his ostentatious worship of 'Mahound' marks him out as the kind of exotic infidel who loomed so large in the medieval imagination after the Crusades. His persistent diabolical oaths reveal his affiliation with a succession of wicked characters in the cycle: Satan and his tributary devils, Pharaoh, Judas, Annas, Caiaphas, Pilate, and the Herod of the Passion.

The conflict between the knights and the mothers was probably presented in the street, close to the audience. The York dramatist on the whole avoided the grotesque effect found in other cycles, where the women confronted the soldiers with coarse invective, whilst their keening and screaming after the massacre ran the risk of becoming as much a commonplace as Herod's ranting. Instead, the women are here presented in a largely lyrical and passive vein, clearly intended to prefigure the Virgin's *planctus Mariae* of *The Death of Christ*, and also to echo her tone in *The Flight into Egypt*. The episode stands at a central point in the cycle, looking back towards the Old Testament sacrificial types, Abel and Isaac, and forward to the acute pathos and distress of the Crucifixion. Modern productions reveal it to be a most appalling spectacle in performance.

HEROD: Poor beausires about,
  Pain of limb and land,
  Stint of your stevens stout
  And still as stone ye stand,

1 *beausires* good men   *about* hereabouts   2 Upon threat to limb and land
3 *Stint* Cease   *stevens stout* loud shouting

And my carping record.   5
Ye ought to dare and doubt,
And lere to lof and lout
To me, your lovely lord.

Ye owe in field and town
To bow at my bidding,   10
With reverence and renown,
As falls for swilk a king,
The lordliest alive.
Who hereto is not boun,
By almighty Mahound,   15
To death I shall him drive.

So bold look no man be
For to ask help nor held
But of Mahound and me,
That has this world in wield,   20
To maintain us amell.
For well of wealth are we,
And my chief help is he;
Hereto what can ye tell?

1 COUNSELLOR: Lord, what you likes to do,   25
All folk will be full fain
To take intent thereto,
And none grudge thereagain.
That full well wit shall ye,
And if they would not so   30
We should soon work them woe,
IIEROD: Yea, fair sirs, so should it be.

2 COUNSELLOR: Lord, the sooth to say,
Full well we understand

---

5 *carping* speaking   *record* attend to   6 *dare* fear   *doubt* worry   7 *lere*
learn   *lof* give worship   *lout* bow down   9 *owe* ought   10 *bidding* request
11 *renown* a sense of respect   12 *falls for* befits   *swilk* such   14 Who is not
prepared to do this   15 *Mahound* Muhammad (intended diabolically)   18 *held*
favour   19 *But* Except   20 *in wield* in our power   21 To rule between
the two of us   22 *well* source   24 *Hereto* To this end   25 *you likes* it pleases
you   26 *fain* eager   27–8 To pay attention to that, and none to object
against it   29 *wit* know   31 *work them woe* cause them distress   33 *sooth*
truth

Mahound is God veray,   35
And ye are lord of ilka land.
Therefore, so have I sele,
In rede we wait alway
What mirth most mend you may.
HEROD: Certes, ye say right well.   40

But I am noyed of new,
That blithe may I not be,
For three kings, as ye know,
That came through this country,
And said they sought a swain.   45
1 COUNSELLOR: That rule I hope them rue,
For had their tales been true
They had come this way again.

2 COUNSELLOR: We heard how they you hight,
If they might find that child   50
For to have told you right,
But certes, they are beguiled.
Swilk tales are not to trow,
Full well wot ilka wight,
There shall never man have might   55
Nor mastery unto you.

1 COUNSELLOR: Them shames so, for certain,
That they dare meet you no more.
HEROD: Wherefore should they be fain
To make swilk fare before,   60
To say a boy was born
That should be most of main?
These gadlings shall again,
If that the devil had sworn.

35 *God veray* the true God   36 *ilka* every   37 as I prosper   38 *rede*
counsel   *wait alway* are always in attendance [to see]   39 What pleasure may
best cheer you   40 *Certes* Certainly   41–2 But I am vexed at the moment,
and cannot be happy   43 *For* Because of   45 *swain* boy   46 I believe
they will repent that deed   49 *hight* promised   51 *right* accordingly   53 *to*
trow to be believed   54–5 Each man knows very well that nobody shall ever have
power or mastery over you   57 They are so ashamed   60 To mention
such a business beforehand   62 *main* power   63 *gadlings* fellows   *shall*
again shall [go forth and look] again   64 Even though the devil had sworn otherwise

For by well never they wot,   65
Whether they work well or wrong,
To frayne gart them thus-gate
To seek that gadling gang,
And swilk carping to kith.

2 COUNSELLOR: Nay lord, they lered over-late   70
Our bliss shall never abate,
And therefore, lord, be blithe.

MESSENGER: Mahound without peer,
My lord, you save and see.
HEROD: Messenger, come near,   75
And beausire, well thee be.
What tidings? Tells thou any?
MESSENGER: Yea lord, since I was here
I have sought sides sere,
And seen marvels full many.   80

HEROD: And of marvels to mean
That were most mirth to me.
MESSENGER: Lord, even as I have seen
The sooth soon shall ye see,
If ye will, hear in hie: 85
I met two towns between
Three kings with crowns clean,
Riding full royally.

HEROD: Ah, my bliss, boy, thou bourds too broad.
MESSENGER: Sir, there may no botment be.   90
HEROD: Oho, by sun and moon,
Then tide us tales tonight.
Hopes thou they will come soon
Hither, as they have hight,
For to tell me tidand?   95

65–9 Whether they have done well or not since, their intentions were not good. They
certainly sought to go forth and look for that little wretch, and to make known what
was said [of him] (?). (Uncertain, passage corrupt in MS.)   70 *lered over-late*
learned too late   71 *abate* diminish   73–4 May the peerless Muhammad, lord,
save and preserve you   76 *well . . . be* a blessing on you   79 I have gone
everywhere   81 *mean* call to mind   82 That would delight me most   85 *in
hie* straight away   86 Midway between two towns I met   87 *clean* perfect
89 *my bliss* expression of consternation   you speak out of turn   90 *botment*
amendment   92 Then we shall hear news tonight   93 *Hopes thou* Do you
think   95 *tidand* news

MESSENGER: Nay lord, that dance is done.
HEROD: Why, whither are they gone?
MESSENGER: Ilkone into their own land.

HEROD: How says thou, lad? Let be.
MESSENGER: I say, forth they are passed.   100
HEROD: What, forth away from me?
MESSENGER: Yea lord, in faith full fast,
    For I heard and took heed
    How that they went all three
    Into their own country.   105
HEROD: Ah, dogs, the devil you speed.

MESSENGER: Sir, more of their meaning
    Yet well I understood,
    How they had made offering
    Unto that freely food   110
    That now of new is born.
    They say he should be king
    And wield all earthly thing.
HEROD: Alas, then am I lorn.

    Fie on them, faitours, fie!   115
    Will they beguile me thus?
MESSENGER: Lord, by their prophecy
    They named his name Jesus.
HEROD: Fie on thee, lad, thou lies.
2 COUNSELLOR: Hence tite but thou thee hie,   120
    With dole here shall thou die,
    That wrays him on this wise.

MESSENGER: Ye wite me all with wrong,
    It is thus and well war.
HEROD: Thou lies, false traitor strong,   125
    Look never thou nigh me near.

---

96 *that business is over*   98 *Ilkone* Each one   99 *Let be* i.e. Surely this is not
true   106 *may the devil help you*   107 *meaning* purpose   110 *freely food*
noble child   111 *of new* newly   113 *wield* govern   114 *lorn* destroyed
115 *Fie* A curse   *faitours* impostors   116 *beguile* deceive   119 *lad* wretch
120 *Unless you go away from here quickly*   121 *dole* pain   122 *That pro-
claims him* (i.e. Jesus) *in this way*   123–4 *You blame me unjustly, it is* [not only]
like this, but worse   125 *false . . . strong* bold, deceitful traitor   126 *nigh*
approach

Upon life and limb
May I that faitour fang,
Full high I shall gar him hang,
Both thee, harlot, and him.   130

MESSENGER: I am not worthy to wite,
    But farewell all the heap.
1 COUNSELLOR: Go, in the devil's despite,
    Or I shall gar thee leap
    And dear aby this brew.   135
HEROD: Alas, for sorrow and site,
    My woe no wight may write;
    What devil is best to do?

2 COUNSELLOR: Lord, amend your cheer
    And take no needless noy,   140
    We shall you leally lere
    That lad for to destroy,
    By counsel if we can.
HEROD: That may ye not come near,
    For it is past two year   145
    Since that this bale began.

1 COUNSELLOR: Lord, therefore have no doubt,
    If it were four or five.
    Gar gather in great rout
    Your knights keen belive,   150
    And bid them ding to dead
    All knave children kept in clout;
    In Bethlehem and all about,
    To lait in ilka stead.

2 COUNSELLOR: Lord, save none, for your sele,   155
    That are of two year age within,

127 *Upon* On pain of   128 *fang* catch   129 *gar . . . hang* cause him to be
hanged   130 *harlot* knave   131 *to wite* of blame   132 *all the heap*
the whole lot of you   133 by the devil's malice   134 *gar . . . leap* make
you jump   135 *dear aby* pay dearly for   *brew* trouble   136 *site* distress
137 *write* record   139 Cheer up   140 And don't become needlessly vexed
141 *leally lere* loyally instruct   144 You cannot manage that   146 *bale* trouble
147 have no fear of that   149 Gather together in a great crowd   150 *keen*
ready for action   *belive* in haste   151 *ding to dead* strike dead   152 *knave*
boy   still in swaddling clothes   154 *lait* seek out   *stead* place   155 *for
. . . sele* to preserve your happiness

Then shall that foundling feel
Belive his bliss shall blin,
With bale when he shall bleed.
HEROD: Certes, ye say right well,   160
And as ye deem ilk deal
Shall I gar do indeed.

Sir knights, courteous and hend,
Though the note is now all new,
Ye shall find me your friend   165
And ye this time be true.
1 SOLDIER: What say ye lord? Let see.
HEROD: To Bethlehem bus ye wend,
That shrew with shame to shend
That means to master me.   170

And about Bethlehem both
Bus you well speer and spy,
For else it will be wothe
That he loses this Jewry,
And certes that were great shame.   175
2 SOLDIER: My lord, that were us loathe;
And he escaped, it were scathe,
And we well worthy blame.

1 SOLDIER: Full soon he shall be sought,
That make I mine avow.   180
1 COUNSELLOR: I bid for him you laught,
And let me tell you how
To work when ye come there:
Because ye ken him not,
To death they must be brought,   185
Knave-children, less and more.

---

157 *foundling feel* brat perceive   158 *blin* cease   159 *bale* pain   161–2 And
whatever you suggest I shall certainly try to do   162 *hend* worthy   164 Though
this business has arisen suddenly   166 *And* If   167 *Let see* Tell us   168 *bus*
must   169 *shrew* evil creature   170 *master* overcome   172 *speer* enquire
173 there will be a danger   174 *loses* destroys   *Jewry* kingdom of the Jews
176 *us loathe* opprobrious to us   177 *scathe* harm   178 *worthy* worthy [of]
181 *laught* sieze   184 *ken* know   186 *less . . . more* all of them

HEROD: Yea, all within two year,
　　That none for speech be spared.
2 SOLDIER: Lord, how ye us lere
　　Full well we take reward,　　　　　　　　　　　　190
　　And certes we shall not rest.
1 SOLDIER: Come forth, fellows in fere,
　　Lo, foundlings find we here

　　　　.　　.　　.　　.　　.

1 WOMAN: Out on you, thieves, I cry,
　　Ye slay my seemly son.　　　　　　　　　　　　195
2 SOLDIER: These brolls shall dear aby
　　This bale that is begun,
　　Therefore lay from thee fast.
2 WOMAN: Alas for dole, I die,
　　To save my son shall I,　　　　　　　　　　　　200
　　Ay-whiles my life may last.

1 SOLDIER: Ah, dame, the devil thee speed
　　And me, but it be quit.
1 WOMAN: To die I have no dread
　　I do thee well to wit,　　　　　　　　　　　　205
　　To save my son so dear.
1 SOLDIER: Asarmes, for now is need;
　　But if we do yon deed
　　These queans will quell us here.

2 WOMAN: Alas, this loathly strife,　　　　　　　　210
　　No bliss may be my beet.
　　The knight upon his knife
　　Hath slain my son so sweet,
　　And I had but him alone.
1 WOMAN: Alas, I lose my life,　　　　　　　　　215
　　Was never so woeful a wife
　　Ne half so will of wone;

---

188 *speech* special pleading　　　190 *take reward* pay heed　　　192 *in fere* together
193+ *Line missing in MS*　　194 *Out* A curse　　196 *brolls* brats　　　198 *lay
from thee* let go　　　199 *dole* grief　　201 *Ay-whiles* As long as　　203 *but . . . quit*
but [we shall] be even (he is returning a blow)　　205 I let you know plainly
207 *Asarmes* To arms　　　208 *But if* Unless　　209 *queans* shrewish women　　*quell*
destroy　　　210 *loathly* ghastly　　　211 No happiness could ever comfort me now
217 *Ne* Ever　　*will of wone* distraught

And certes, me were full loath
That they thus harmless yode.

1 SOLDIER: The devil might speed you both,   220
False witches, are ye wood?

2 WOMAN: Nay, false lurdans, ye lie.

1 SOLDIER: If ye be wood or wroth
Ye shall not scape from scathe;
Wend we us hence in hie.   225

1 WOMAN: Alas that we were wrought
In world women to be,
The bairn that we dear bought
Thus in our sight to see
Dispiteously spill.   230

2 WOMAN: And certes, their note is nought,
The same that they have sought
Shall they never come till.

1 SOLDIER: Go we to the king.
Of all this conteck keen   235
I shall not let for nothing
To say as we have seen.

2 SOLDIER: And certes, no more shall I;
We have done his bidding
How so they wrest or wring,   240
We shall say soothfastly.

1 SOLDIER: Mahound, our god of might,
Save thee, Sir Herod the king.

1 COUNSELLOR: Lord, take keep to your knight,
He will tell you now tiding   245
Of bourds where they have been.

HEROD: Yea, and they have gone right

218–19 I would not wish, certainly, that they should go away thus unharmed
221 *wood* mad   222 *lurdans* scoundrels   223 *wroth* enraged   224 *scape*
escape   225 *Wend . . . us* Let us go   226 *wrought* born   228 The
child we paid so dearly for (i.e. in childbirth)   230 Cruelly killed   231 *their*
. . . *nought* their task has been fruitless   232 *same* one   233 *till* to   235 *conteck*
keen fierce fighting   236 *let* forbear   *for nothing* on any account   240 However
they may wring their hands   241 *soothfastly* truthfully   244 *take keep* pay
attention   246 *bourds* sport   247–8 Yes, if they have done well, and kept
the promise they made to us

And hold that they us hight,
Then shall solace be seen.

2 SOLDIER: Lord, as ye deemed us to doon   250
In countries where we came—
HEROD: Sir, by sun and moon,
Ye are welcome home
And worthy to have reward.
Have ye got us this gome?   255
1 SOLDIER: Where we found fele or fone,
Witness we will that none was spared.

2 SOLDIER: Lord, they are dead ilkone,
What would ye we did more?
HEROD: I ask but after one   260
The kings told of before,
That should make great mastery;
Tell us if he be ta'en.
1 SOLDIER: Lord, tokening had we none
To know that brothel by.   265

2 SOLDIER: In bale we have them brought
About all Bethlehem town.
HEROD: Ye lie, your note is nought,
The devils of hell you drown.
So may that boy be fled,   270
For in waste have ye wrought.
Ere that same lad be sought
Shall I never bide in bed.

1 COUNSELLOR: We will wend with you then
To ding that dastard down.   275
HEROD: Asarme every-ilk man
That holds of Mahound.
Were they a thousand score
This bargain shall they ban.
Come after as ye can,   280
For we will wend before.

249 *solace* rejoicing   250 *deemed . . . doon* told us to do   255 *gome* child
256 *fele or fone* many or few   258 *ilkone* all of them   264 *tokening* sign
265 *brothel* wretch   271 For you have wasted your time   272 *Ere* Before
sought found   273 *bide in* go to   275 *dastard* wretch   276 *every-ilk*
each and every   277 *holds of* believes in   279 They will curse this state of
affairs   281 *before* ahead

THE SMITHS

The Temptation

The adult life and ministry of Christ are not major objects of attention in the cycles. Such was the influence of the late medieval contemplative tradition that the greatest emphasis was given to events surrounding the Nativity and Passion, especially the sufferings of Christ. *The Temptation*, however, plays an important part in establishing a thematic chain from man's Fall to his Redemption.

Patristic teachings enlarged on the Gospel accounts in such a way as to suggest that Christ was tempted in the three sins through which Adam fell: gluttony, vainglory, and pride. The York dramatist shows some awareness of this tradition by causing Satan to define the nature of his temptations clearly to the audience and by repeating the word 'fall'. Satan's villainous intimacy with the audience is reminiscent of his part in *The Fall of Man*, and is seen again when he visits Pilate's wife later in the cycle. A further and more subtle theological point underlies the action: as Satan points out, it is important for him to know whether Christ is human or divine. This raises the issue of the 'doctrine of divine duplicity'. It was argued that, since man fell because he disobeyed God, Satan had the right to keep him until his redemption could be achieved by just means. Satan ensnared man by guile when he disguised himself as a serpent, and therefore God too could employ deceit to defeat Satan by disguising himself in man's flesh. This view of the Redemption presents sacral history as a battle of wits, with the Temptation forming a strong link between the Fall and the Harrowing of Hell. The York cycle gives some prominence to the theme here, later in *The Dream of Pilate's Wife* and in *The Harrowing of Hell* itself. At the end of *The Temptation* Satan leaves for hell, ironically predicting the Crucifixion: 'high may he hang'. He evidently does not yet understand that Christ's death will be his own undoing. It is not clear whether he is now satisfied about Christ's divinity; but, by the time he re-appears in the cycle, he has worked out all the implications of the trap.

The play is written in a six-line stanza, aaa$_4$b$_2$a$_4$b$_2$, which also appears in *The Resurrection* in this selection.

DEVIL: Make room belive, and let me gang!
    Who makes here all this throng?
    Hie you hence, high might you hang
    Right with a rope.

---

1 *belive* quickly   *gang* pass   2 *throng* commotion   3 *Hie* Go quickly

I dread me that I dwell too long 5
To do a jape.

For sithen the first time that I fell
For my pride from heaven to hell,
Ever have I mustered me amell
Among mankind, 10
How I in dole might gar them dwell
There to be pined.

And certes, all that hath been sithen born
Have come to me, midday and morn,
And I have ordained so them forne 15
None may them fend,
That from all liking are they lorn
Without end.

And now some men speak of a swain,
How he shall come and suffer pain 20
And with his death to bliss again
They should be bought.
But certes, this tale is but a train,
I trow it nought.

For I wot ilka deal bedene 25
Of the miting that men of mean,
How he has in great barrat been
Sithen he was born,
And suffered mickle tray and teen
Both even and morn. 30

And now it is brought so about
That lurdan that they lof and lout

---

5 I am afraid I have delayed too long   6 *jape* evil deed   7 *sithen* since
9 *mustered me amell* manifested myself in the midst   11 To see how I might bring
them into misery (i.e. hell)   12 *pined* afflicted   13 *certes* certainly   14 *midday*
. . . *morn* all the time   15–18 And I have so arranged things for them that now
they are defenceless, [and] utterly deprived of happiness for ever   19 *swain* fellow
22 *bought* redeemed   23 *train* deceit   24 *trow* believe   *nought* not at all
25 For I indeed know everything   26 *miting* nonentity   *of mean* speak of
27 *barrat* trouble   29 *mickle . . . teen* great trouble and affliction   30 Both
evening and morning (i.e. all the time)   32 *lurdan* wretch   *lof* praise   *lout*
reverence

To wilderness he is went out,
Without mo;
To dere him now have I no doubt,   35
Betwixt us two.

Before this time he has been tent
That I might get him with no glent,
But now since he alone is went
I shall assay,   40
And gar him to some sin assent
If that I may.

He has fasted—that mars his mood—
These forty days without food.
If he be man in bone and blood   45
Him hungers ill;
In gluttony then hold I good
To wit his will.

For so it shall be known and kid
If Godhead be in him hid,   50
If he will do as I him bid
When I come nar.
There was never deed that ever he did
That grieved him war.

Thou witty man and wise of rede,   55
If thou can aught of Godhead,
Bid now that these stones be bread,
Betwixt us two;
Then may they stand thyself in stead,
And other mo.   60

For thou hast fasted long I ween;
I would now some meat were seen

34 Alone   35 *dere* harm   36 Between you and me   37 *tent* protected
38 So that by no subterfuge could I get him   40 *assay* put him to the test
41 And cause him to commit some sin   43 —that impairs his frame of mind—
46 He is very hungry   47 I consider it profitable   48 To learn his desire
49 *kid* revealed   51 *bid* command   52 *nar* nearer   54 That harmed
him worse   55 *witty* intelligent   *rede* counsel   56 If you are in any way
possessed of Godhead   59–60 Then may they provide for you and others in
addition   61 *ween* believe   62 *meat* food

For old acquaintance us between,
Thyself wot how.
There shall no man wit what I mean   65
But I and thou.

JESUS: My Father, that all site may slake,
    Honour evermore to thee I make
    And gladly suffer I for thy sake
    Swilk villainy,   70
    And thus temptations for to take
    Of mine enemy.

Thou waried wight, thy wits are wood,
For written it is, whoso understood,
A man lives not in main and mood   75
    With bread alone,
But God's words are ghostly food
    To men ilkone.

If I have fasted out of skill,
Wit thou me hungers not so ill   80
That I ne will work my Father's will
    In all degree;
Thy bidding will I not fulfil,
    That warn I thee.

DEVIL: Ah, slike carping never I kenned,   85
    Him hungers not, as I wend.
    Now since thy Father may thee fend
    By subtle sleight,
    Let see if thou alone may lend
    There upon height,   90

Upon the pinnacle perfectly.

---

63 *For* For the sake of   64 You yourself know how it is   65 No one shall
know about what I speak of   67 *site* sorrow   *slake* assuage   70 *Swilk*
Such   71 *take* endure   73 *waried* cursed   *wight* creature   *wood* mad
74 *whoso* [for] whoever   75 in health and strength   77 *ghostly* spiritual
78 *ilkone* each one   79 *out of skill* unreasonably   80 Understand you do
not make me so hungry   81 *ne will* do not want to   82 In every respect
85 *slike* such   *carping* words   *kenned* heard [before]   86 He is not, as I
believed, hungry   87 *fend* protect   88 *sleight* contrivance   89 *lend*
remain

Then the angels sing, 'Come Creator'.

Aha, now go we well thereby;
I shall assay in vainglory
To gar him fall,
And if he be God's son mighty,   95
Wit I shall.

Now list to me a little space:
If thou be God's son, full of grace,
Show some point here in this place
To prove thy might.   100
Let see, fall down upon thy face
Here in my sight.

For it is written, as well is kenned,
How God shall angels to thee send,
And they shall keep thee in their hend   105
Whereso thou goes,
That thou shall on no stones descend
To hurt thy toes.

And since thou may without wothe
Fall and do thyself no scathe,   110
Tumble down to ease us both
Here to my feet;
And but thou do I will be wroth,
That I thee hete.

JESUS: Let be, warlock, thy words keen,   115
For written it is, without ween,
Thy God thou shall not tempt with teen
Nor with discord,
Ne quarrel shall thou none maintain
Against thy Lord.   120

---

93 *vainglory* inordinate pride   94 *gar* make   97 *list* listen   *space* while
99 *point* indication   103 *kenned* known   105 *keep* look after   *hend* hands
106 *Whereso* Wherever   109 *wothe* peril   110 *scathe* damage   111 *ease*
satisfy   113 *And but* Unless   114 *hete* promise   115 Scoundrel, abandon
your provocative words   116 *ween* doubt   117 *teen* deceit   119 Nor
shall you persist in any quarrel

And therefore, trow thou, without train,
That all thy gauds shall nothing gain;
Be subject to thy sovereign
Early and late.
DEVIL: What, this travail is in vain   125
By aught I wot.

He proves that he is mickle of price,
Therefore it is good I me advise,
And since I may not in this wise
Make him my thrall,   130
I will assay in covetise
To gar him fall,

For certes, I shall not leave him yet.
Who is my sovereign, this would I wit.
Myself ordained thee there to sit,   135
This wot thou well,
And right even as I ordained it
Is done ilk deal.

Then may thou see, since it is so,
That I am sovereign of us two,   140
And yet I grant thee ere I go,
Without fail,
That if thou will assent me to
It shall avail.

For I have all this world to wield,   145
Tower and town, forest and field;
If thou thine heart will to me hield
With words hend,
Yet will I bainly be thy bield
And faithful friend.   150

---

122 *gauds* deceitful tricks   *nothing gain* be of no avail   123 *sovereign* i.e. God
124 At all times   125 *travail* effort   126 For all I know   127 of
great worth   128 *me advise* consider   129 *wise* manner   139 *thrall*
slave   131 *covetise* covetousness   134 I should like to know   137–8 And
just as I decreed it, everything is done   141 *ere* before   143 *assent me to*
come to an agreement with me   144 *avail* be the better [for you]   145 *wield*
command   147 *hield* incline   148 *hend* gracious   149 I shall readily
be your support

Behold now sir, and thou shalt see
Sere kingdoms and sere country;
All this will I give to thee
For evermore,
And thou fall and honour me   155
As I said ere.

JESUS: Cease of thy saws, thou Satanas,
I grant nothing that thou me asks,
To pine of hell I bid thee pass
And wightly wend,   160
And won in woe, as thou ere was,
Without end.

None other might shall be thy meed,
For written it is, who right can read,
Thy Lord God thee ought to dread   165
And honour ay,
And serve him in word and deed
Both night and day.

And since thou does not as I thee tell
No longer list me let thee dwell,   170
I command thee thou hie to hell
And hold thee there,
With fellowship of fiends fell
For evermore.

DEVIL: Out! I dare not look, alas,   175
It is war than ever it was.
He musters what might he has,
High mote he hang.
Follow fast, for me bus pass
To pains strong.   180

152 *sere* divers, many   155 *And* If   157 *saws* words   *Satanas*
Satan   159–60 I command you, be off to the punishment of hell, and leave in
haste   161 *won* remain   163 *None* No   *might* powers   *meed* reward
164 *who . . . read* whosoever may correctly interpret it   170 *list me* do I desire to
172 *hold thee* stay   173 *fell* horrible   175 *Out!* diabolical expletive   176 *war*
worse   177 *musters* displays   178 *mote* may   179–80 for I must be
off to dreadful torment

1 ANGEL: Ah, mercy Lord, what may this mean?
    Me marvels that ye thole this teen
    Of this foul fiend cant and keen
    Carping you till,
    And ye his wickedness, I ween,   185
    May waste at will.

    Methink that ye were straitly stead,
    Lord, with this fiend that now is fled.
JESUS: Mine angel dear, be not adread,
    He may not grieve;   190
    The Holy Ghost me has led,
    Thus shall thou leve.

    For when the fiend shall folk see,
    And sails them in sere degree,
    Their mirror may they make of me   195
    For to stand still,
    For overcome shall they not be
    But if they will.

2 ANGEL: Ah, Lord, this is a great meekness
    In you, in whom all mercy is,   200
    And at your will may deem or dress
    As is worthy;
    And three temptations take express,
    Thus sufferantly.

JESUS: My blessing have they with my hand   205
    That with swilk grief is not grutchand,
    And also that will stiffly stand
    Against the fiend.
    I know my time is fast comand,
    Now will I wend.   210

---

182 I am amazed that you endure this affliction   183 *cant* bold   *keen* malicious
184 *till* to   186 *waste* dispel   187 *straitly stead* hard pressed   189 *adread*
afraid   192 *leve* believe   193–4 For when the fiend approaches people,
and assails them in sundry ways   196 *stand still* resist stoutly   198 Unless
they want to be   201 *deem* judge   *dress* direct   203 *express* deliberately
204 *sufferantly* submissively   206 Who under such temptation do not complain
207 *stiffly* solidly   209 *comand* coming

THE SKINNERS

The Entry into Jerusalem

As Jesus himself points out in the course of the play (lines 4, 461–7), the *Entry into Jerusalem* initiates the sequence of events leading to the Passion. It was also important in itself as the fulfilment of one of the great Messianic prophecies, which is quoted prominently near the beginning (lines 24–8). As related in the Bible, the episode is not inherently dramatic, and in order to make it more so the York dramatist arrived at a new combination of characters and incidents, some of them traditional, and some of his own invention. The errand of the two disciples to fetch the ass and her foal serves to emphasize that the animal is 'common', that is, for the use of the poorest in the medieval community. This scene also introduces the Porter, who forms a link with the eight citizens, and prompts their discussion of Christ's miracles and the prophecies of his coming. The dramatist also brought in typical episodes from Christ's ministry: the healing of the Blind Man and the Lame Man, and the story of Zacheus in the sycamore tree. The physical infirmities of the first two were often interpreted as betokening fallen mankind's flawed spiritual state, and the imagery of Christ as a healer is found throughout the play.

Jesus must have ridden on the ass in the street amongst the audience, who were thus deftly drawn into the illusion of the play, and given a role as the crowd that lined the route into Jerusalem. The citizens probably awaited him on the pageant-wagon, and the tableau at the end, with its ordered arrangement of formal greetings, suggests that the dramatist had in mind the conventions of the contemporary royal entry into the medieval town. In the last line of the play, the local audience must have had a strong sense that the King of Heaven was being welcomed as much to medieval York as to the biblical Jerusalem.

The stanza is the same as that used in the *Nativity*, and the citizens' 'Hail' speeches at the end echo the 'Hail' lyrics of Joseph and Mary. Similar speeches are given by the Three Kings in *Herod and the Magi*, and the form is later gruesomely parodied by the soldiers who torture Christ after his second appearance before Pilate. The two stage directions calling for music do not specify the pieces that were sung, but they are likely to have been drawn from the liturgy of Palm Sunday. There seems to be no obvious connection between the content or presentation of the play and the daily activity of the Skinners, who dressed animal skins, pelts and furs.

JESUS: To me take tent and give good heed
  My dear disciples that be here,
  I shall you tell that shall be indeed:
  My time to pass hence it draweth near,
  And by this skill,   5
  Man's soul to save from sorrows sere
  That lost was ill.

  From heaven to earth when I descend
  Ransom to make I made promise,
  The prophecy now draws to end,   10
  My Father's will forsooth it is
  That sent me hither.
  Peter, Philip, I shall you bless,
  And go together

  Unto yon castle that is you again,   15
  Go with good heart and tarry nought,
  My commandment to do be ye bain.
  As I you charge look it be wrought:
  There shall ye find
  An ass this feast as ye had sought.   20
  Ye her unbind

  With her foal, and to me them bring,
  That I on her may sit a space,
  So the prophecy's clear meaning
  May be fulfilled here in this place: 25
  'Daughter Sion,
  Lo, thy Lord comes riding an ass
  Thee to upon'.

  If any man will you gainsay,
  Say that your lord has need of them   30
  And shall restore them this same day
  Unto what man will them claim;

1 *take tent* pay attention   3 I shall tell you what is surely to happen   5 And for this reason   6 *sere* manifold   7 That was lost through evil   8 *descend* descended   11 *forsooth* truly   14 *And* Now   15 *you again* in front of you 16 *mought* not at all   17 *bain* willing   18 *charge* instruct   *wrought* done 23 *a space* for a while   26–8 'Tell ye the Daughter of Sion, Behold, thy King cometh unto thee, meek, and riding upon an ass.' (Matthew 21: 5.)   29 *gainsay* oppose   32 *what man* whoever

Do thus this thing.
Go forth ye both and be ay bain
In my blessing.   35

PETER: Jesu, master, even at thy will
  And at thy list us likes to do.
  Yon beast which thou desires thee till
  Even at thy will shall come thee to,
  Unto thine ease.   40
  Certes, Lord, we will thither all go
  Thee for to please.

PHILIP: Lord, thee to please we are full bain
  Both night and day to do thy will.
  Go we, brothers, with all our main   45
  My Lord's desire for to fulfil,
  For prophecy
  Us bus it do to him by skill
  Thereto duly.

PETER: Yea, brother Philip, behold gradely,   50
  For as he said we should soon find,
  Methink yon beasts before mine eye
  They are the same we should unbind.
  Therefore freely
  Go we to him that them gan bind,   55
  And ask meekly.

PHILIP: The beasts are common, well I know,
  Therefore us needs to ask less leave;
  And our master keeps the law
  We may them take titer, I prove.   60
  For nought we let,
  For well I wot our time is brief,
  Go we them fetch.

---

34 *ay* always   37 *list* pleasure   *us likes* we are willing   38 *thou . . . till*
you ask for   40 At your convenience   41 *Certes* Indeed   45 *main*
strength   47–9 Because of the prophecy, we must needs duly oblige him in a
reasonable manner   50 *gradely* plainly   55 *gan* did   57 *common* for
the use of the community   58 We have little need to ask permission   59 *And*
If   60–1 I declare we may take them the more readily. Let nothing prevent us.
62 *wot* know   63 Let us go and take them

PORTER: Say, what are ye that make here mastery,
    To loose these beasts without livery?   65
    You seem too bold, since nought that ye
    Have here to do; therefore rede I
    Such things to cease,
    Or else ye may fall in folly
    And great disease.   70

PETER: Sir, with thy leave, heartily we pray
    This beast that we might have.
PORTER: To what intent first shall ye say,
    And then I grant what ye will crave
    By good reason.   75
PHILIP: Our master, sir, that all may save,
    Asks by chesoun.

PORTER: What man is that ye master call,
    Swilk privilege dare to him claim?
PETER: Jesus, of Jews king and ay be shall,   80
    Of Nazareth, prophet by name.
    This same is he,
    Both God and man without blame,
    This trust well we.

PORTER: Sirs, of that prophet heard I have,   85
    But tell me first plainly, where is he?
PHILIP: He comes at hand, so God me save,
    That Lord we left at Bethpagé,
    He bides us there.
PORTER: Sir, take this beast with heart full free,   90
    And forth ye fare.

    And if ye think it be to doon,
    I shall declare plainly his coming
    To the chief of the Jews, that they may soon
    Assemble sam to his meeting;   95
    What is your rede?

64 Tell me, who are you who are behaving so boldly?   65 *livery* permission
66–7 *since . . . do* since this is no concern of yours   *rede* advise   70 *disease*
offence   73 First tell me for what purpose   75 Given that it is reasonable
77 *by chesoun* for a good reason   79 *Swilk* Such   83 *without blame* in perfection
84 We truly believe   89 *bides* awaits   90 *with . . . free* by all means   91 And
go on your way   92 *to doon* necessary   95 Gather together to meet him

PETER: Thou says full well in thy meaning,
  Do forth thy deed.

  And soon this beast we shall thee bring
  And it restore as reason will.   100
PORTER: These tidings shall have no laining,
  But be the citizens declared till
  Of this city.
  I suppose fully that they will
  Come meet that free.   105

  And since I will they warned be,
  Both young and old in ilka state,
  For his coming I will them see
  To let them wit, without debate.
  Lo, where they stand,   110
  The citizens chief without debate
  Of all this land.

  He that is ruler of all right
  And freely shaped both sand and sea,
  He save you, lordings, gaily dight,   115
  And keep you in your seemly
  And all honour.
1 CITIZEN: Welcome porter, what novelty?
  Tell us this hour.

PORTER: Sirs, novelty I can you tell   120
  And trust them fully as for true:
  Here comes of kind of Israel
  At hand the prophet called Jesu,
  Lo, this same day,
  Riding on an ass. These tidings new   125
  Conceive ye may.

---

97 *thy meaning* what you suggest   98 Do so   100 *as . . . will* as is reasonable
101 *laining* concealment   102–3 But be revealed to the citizens of this city
105 *free* worthy person   106 *I . . . be* I desire that they should be told   107 *in
. . . state* of every degree   108 *For* Before   109 *wit* know   111 *without
debate* without a doubt   114 *freely shaped* graciously created   115 *lordings*
my lords   *dight* dressed   116 *seemlity* proper condition   118 *novelty* news
119 *this hour* at once   122 *kind* race   126 *Conceive* Understand

2 CITIZEN: And is that prophet Jesu near?
   Of him I have heard great ferlies told.
   He does great wonders in countries sere,
   He heals the sick, both young and old,   130
   And the blind gives them their sight.
   Both dumb and deaf, as himself would,
   He cures them right.

3 CITIZEN: Yea, five thousand men with loaves five
   He fed, and ilkone had enough.   135
   Water to wine he turned rife,
   He gart corn grow without plough
   Where ere was none.
   To dead men also he gave life,
   Lazar was one.   140

4 CITIZEN: In our temple if he preached
   Against the people that lived wrong,
   And also new laws if he teached
   Against our laws we used so long,
   And said plainly   145
   The old shall waste, the new shall gang,
   That we shall see.

5 CITIZEN: Yea, Moses' law he could ilk deal,
   And all the prophets on a row,
   He tells them so that ilka man may feel,   150
   And what they say entirely know
   If they were dim.
   What the prophets said in their saw,
   All longs to him.

6 CITIZEN: Emmanuel also by right   155
   They call that prophet by this skill,

128 *ferlies* wonders   129 *sere* various   132 *as . . . would* according to his inclination   133 *right* completely   135 *ilkone* each one   136 *rife* in abundance   137 *gart* caused   138 *ere* previously   140 *Lazar* Lazarus 144 Against old-accustomed laws   146 *waste* decline *gang* prosper   148 *could . . . deal* knew thoroughly   150 *tells* expounds *ilka* every *feel* perceive 151 *entirely* clearly   152 *dim* obscure   153 *saw* sayings   154 *longs* pertains   156 *by . . . skill* for this reason

He is the same that ere was hight
By Isaiah before us till,
That said full clear:
Lo, a maiden that knew never ill   160
A child should bear.

7 CITIZEN: David spoke of him, I ween,
And left witness, ye know ilkone,
He said the fruit of his corse clean
Should royally reign upon his throne,   165
And therefore he
Of David's kin and other none
Our king shall be.

8 CITIZEN: Sirs, methinks ye say right well,
And good examples forth ye bring,   170
And since we thus this matter feel,
Go we him meet as our own king,
And king him call.
What is your counsel in this thing
Now say ye all.   175

1 CITIZEN: Against reason I will not plead,
For well I wot our king he is.
Whoso against his king list threat,
He is not wise, he does amiss.
Porter, come near.   180
What knowledge hast thou of his coming?
Tell us all here,

And then we will go meet that free,
And him honour as we well owe
Worthily to our city,   185
And for our sovereign lord him know,
In whom we trist.
PORTER: Sirs, I shall tell you all on row,
And ye will list.

157–9 He is the one who once was promised to us by Isaiah, who said very clearly
160 *knew . . . ill* was without sin   162 *ween* know   164 *fruit* offspring   *corse clean* pure body   167 *other none* of no other   174 *thing* matter   178 *list threat* is inclined to offend   184 *well owe* certainly should   186 *know* acknowledge   187 *trist* trust   188 *on row* in order   189 *list* listen

Of his disciples, two this day,   190
Where that I stood, they fair me gret,
And on their master's half did pray
Our common ass that they might get
But for a while,
Whereon their master soft might sit   195
Space of a mile.

And all this matter they me told
Right wholly as I say to you,
And the ass they have right as they would
And soon will bring again, I trow,   200
So they behest.
What ye will do, advise you now,
Thus think me best.

2 CITIZEN: Truly, as for me I say,
I rede we make us ready boun   205
Him to meet goodly this day,
And him receive with great renown,
As worthy is.
And therefore, sirs, in field and town
Ye fulfil this.   210

PORTER: Yea, and your children with you take,
Though all in age that they be young,
Ye may fare the better for their sake
Through the blessing of so good a king,
This is no doubt.   215
3 CITIZEN: I can thee thank for thy saying,
We will him lout.

And him to meet I am right bain
On the best manner that I can,
For I desire to see him fain   220
And him honour as his own man,

191 *fair . . . gret* greeted me politely   192 *half* behalf   195 *soft* comfortably
196 *Space* For the distance   200 *trow* believe   201 *behest* promised
202 *advise you* consider   203 So I would advise   205 *boun* to go   206 *goodly*
in a seemly fashion   210 Proceed in this way   212 *Though all* Even though
215 There can be no doubt about this   216 *can* do indeed   *saying* suggestion
217 *lout* worship   219 *On* In   220 *fain* eagerly   221 And to him
honour as one of his subjects

Since the sooth I see.
King of Jews we call him then,
Our king is he.

4 CITIZEN: Our king is he—that is no lease—   225
Our own law to it cords well,
The prophets all bore full witness
Which of him secret gan tell,
And thus would say:
Among yourselves shall come great sele   230
Through God verray.

5 CITIZEN: This same is he, there is none other,
Was us behest full long before,
For Moses said, as our own brother
A new prophet God should restore.   235
Therefore, look ye
What ye will do, without more;
Our king is he.

6 CITIZEN: Of Judah comes our king so gent,
Of Jesse, David, Solomon;   240
Also by his mother's kin take tent,
The genealogy bears witness on,
This is right plain.
Him to honour, right as I can
I am full bain.   245

7 CITIZEN: Of your clean wit and your conceit
I am full glad in heart and thought,
And him to meet without let
I am ready, and feign will nought,
But with you sam   250
Go him again us bliss hath brought,
With mirth and game.

---

222 *sooth* truth   225 *lease* lie   226 *cords* agrees   228 *secret* a mysterious
thing   230 *sele* joy   231 *God verray* the true God   233 Who was
promised to us many years ago   236 *look ye* consider   237 *without more*
without more ado   239 *gent* worthy   241 *by* to   242 *on* to it   246 *clean
wit* pure thoughts   *conceit* intent   248 *let* delay   249 *feign . . . nought*
will not delay   250 *sam* together   251 Go to him that has brought us joy
252 *game* rejoicing

8 CITIZEN: Your arguments they are so clear
    I can not say but grant you till,
    For when I of that counsel hear   255
    I covet him with fervent will
    Once for to see;
    I trow from thence I shall
    Better man be.

1 CITIZEN: Go we then with procession   260
    To meet that comely as us owe,
    With branches, flowers and orison.
    With mightful songs here on a row
    Our children shall
    Go sing before, that men may know.   265
2 CITIZEN: To this grant we all.

PETER: Jesu, Lord and master free,
    As thou command so have we done.
    This ass here we have brought to thee;
    What is thy will thou show us soon   270
    And tarry nought,
    And then shall we without hone
    Fulfil thy thought.

JESUS: I thank you, brothers, mild of mood.
    Do on this ass your clothes ye lay,   275
    And lift me up with hearts good
    That I on her may sit this day
    In my blessing.
PHILIP: Lord, thy will to do alway,
    We grant this thing.   280

JESUS: Now my brothers, with good cheer
    Give good intent, for ride I will
    Unto yon city ye see so near.

---

254 I cannot but agree with you   256 *covet* yearn for   *will* desire   257 To
see him but once   261 *comely* gracious one   *owe* ought   262 *orison* worship
263 *mightful* loud   *on . . . row* in due order   265 *before* in front   266 *grant*
agree   267 *free* worthy   268 *command* commanded   271 *tarry* linger
272 *hone* delay   273 *thought* will   280 *grant . . . thing* agree to do this
282 *Give . . . intent* Pay close attention

Ye shall me follow sam and still
As I ere said.   285
PHILIP: Lord, as thee list, we grant thee till,
And hold us paid.

Then they sing.

BLIND MAN: Ah, Lord, that all this world has made,
Both sun and moon, night and day,
What noise is this that makes me glad?   290
From whence it should come I cannot say,
Or what it mean.
If any man walk in this way
Tell him me bedene.

POOR MAN: Man, what ails thee to cry?   295
Where would thou be? Thou say me here.
BLIND MAN: Ah, sir, a blind man am I
And ay has been of tender year,
Since I was born.
I heard a voice with noble cheer   300
Here me before.

POOR MAN: Man, will thou aught that I can do?
BLIND MAN: Yea, sir, gladly would I wit
If thou could aught declare me to
This mirth I heard, what mean may it   305
Or understand?
POOR MAN: Jesu the prophet full of grace
Comes here at hand,

And all the citizens they are boun
Go him to meet with melody,   310
With the fairest procession
That ever was seen in this Jewry;
He is right near.

284 *sam and still* all together   286–7 Lord, we are pleased to agree to what you
say   294 Let him tell me quickly   295–6 Man, what causes you to cry
out like this? Tell me quickly what you want.   298 *of . . . year* from my earliest
years   300 *noble cheer* a gracious sound   301 In front of me here   302 *will*
. . . do? is there anything I can do for you?   304 *aught declare* in any way explain
306 *understand* signify   309 *boun* ready

BLIND MAN: Sir, help me to the street hastily,
    That I may hear   315

    That noise, and also that I might through grace
    My sight of him to crave I would.
POOR MAN: Lo, he is here at this same place.
    Cry fast on him, look thou be bold,
    With voice right high.   320
BLIND MAN: Jesu, the son of David called,
    Thou have mercy.

    Alas, I cry, he hears me nought,
    He has no ruth of my misfare.
    He turns his ear, where is his thought?   325
POOR MAN: Cry somewhat louder, look thou not spare,
    So may thou spy.
BLIND MAN: Jesu, the salver of all sore,
    To me give good eye.

PHILIP: Cease, man, and cry not so,   330
    The voice of the people goes thee by.
    Thee owe sit still and tent give to,
    Here passes the prophet of mercy—
    Thou does amiss.
BLIND MAN: Ah, David's son, to thee I cry,   335
    The king of bliss.

PETER: Lord, have mercy, and let him go,
    He can not cease of his crying.
    He follows us both to and fro,
    Grant him his boon and his asking   340
    And let him wend.
    We get no rest ere that this thing
    Be brought to end.

JESUS: What would thou, man, I to thee did
    In this present? Tell openly.   345

317 *crave* ask   319 *fast on* earnestly to   320 *high* loud   322 Be merciful
324 *ruth of* pity for   *misfare* misfortune   325 He ignores me, what is he think-
ing of?   326 *look . . . spare* do not stint   327 *spy* see   328 *salver . . .
sore* remedy for all afflictions   331 *goes . . . by* drowns yours   332 You
should sit still and pay attention   340 *boon* request *asking* plea   341 *wend*
go   345 *In . . . present* Before these people

BLIND MAN: Lord, my sight is from me hid,
  Thou grant me it, I cry mercy,
  This would I have.
JESUS: Look up now with cheer blithely,
  Thy faith shall thee save. 350

BLIND MAN: Worship and honour ay to thee
  With all the service that can be done,
  The king of bliss, lofed mote he be
  That thus my sight hath sent so soon,
  And by great skill. 355
  I was ere blind as any stone:
  I see at will.

LAME MAN: Ah, well were them that ever had life,
  Old or young whether it were,
  Might wield their limbs without strife, 360
  Go with this mirth that I see here,
  And continue;
  For I am set in sorrows sere
  That ay are new.

Thou Lord that shaped both night and day, 365
  For thy mercy have mind on me
  And help me, Lord, as thou well may
  . . . . . .
I may not gang,
  For I am lame, as men may see,
  And have been long. 370

For well I wot, as known is rife,
  Both dumb and deaf thou grantest them grace,
  And also the dead that thou hast given life;
  Therefore grant me, Lord, in this place
  My limbs to wield. 375

349 *cheer blithely* a happy countenance   353 *lofed . . . be* may he be praised
358–62 Ah, they were surely fortunate in this life, whether they were old or young,
who could use their limbs without difficulty. They might follow this joyful procession
before me, and always be healthy   363 *set* plunged   364 That forever
renew themselves   366 *have . . . on* attend to   367+ *Line missing in MS*
368 *gang* walk   371 *rife* everywhere   375 Power over my limbs

JESUS: My man, rise, and cast thy crutches good space
  Here in the field.

  And look in truth thou steadfast be,
  And follow me forth with good meaning.
LAME MAN: Lord, lo my crutches, where they flee, 380
  As far as I may let them fling
  With both my hend.
  That ever we have meeting
  Now I defend,

  For I was halt of limb and lame 385
  And I suffered teen and sorrows enough.
  Ay-lasting Lord, lofed be thy name,
  I am as light as bird on bough.
  Ay be thou blessed,
  Such grace hast thou showed me now, 390
  Lord, as thee list.

ZACHEUS: Since first this world was made of nought
  And all thing set in equity,
  Such ferly thing was never none wrought
  As men this time may see with eye. 395
  What may it mean?
  I can not say what it may be,
  Comfort or teen.

  And chiefly of a prophet new
  That mickle is profit, and that of late 400
  Both day and night they him asue,
  Our people sam through street and gate
  .   .   .   .
  Our old laws as now they hate
  And his keep yare.

376 *cast . . . space* throw your crutches a good distance away   378 *steadfast* loyal
379 *meaning* intentions   382 *hend* hands   384 *defend* forbid   385 *halt
of* crippled in   386 *teen* anguish   387 *Ay-lasting* Eternal   *lofed* praised
391 *thee list* it pleases you   393 *equity* a state of righteousness   394 *Such
an amazing thing never happened*   398 *teen* trouble   399–402 The chief
[marvel] is a wonderful new prophet, and recently the people have begun continually to
follow him along the streets and highways   402+ *Line missing in MS*   404 *yare*
willingly

Men from death to life he raise,   405
The blind and dumb gives speech and sight,
Greatly therefore our folk him praise,
And follow him both day and night
From town to town.
They call him prophet, by right   410
As of renown.

And yet I marvel of that thing,
Of publicans since prince am I,
Of him I could have no knowing
If all I would have come him nigh,   415
Early and late;
For I am low, and of men high
Full is the gate.

But since no better may befall,
I think what best is for to do.   420
I am short, ye know well all,
Therefore yon tree I will go to
And in it climb.
Whether he come or pass me fro
I shall see him.   425

Ah, noble tree, thou sycamore,
I bless him that thee on the earth brought.
Now may I see both here and there
That under me hid may be nought.
Therefore in thee   430
Will I bide in heart and thought,
Till I him see.

Until the prophet come to town
Here will I bide, what so befall.
JESUS: Do, Zacheus, do fast come down.   435
ZACHEUS: Lord, even at thy will hastily I shall,
    And tarry nought.

---

405 *raise* raises   413 *publicans* tax-collectors   *prince* chief   414 *Of* With
knowing acquaintance   415–16 Even though I would frequently have been near
him   417 *low* short   *high* tall   418 *gate* street   419 *no . . . befall*
it can't be helped   424 *pass . . . fro* go away from me   429 *hid . . . nought*
nothing can be concealed

To thee on knees, Lord, here I fall,
For sin I wrought.

And welcome, prophet traist and true, 440
With all the people that to thee long.
JESUS: Zacheus, thy service new
Shall make thee clean of all the wrong
That thou hast done.
ZACHEUS: Lord, I let not for this throng 445
Here to say soon

Me shames with sin, but ought to mend.
My sin forsake therefore I will,
Half my good I have unspent
Poor folk to give it till, 450
This will I fain.
Whom I beguiled, to him I will
Make asith again.

JESUS: Thy clear confession shall thee cleanse,
Thou may be sure of lasting life. 455
Unto thy house, without offence,
Is granted peace, without strife.
Farewell, Zaché.
ZACHEUS: Lord, thee lout ay man and wife,
Blessed might thou be. 460

JESUS: My dear disciples, behold and see,
Unto Jerusalem we shall ascend.
Man's son shall there betrayed be
And given into his enemies' hend,
With great despite. 465
Their spitting on him there shall they spend,
And smartly smite.

---

439 *wrought* did   440 *traist* trustworthy   441 *that . . . long* who accompany you
445 *let . . . throng* do not hesitate in spite of all these people   446 *soon* readily
447 I am ashamed of [my] sin, and should amend my life   449–50 Half of my
assets to give to the poor   451 *fain* gladly   452–3 I will make reparation to
whoever I have cheated   455 *lasting* eternal   459 Lord, may you eternally be
worshipped by all   465 *despite* hatred   466 *spend* discharge   467 *smartly*
fiercely

Peter, take this ass me fro
And lead it where thou ere it took.
I mourn, I sigh, I weep also,   470
Jerusalem, on thee to look.
And so may thou rue
That ever thou thy king forsook,
And was untrue.

For stone on stone shall none be left,   475
But down to the ground all shall be cast,
Thy game, thy glee, all from thee reft,
And all for sin that thou done hast.
Thou art unkind;
Against thy king thou hast trespassed,   480
Have this in mind.

PETER: Porter, take here thine ass again,
At hand my Lord comes on his feet.
PORTER: Behold where all the burgesses bain
Come with worship him to meet.   485
Therefore I will
Let him abide here in this street,
And lout him till.

1 CITIZEN: Hail, prophet proved without peer,
Hail, prince of peace shall ever endure,   490
Hail, king comely, courteous and clear,
Hail, sovereign seemly, to sinful sure;
To thee all bow.
Hail, Lord lovely, our cares may cure,
Hail, king of Jews.   495

2 CITIZEN: Hail, flourishing flower that never shall fade,
Hail, violet vernant with sweet odour,
Hail, mark of mirth, our medicine made,
Hail, blossom bright, hail, our succour,

---

472 *rue* repent   477 *reft* taken away   479 *unkind* degenerate   480 *tres-*
passed sinned   483 *At hand* Near by   488 Pay homage to him   489 *peer*
equal   491 *comely* gracious   *clear* pure   492 *seemly* worthy   *to . . . sure*
true helper of sinners   494 *our . . . cure* remedy for our afflictions   497 *vernant*
blooming   498 *mark* object   *mirth* joy   *medicine* salvation

Hail, king comely. 500
Hail, menskful man, we thee honour
With heart freely.

3 CITIZEN: Hail, David's son, doughty in deed,
Hail, rose ruddy, hail beryl clear,
Hail, well of wealth, may make us meed, 505
Hail, salver of our sores sere,
We worship thee.
Hail, hendful, with solace sere
Welcome thou be.

4 CITIZEN: Hail, blissful babe, in Bethlehem born, 510
Hail, boot of all our bitter bales,
Hail, segge that shaped both even and morn,
Hail, talker tristful of true tales,
Hail, comely knight.
Hail, of mood that most prevails 515
To save the tight.

5 CITIZEN: Hail, diamond with druery dight,
Hail, jasper gentle of Jewry,
Hail, lily lovesome, leamed with light,
Hail, balm of boot, moist and dry, 520
To all has need.
Hail, bairn most blessed of mild Mary,
Hail, all our meed.

6 CITIZEN: Hail, conqueror, hail, most of might,
Hail, ransomer of sinful all, 525
Hail, pitiful, hail lovely light,
Hail, to us welcome be shall,
Hail, king of Jews.

---

501 *menskful* exalted   502 *freely* glad   503 *doughty in deed* courageous
504 *ruddy* red   505 *well . . . meed* source of good things, who may grant us
reward   506 *salver . . . sere* remedy for our various afflictions   508 *hendful*
worthy one   *solace sere* abundant joy   511 *boot . . . bales* salvation from all our
grievous troubles   512 *segge* being   513 *tristful* trustworthy   515 *mood*
will   *most* surely   516 *the tight* those in captivity   517 *with . . . dight*
adorned with ornamentation   519 *lovesome* worthy of love   *leamed* shining
520 *balm . . . boot* beneficent ointment   521 To all who have need   525 *sinful*
all all sinners   526 *pitiful* one who is filled with pity

Hail, comely corse that we thee call,
With mirth that news.   530

7 CITIZEN: Hail, sun ay shining with bright beams,
Hail, lamp of life shall never waste,
Hail, liking lantern that lovely leams,
Hail, text of truth, the true to taste.
Hail, king and sire,   535
Hail, maiden's child that mensked her most,
We thee desire.

8 CITIZEN: Hail, doomsman dreadful, that all shall deem,
Hail, quick and dead, that all shall lout,
Hail, whom worship most will seem,   540
Hail, whom all thing shall dread and doubt.
We welcome thee;
Hail and welcome of all about
To our city.

   Then they sing.

529 *comely corse* fair creature   530 *news* continues   532 *waste* go out
533 *liking* fair   *lovely leams* shines beautifully   534 *text* very word   *taste*
put to the test   536 *mensked* honoured   538 *doomsman dreadful* stern judge
deem judge   539 *quick* living   540 *most . . . seem* will be most fitting for
541 *doubt* fear   543 *all about* everybody here

THE CUTLERS

The Conspiracy

The underlying theological structure of the Corpus Christi cycle made it inevitable that the Passion be treated with much more amplitude and detail than any other subject. The events leading up to the Crucifixion were set in motion by the conspiracy of the Jews with Pontius Pilate and Judas Iscariot, the subject of the following play, and the first of several pageants in the Passion sequence which have been attributed by J. W. Robinson and others to a single anonymous dramatist known as the 'York Realist'.

The Realist's work is easily distinguishable in various ways from the bulk of the cycle. He wrote in vigorous and distinctive alliterative verse, originally an Anglo-Saxon epic medium, which had achieved renewed currency during the fourteenth century in both rhymed and unrhymed form with masterpieces such as *Piers Plowman*, *Sir Gawain and the Green Knight*, and *Pearl*. The Realist's plays share with these works a range of poetic diction and a suiting of character and incident to different registers in the alliterative style which distinguish them from much of the other writing in the cycle. Of the eight plays usually attributed to him, six are included in the present selection: the *Conspiracy*, *Christ before Annas and Caiaphas*, *Christ before Pilate 1*, *Christ before Herod*, *Christ before Pilate 2*, and the *Death of Christ*. All his compositions are pervaded by a powerful sense of atmosphere, and often achieve great emotional intensity in their realization of dialogue, character, and action. Like all great dramatists, the Realist creates an internally consistent and recognizable 'world' in each of his plays. His selection and arrangement of the biblical material owe something to two fourteenth-century vernacular poems, the *Northern Passion* and the *Gospel of Nicodemus*, but several characters and scenes appear to be original inventions.

The *Conspiracy* introduces the principal human characters in the York Passion sequence: the elusive Pilate; the malicious and subtly differentiated High Priests Annas and Caiaphas; and above all Judas, who in an insinuating soliloquy explains his motives to the audience and establishes himself as a very early example of a familiar type of English stage villain. His subsequent encounter with the Porter, who instinctively perceives Judas's evil nature, is shot with symbolism and verbal hints of his diabolical affiliations, which were doubtless emphasized by visual means in performance.

The fourteen-line stanza of the *Conspiracy* also appears in its alliterative form in another of the Realist's compositions, *Christ before Herod*. Earlier in the cycle a similarly shaped stanza is found in the *Flood*, but there the line is scanned syllabically, rather than accentually. The owners of the *Conspiracy*, the Cutlers, made knives.

PILATE: Under the royalest roy of rent and renown,
　Now am I regent of rule of this region in rest;
　Obey unto bidding bus bishops me boun,
　And bold men that in battle make breasts to burst.
　To me betaught is the tent this tower-begone town,　　　　　5
　For traitors tite will I taint, the truth for to trist.
　The dubbing of my dignity may not be done down,
　Neither with duke nor douzepers, my deeds are so dressed.
　My desire must daily be done
　With them that are greatest of game,　　　　　10
　And thereagainst find I but fone,
　Wherefore I shall better their boon—
　But he that me grieves for a groan,
　Beware, for boistous I am.

　Pounce Pilate of three parts then in my proper name;　　　　　15
　I am a perilous prince to prove where I pear.
　Among the philosophers first there fanged I my fame,
　Wherefore I feel to affect I find not my fere.
　He shall full bitterly ban that bide shall my blame,
　If all my blee be as bright as blossom on briar,　　　　　20
　For soon his life shall he lose, or left be for lame,
　That louts not to me lowly, nor list not to lere.
　And thus since we stand in our state
　As lords with all liking in land,
　Do let us wit if ye wot　　　　　25
　Either, sirs, of bale or debate
　That needs for to be handled full hot,
　Since all your help hangs in my hand.

1 *roy* king　　*of rent* having revenue　　2 *regent of rule* deputy ruler　　*rest* peace
3 Bishops who are my subjects must obey my command　　4 *breasts* breastplates
5 *betaught* entrusted　　*tent* care [of]　　*tower-begone* turreted　　6 *tite* swiftly
taint convict　　*the . . . trist* to be sure　　7 *dubbing . . . dignity* rights by virtue of
my title　　8 *with* by　　*douzepers* famous knights　　*deeds . . . dressed* actions are
so sure　　10 *greatest of game* the noblest of all　　11 *fone* few　　12 *better
. . . boon* enhance their rewards　　13 But he who vexes me by complaining
14 *boistous* savage　　16 *prove* encounter　　*pear* appear　　17 *fanged* acquired
18 Wherefore I aspire to the opinion that I have no equal　　19 *ban* curse　　*bide*
suffer　　*blame* censure　　20 *If all* Even though　　*blee* countenance　　22 *louts*
bows down　　*lowly* humbly　　*nor . . . lere* or who is not inclined to learn　　24 *liking
in land* pleasure at our disposal　　25 *wit* know　　*wot* have evidence　　26 *bale*
trouble　　*debate* dispute　　27 *handled . . . hot* dealt with urgently

CAIAPHAS: Sir, and for to certify the sooth in your sight,
    As to you for our sovereign seemly we seek.   30
PILATE: Why, is there any mischief that musters his might,
    Or malice through mean men us musters to meek?
ANNAS: Yea, sir, there is a rank swain whose rule is not right,
    For through his rumour in this realm hath raised mickle reek.
PILATE: I hear well ye hate him; your hearts are on height,   35
    And heed if I help would his harms for to eke.
    But why are ye barely thus brath?
    Be ruly, and ray forth your reason.
CAIAPHAS: To us, sir, his lore is full loath.
PILATE: Beware that ye wax not too wrath.   40
ANNAS: Why sir, to skift from his scathe
    We seek for your succour this season.

PILATE: And if that wretch in our ward have wrought any wrong,
    Since we are warned, we would wit and wis ere we wend.
    But and his saw be lawful, ledge not too long,   45
    For we shall leave him, if us list, with love here to lend.
1 CLERK: And if that false faitour your furtherance may fang,
    Then feel I well that our folk mun fail of a friend.
    Sir, the strength of his steven ay still is so strong,
    That but he shortly be shent, he shape us to shend;   50
    For he kens folk him for to call
    Great God's son—thus grieves us that gome—
    And says that he sitting be shall
    In high heaven, for there is his hall.
PILATE: And friends, if that force to him fall,   55
    It seems not ye shall him consume.

---

29 *and* now   *sooth* truth   30 *seemly we seek* we apply to you in a fitting manner   31 *mischief . . . might* miscreant who is asserting himself   32 Or wickedness done by evil men that we ought to suppress   33 *rank swain* rebellious fellow   *rule* behaviour   34 *hath . . . reek* great disturbance has arisen   35 *on height* filled with malice   36 *heed* seek to know   *harms . . . eke* aggravate his misfortunes   37 Why are you so utterly enraged?   38 *ruly* moderate   *ray* set   39 *lore* teaching   *full loath* most offensive   40 *wax . . . wrath* do not become overwrought   41 *skift* escape   *scathe* malefactions   42 *succour . . . season* help at this time   43 *ward* jurisdiction   44 *wis* understand   *wend* go   45 *and* if   *saw* sayings   *ledge* accuse   46 For we shall permit him, if it pleases us, to live here unmolested   47 *faitour* liar   *furtherance* favour   *fang* acquire   48 *mun . . . of* must lose   49 *steven* teaching   *ay . . . is* remains   50 That unless he is quickly put down he is likely to overthrow us   51 *kens* tells   52 *thus . . . gome* so this fellow provokes us   55 *if . . . fall* if he should have that power   56 *consume* destroy

But that himself is the same ye said should descend,
Your seed and you then all for to succour.
CAIAPHAS: Ah, soft sir, and cease,
For of Christ when he comes no kin shall be kenned,
But of this caitiff's kindred we know the increase.   60
He likens him to be like God, ay-lasting to lend,
To lift up the laby, to lose or release.
PILATE: His masteries should move you your mood for to
    amend.
ANNAS: Nay, for swilk miss, from malice we may not us mese,
For he says he shall deem us, that dote,   65
And that, to us, is dain or despite.
PILATE: To noy him now is your note,
But yet the law lies in my lot.
1 CLERK: And if ye will wit, sir, ye wot
That he is well worthy to wite.   70

For in our temple has he taught by times more than ten,
Where tables full of treasure lay to tell and to try,
Of our chief money-changers—but, cursedly to ken,
He cast them over, that caitiff, and counted nought thereby.
CAIAPHAS: Lo sir, this is a perjury to print under pen,   75
Wherefore make ye that *appostita*, we pray you, to ply.
PILATE: How mean ye?
CAIAPHAS: Sir, to mort him for moving of men.
PILATE: Then should we make him to mourn but through your
    mastery.
Let be, sirs, and move that no more;
But what in your temple betid?   80

---

57 *himself* he   58 *seed* offspring   *succour* redeem   *soft sir* do not be hasty,
sir   59 *kenned* known   60 *caitiff's* wretch's   *increase* pedigree
61 *ay-lasting . . . lend* to live for ever   62 *laby* burden   *lose* destroy   63 His
assertions should incline you to improve your dispositions   64 No, given such
wickedness, we cannot restrain ourselves from hatred   65 *deem* judge   *dote*
fool   66 *dain* insult   *despite* malice   67 *noy* harass   *note* business
68 *lot* dispensation   69 *wit* consider   *wot* will find   70 *wite* blame
71 *by . . . ten* more than ten times   72 *tell . . . try* count and sort   73 *cursedly*
. . . *ken* to be frank about his wickedness   74 *cast* throw   *counted . . . thereby*
thought nothing of it   75 *perjury* offence   *print . . . pen* commit to writing
76 *appostita* apostate, renegade   *ply* submit   77 *mort* put to death   *moving*
. . . *men* subversion   78 *mastery* arbitrary power   79 That is enough, sirs,
say no more about it   80 *betid* happened

1 SOLDIER: We! There, sir, he skelped out of score
    That stately stood selling their store.
PILATE: Then felt he them faulty before,
    And made the cause well to be kid.

But what taught he that time? Swilk tales as thou tells?   85
1 SOLDIER: Sir, that our temple is the tower of his throned
        sire,
    And thus to pray in that place our prophets compel,
    To him that has poustie of prince and of empire;
    And they make *domus domini* that dealing there dwells
    The den of derfness as oft that they desire.   90
PILATE: Lo, is he not a mad man that for your meed mells,
    Since ye imagine amiss that makeless to mire?
    Your rancour is raking full raw.
CAIAPHAS: Nay, nay sir, we rule us but right.
PILATE: Forsooth, ye are over-cruel to know.   95
CAIAPHAS: Why, sir? For he would lose our law,
    Heartily we him hate as we owe,
    And thereto should ye maintain our might.

For why, upon our Sabbath day the sick makes he safe,
    And will not cease for our saws to sink so in sin.   100
2 SOLDIER: Sir, he covers all that come recoverance to crave
    But in a short continuance, that kens all our kin.
    But he holds not our holy days, hard hap might him have,
    And therefore hanged be he, and that by the halse.
PILATE: Ah, ho, sir, now, and hold in.
    For though ye gang thus giddy him guiltless to grave,   105
    Without ground you gain not swilk grief to begin;

---

81 *We* expression of outrage   *skelped* beat   *out . . . score* unreasonably   82 Those
who stood selling their goods in an orderly fashion   83 *faulty* guilty of offences
84 *kid* known   85 *Swilk* Such   86 *throned sire* enthroned Father   87 *compel*
oblige [us]   88 *poustie of* power over   89–90 And those who carry on
trade there make the house of the Lord into a den of iniquity as often as they like
91 *for . . . mells* acts for your benefit   92 Since you plan maliciously to destroy
that innocent man   93 *raking* rushing forward   *raw* viciously   94 *rule .*
. . right proceed correctly   96 *lose* overthrow   97 *owe* ought   98 *maintain*
. . . might back up our power   99 *safe* well   100 And for all that we can
say does not hesitate to fall into sin   101 he cures all who come to seek healing
102 *continuance* time   103 *But* But because   *holds* observes   *hard hap* ill-
fortune, a curse   104 *halse* neck   *hold in* restrain yourself   105–6 For
though you rush thoughtlessly to condemn him even though he is innocent, without
evidence it is not to your advantage to venture upon such a troublesome business

And look your ledging be leal,
Without any trifles to tell.
ANNAS: For certain our saws dare we seal.
PILATE: And then may we profit our peal.   110
CAIAPHAS: Sir, but his faults were fele,
We meant not of him for to mell.

For he perverts our people that proves his preaching,
And for that point ye should press his poustie to pair.
2 CLERK: Yea, sir, and also that caitiff he calls him our king,   115
And for that cause our commons are cast in care.
PILATE: And if so be, that bourd to bale will him bring,
And make him boldly to ban the bones that him bare.
For-why that wretch from our wrath shall not wring,
Ere there be wrought on him wrake.
1 CLERK: So would we it were,   120
For so should ye sustain your sele,
And mildly have mind for to meek you.
PILATE: Well wit ye, this work shall be well,
For kenned shall that knave be to kneel.
2 CLERK: And so that our force he may feel,   125
All sam for the same we beseech you.

JUDAS: *Ingenti pro inuria*—him Jesus, that Jew,
Unjust unto me, Judas, I judge to be loath.
For at our supper as we sat, the sooth to pursue,
With Simon Leprous, full soon my skift came to scathe.   130
To him there brought one a box, my bale for to brew,
That bainly to his bare feet to bow was full brath.
She annointed them with an ointment that noble was and new,
But for that work that she wrought I waxed wonder wrath.

107 *ledging . . . leal* allegations are true   108 *trifles . . . tell* lies added   109 *saws words   seal* certify for true   110 *profit . . . peal* allow the case to go forward
111 *Sir*, if his faults were not numerous   112 *of . . . mell* to concern ourselves
with him   113 *proves* hear   114 *press* act firmly   *pair* impair   116 *cast . . . care* troubled   117 *bourd* trick, prank   119 *For-why* Wherefore   *wring* slip away   120 *Ere* Before   *wrake* vengeance   121 *sele* prosperity   122 If
you prudently decide to agree   123 *be well* proceed satisfactorily   124 *kenned* taught   126 *sam* together   *the same* such an outcome   127 'On account
of a great injury'   128 *loath* opprobrious   129 *the . . . pursue* to tell the
truth   130 *skift . . . scathe* evil plan was hatched   131 *my . . . brew* which
angered me   132 Who was willing and eager to bow to his bare feet   134 *I . . . wrath* I was extremely enraged

And this—to discover—was my skill: 135
For of his pence, purser was I,
And what that me taught was until,
The tenth part that stole I ay still.
But now for me wants of my will,
That bargain with bale shall he buy. 140

That same ointment, I said, might sam have been sold
For silver pence in a sum three hundred, and fine
Have been departed to poor men as plain pity would;
But for the poor, ne their part pricked me no pine—
But me teened for the tenth part, the truth to behold, 145
That thirty pence of three hundred so tite I should tine.
And for I miss this money, I mourn on this mould,
Wherefore for to mischieve this master of mine
Therefore fast forth will I flit,
The princes of priests until, 150
And sell him full soon ere that I sit,
For thirty pence in a knot knit.
Thusgates full well shall he wit
That of my wrath wreak me I will.

Do open, porter, the port of this proud place, 155
That I may pass to your princes to prove for your prow.
PORTER: Go hence, thou glowering gadling, God give thee ill
grace,
Thy glifting is so grimly thou gars my heart grow.
JUDAS: Good sir, be toward this time, and tarry not my trace,
For I have tidings to tell.
PORTER: Yea, some treason, I trow, 160
For I feel by a figure in your false face

135 *my skill* the reason   136–40 For I was the keeper of his money, and whatever
was given to me, I always stole the tenth part. But now, because I lack what I want, he
will pay for that transaction with trouble   142 *fine* subsequently   143 *departed*
distributed   *would* demanded   144 *ne . . . pine* concern for them did not
affect me   145 *me teened* I was agrieved   *the . . . behold* to speak truly   146 *tine*
lose   147 *mourn . . . mould* go about with a grudge   148 *mischieve* injure
149 *flit* go   150 To the high priests   151 *sit* rest   152 *in . . . knit*
in a sealed bargain   153 *Thusgates* In this way   154 *wreak . . . will* I will
avenge myself   155 *port* door   156 *prove* act   *prow* good   157 *gadling*
rascal   158 Your glaring is so offensive you cause my heart to swell [with indig-
nation]   159 *toward* helpful   *tarry* hinder   *trace* course of action   160 *trow*
suppose   161 *feel* sense   *figure* expression

It is but folly to fast affection in you.
For Mars he hath morticed his mark,
After all lines of my lore,
And says ye are wicked of work   165
And both a strong thief and a stark.

JUDAS: Sir, thus at my beard and ye bark,
It seems it shall sit you full sore.

PORTER: Say, beetle-browed briber, why blows thou such boast?
Full false in thy face in faith can I find.   170
Thou art cumbered in cursedness and cairs to this coast,
To mar men of might hast thou marked in thy mind.

JUDAS: Sir, I mean of no malice, but mirth move I most.

PORTER: Say, unhanged harlot, I hold thee unhend,
Thou lookest like a lurdan his livelihood had lost.   175
Woe shall I work thee away but thou wend.

JUDAS: Ah, good sir, take tent to my talking this tide,
For tidings full true can I tell.

PORTER: Say, brethel, I bid thee abide,
Thou chatterest like a churl that can chide.   180

JUDAS: Yea, sir, but and the truth should be tried,
Of mirth are these matters I mell;

For through my deeds your douzepers from dere may be
   drawn.

PORTER: What, deems thou till our dukes that dole should be
   dight?

JUDAS: Nay, sir, so said I not.   184a
If I be called to council, that cause shall be known   185
Among that comely company, to clerk and to knight.

PORTER: Bide me here, beausire, or more blore be blown,

---

162 *fast* place   163 *morticed* fixed   164 According to the principles of my
understanding   166 *strong* bold   *stark* thoroughgoing [one]   168 *sit* . . .
sore be the worse for you   169 *briber* villain   *blows thou* do you give vent to
170 *Full false* Deep treachery   171 You came to this place burdened with malice
172 *mar* injure   *marked . . . mind* undertaken   173 *mean* intend   *but* . . .
most but rather I have good things to tell   174 *harlot* miscreant   *unhend* unworthy   175 *lurdan* wretch [who]   176 I shall do you mischief unless you
go away   177 *take tent* pay heed   *this tide* at this time   179 *brethel* scoundrel
180 *chide* wrangle 181 *tried* put to the test   182–3 What I have to say is good
news, for through my actions can your leaders be saved from harm   184 What,
do you know of harm intended to our leaders?   184a Extra-metrical line.
186 *comely* worthy   187 *Bide* Await   *beausire* my fine fellow   *blore* boasting

And I shall busk to the bench where banners are bright
And say unto our sovereigns, ere seed more be sown,
That swilk a segge as thyself sues to their sight.   190
My lord now, of wit that is well,
I come for a case to be kid.
PILATE: We! Speak on, and spare not thy spell.
CAIAPHAS: Yea, and if us mister to mell,
Since ye bear of beauty the bell,   195
Blithely shall we bow as ye bid.

PORTER: Sir, without abating, there hoves as I hope
A hind, hilt-full of ire, for hasty he is.
PILATE: What comes he for?
PORTER: I ken him not, but he is clad in a cope.
He cairs with a keen face, uncomely to kiss.   200
PILATE: Go get him, that his grief we gradely may grope,
So no open language be going amiss.
PORTER: Come on belive to my lord, and if thee list to leap,
But utter so thy language that thou let not their bliss.
JUDAS: That lord, sirs, might sustain your sele   205
That flower is of fortune and fame.
PILATE: Welcome. Thy words are but well.
CAIAPHAS: Say, hearest thou, knave? Can thou not kneel?
PILATE: Lo, here may men fault in you feel.
Let be, sir, your scorning, for shame.   210

But beausire, be not abashed to bide at the bar.
JUDAS: Before you, sirs, to be brought, about have I been,
And always for your worship.
ANNAS: Say, wot thou any were?
JUDAS: Of work, sir, that hath wrathed you, I wot what I mean,
But I would make a merchandise, your mischief to mar.   215

188 *busk* hasten   189 *ere . . . sown* before anything more is said   190 *swilk
. . . segge* such a man *sues . . . sight* requests audience   191 *of . . . well* who is
source of all knowledge   193 Aha! Speak on, and say all you have to   194 *if
. . . well* if it is necessary for us to concern ourselves   196 *bow* act
197–8 Sir, to tell you all, there comes a fellow who, it seems, is brimming with anger
and in great haste   199 *cope* cloak   200 *cairs* comes   *keen* malicious
201 *that . . . grope* that we may immediately enquire into his grievance   202 *open
language* careless talk   *amiss* astray   203 *belive* quickly   *and . . . leap* if you
really are in haste   204 *let* disrupt *bliss* equanimity   210 *Let be* Leave off
211 *abashed* afraid   212 *about* busy   213 *always* entirely   *worship* benefit
were danger   214 *wrathed* enraged   *I . . . mean* I know what I know
215 *merchandise* bargain   *your . . . mar* to end the threat to you

PILATE: And may thou so?

JUDAS: Else mad I such masteries to mean.

ANNAS: Thou kens thou of some cumberance our charge for to
    chare?

  For cousin, thou art cruel.

JUDAS: My cause, sir, is keen.

  For if ye will bargain or buy,

  Jesus this time will I sell you.   220

1 CLERK: My blessing soon have thou forthy—

  Lo, here is a sport for to spy.

JUDAS: And him dare I hight you in hie,

  If ye will be toward, I tell you.

PILATE: What hightest thou?

JUDAS: Judas Iscariot.

PILATE: Thou art a just man   225

  That will Jesus be justified by our judgement.

  But howgates bought shall he be? Bid forth thy bargain.

JUDAS: But for a little beeting to bear from this bent.

PILATE: Now what shall we pay?

JUDAS: Sir, thirty pence and plete, no more then.

PILATE: Say, are ye pleased of this price he presses to present?   230

2 CLERK: Else contrary we our consciences, conceive since we
    can

  That Judas knows him culpable.

PILATE: I call you consent.

  But Judas, a knot for to knit,

  Wilt thou to this covenant accord?

JUDAS: Yea, at a word.

PILATE: Welcome is it.   235

2 SOLDIER: Take thereof, a traitor tite.

1 SOLDIER: Now, lief sir, let no man wit

  How this losel lakes with his lord.

---

216 Otherwise I should be mad to make such assertions   217 *cumberance . . . chare*
trouble that should arouse our concern   218 *cousin* term of mock-endearment
221 *soon* forthwith   *forthy* therefore   222 *spy* discover   223 *hight* promise *in
hie* quickly   224 *toward* co-operative   225 What is your name?   226 Who
should wish Jesus submitted to the justice of our judgement   227 *howgates* in what
way   228 *beeting* reward   *bent* place   229 *and plete* in full   231 *contrary*
violate   *conceive* perceive   232 You are agreed   233 *a . . . knit* to seal a
bargain   234 *covenant* agreement   *accord* consent   236 Look at that, an
eager traitor   237 *lief* dear   238 *losel* villain   *lakes* trifles

PILATE: Why, dwells he with that dochard whose deeds has us
    droved?

1 SOLDIER: That has he done, sir, and does, no doubt is this   240
    day.

PILATE: Then would we know why this knave thus cursedly
    contrived.

2 SOLDIER: Enquire him, since ye can best ken if he gainsay.

PILATE: Say, man, to sell thy master what miss hath he moved?

JUDAS: For of as mickle money he made me delay,
    Of you as I receive shall but right be reproved.   245

ANNAS: I read not that ye reckon us, our rule so to ray—
    For that the false fiend shall thee fang.

1 SOLDIER: When he shall want of a wrast.

1 CLERK: To whom work we wittingly wrong.

2 CLERK: Till him but ye hastily hang.   250

CAIAPHAS: Your language ye lay out too long.
    But Judas, we truly thee trast,

    For truly thou must learn us that losel to latch,
    Or of land through a lirt that lurdan may leap.

JUDAS: I shall you teach a token him tite for to tache,   255
    Where he is thringing in the throng, without any threap.

1 SOLDIER: We know him not.

JUDAS: Take keep then that caitiff to catch
    The which that I kiss.

2 SOLDIER: That comes well thee, curious, I clepe!
    But yet to warn us wisely always must ye watch.
    When thou shall wend forthwith we shall walk a wild heap,   260
    And therefore busy look now thou be.

JUDAS: Yes, yes, a space shall I spy us
    As soon as the sun is set, as ye see.

---

239 *dochard* fool   *whose . . . droved* whose behaviour has vexed us   241 *cursedly*
maliciously   242 *ken* discover   *gainsay* should contradict   243 Tell me,
what offence has your master done, that you should betray him?   244 *mickle*
much   *made . . . delay* withheld from me   245 *right . . . reproved* proper redress
be made   246 I believe you are not taking us seriously, to treat our laws in this
manner (i.e. to betray Christ over a minor debt)   247 *fang* seize   248 *want*
. . . wrast have need of an evil trick   249 *wittingly* knowingly   251 You have too
much to say for yourselves   252 *trast* trust   253 *learn* show [how]   *latch*
capture   254 Or that villain may slip away by means of a trick   255 *teach* show
tache seize upon   256 *thringing* being pressed   *threap* dispute   257 *keep*
care   258 *comes* becomes   *clepe* declare   260 *wend forthwith* go on ahead
walk . . . heap follow in a great crowd   262 *space* opportunity

1 SOLDIER: Go forth, for a traitor are ye.
2 SOLDIER: Yea, and a wicked man.
1 CLERK: Why, what is he?   265
2 CLERK: A losel, sir, but lewty should lie us.

He is trapped full of train, the truth for to trest,
I hold it but folly his faith for to trow.
PILATE: Abide in my blessing, and let your brest,
For it is best for our boot in bale for to bow.   270
And Judas, for our profit, we pray thee be prest.
JUDAS: Yet had I not a penny to purvey for my prow.
PILATE: Thou shalt have deliverance belive at thy list,
So that thou shall have liking our lordship to love.
And therefore, Judas, mend thou thy moan,   275
And take there thy silver all sam.
JUDAS: Yea, now is my great grief over-gone.
1 SOLDIER: Be light, then.
JUDAS: Yes, let me alone,
For tite shall that taint be tone,
And thereto jocund and jolly I am.   280

PILATE: Judas, to hold thy behest, be hend for our hap;
And of us, help and uphold we hight thee to have.
JUDAS: I shall beken you his corse in care for to clap.
ANNAS: And more comfort in this case we covet not to crave.
1 SOLDIER: Fro we may reach that reckless, his ribs shall we   285
    rap,
And make that roy, ere we rest, for running, to rave.
PILATE: Nay, sirs, all if ye scourge him, ye shend not his shape,
For if the sot be sackless, us sits him to save;

266 *lewty* truth   *lie* belie   267 If the truth be known, he is loaded with deceit
268 *trow* believe in   269 *let . . . brest* stop arguing   270 For it is to our
advantage to comply in difficult circumstances   271 *prest* quick   272 *purvey*
provide   *prow* comfort   273 *deliverance* payment   *list* liking   274 *liking*
good reason   *lordship* authority   275 *mend . . . moan* cease complaining
277 *over-gone* subsided   278 *light* happy   279 *taint* traitor   *tone* taken
281 *behest* promise   *be . . . hap* act well for our good   282 *uphold . . . hight*
support we promise   283 I shall show you how he may be captured   284 *we
. . . crave* we do not aspire to have   285 *Fro* When   *reach* seize   *reckless*
fool   286 *roy* fellow   *running* running [to escape pursuit] or perhaps 'letting
of blood'   *rave* writhe in agony   287 *all if* even though   *shend* injure   *shape*
body   288 For if the fool be innocent, we must spare him

Wherefore, when ye go shall to get him,
Unto his body brew ye no bale.   290
2 SOLDIER: Our list is from leaping to let him,
But in your sight, sound shall we set him.
PILATE: Do flit now forth till ye fetch him,
With solace all sam to your sale.

290 *brew . . . bale* do no injury   291 We mean only to prevent him from resisting
arrest   294 Joyfully together to your place

THE BOWERS AND FLETCHERS

Christ before Annas and Caiaphas

Christ before Annas and Caiaphas is attributed to the York Realist, the principal dramatist of the York Passion sequence (see the Headnote to the *Conspiracy*). Like the appearances before Pilate and Herod that follow, it is set at night, and in each play Jesus's principal adversary goes to bed, or rather, is put to bed only to be rudely awakened by a new development in the events. These scenes are of the dramatist's own invention. They are full of details of personal psychology and manners, and taken together powerfully evoke the impression of the one terrible night of Jesus's repeated examinations. In this play, Caiaphas's retirement for the night was probably staged 'within' on the pageant-wagon. Peter's denial is likely to have been presented 'without', close to the audience in the street. It skilfully amalgamates details from the different Gospel accounts. Caiaphas's servant Malcus, whose ear Peter had struck off with his sword, is introduced to recount the story of how Jesus healed the injury (John 18: 26). When Peter has denied his Lord for the third time, Jesus speaks a few words of sad reproach, evidently an expansion on a detail of St Luke's, of how 'the Lord turned, and looked upon Peter' (22: 61).

At line 170 the metre of the play changes. The preceding episodes were written mostly in alliterative quatrains with either three or four stresses to the line. From the turn in the action where the soldiers bring Jesus to Caiaphas's 'hall', the rest of the play is cast in twelve-line stanzas in the long alliterative line (ababababab$_4$cdcd$_3$). Christ's appearance before the High Priests also sets a pattern for the plays which follow, the calm, still, and largely silent figure of Jesus providing a stark contrast with the violent verbosity and frenetic activity of those around him. Some of this is implicit in the Gospels. What is not is the sadistic ferocity of the beating he receives before being passed on to Pilate. The soldiers cruelly elaborate their task by formalizing it as a popular buffeting game called 'pops', a muted modern descendant of which is the children's game Hot Cockles. The brutality of such scenes found some sanction in the tradition of affective meditation on the sufferings of Christ, but here there is a gruesomely festive atmosphere established by the cries of 'Wassail' and the treatment of Christ as the kind of fool that was made the butt of cruel popular entertainment in the period.

York was a city of some strategic importance in the Middle Ages, especially during disputes with the Scots, and the crafts dealing in armour and armaments flourished. Among the craftsmen were the Bowers and Fletchers, who made bows and arrows.

CAIAPHAS: Peace, beausires, I bid no jangling ye make,
 And cease soon of your saws, and see what I say,
 And true tent unto me this time that ye take,
 For I am a lord, learned leally in your lay.

 By cunning of clergy and casting of wit,   5
 Full wisely my words I wield at my will;
 So seemly in seat me seems for to sit
 And the law for to learn you and lead it by skill,
 Right soon.

 What wight so will aught with me   10
 Full friendly, in faith, am I found;
 Come off, do tite let me see,
 How graciously I shall grant him his boon.

 There is neither lord ne lady learned in the law,
 Ne bishop ne prelate that proved is for price,   15
 Nor clerk in the court that cunning will know,
 With wisdom may were him in world is so wise.

 I have the reign and the rule of all royalty,
 To rule it by right, as reason is.
 All doomsmen on dais owe for to doubt me   20
 That has them in bandon, in bale or in bliss;
 Wherefore take tent to my tales, and lout me.

And therefore, sir knights—

 Then they shall say 'Lord'.

---

1 *beausires* my good fellows *jangling* noise 2 *saws* talking 3 *true tent*
careful attention *take* give 4 *learned . . . lay* deeply learned in your laws
5 Through expertise in learning and application of intelligence 7 *me seems for* it
is appropriate for me 8 *learn* teach *lead* expound 10–11 Whoever
has dealings with me, finds me, in truth, most co-operative 12 *Come off* Come
along *tite* quickly 13 *boon* request 14 *ne* nor 15 *that . . . price*
who is so highly regarded 16 *clerk* learned man *cunning* expertise 17 [Who]
so cleverly may defend himself, [nor who] is so wise 18 I have all power and
rule over the entire kingdom 19 *as . . . is* as is reasonable 20 *doomsmen*
judges *owe* ought *doubt* fear 21 *in bandon* under [my] control *in bale*
. . . bliss in all circumstances 22 Wherefore pay attention to what I have to say,
and respect me

I charge you challenge your rights,
To wait both by day and by nights   25
Of the bringing of a boy into bail.

1 SOLDIER: Yes lord, we shall wait if any wonders walk,
And frayne how your folk fare that are forth run.
2 SOLDIER: We shall be bain at your bidding, and it not to-
      balk,
If they present you that boy in a band bound.   30

ANNAS: Why sir, and is there a boy that will not lout to your
      bidding?
CAIAPHAS: Yea sir, and of the curiousness of that carl there is
      carping,
But I have sent for that segge half for hething.
ANNAS: What wonderful works works that wight?
CAIAPHAS: Sick men and sorry he sends siker healing—   35
And to lame men—and blind he sends their sight.

Of crooked cripples that we know
It is to hear great wondering,
How that he heals them all on row,
And all through his false happening.   40

I am sorry of a sight
That eggs me to ire,
Our law he breaks with all his might,
That is most his desire.

Our Sabbath day he will not save,   45
But is about to bring it down,
And therefore sorrow must him have,
May he be catched in field or town,

24 *challenge* be alive to   25 *wait* keep watch   26 *boy* knave   *bail* custody
27 *wonders walk* unusual things are happening   28 *frayne* enquire   *forth run* gone
out   29 *bain* willing   *it . . . to-balk* not shirk in the slightest   30 *band* rope
31 *lout* submit   32 *curiousness* cleverness   *carl* fellow   *carping* talk   33 *segge*
person   *half . . . hething* partly for amusement   34 What extraordinary things
does this man perform?   35 *sorry* distressed   *siker* sure   38 It is most extraordinary to learn   39 *all . . . row* one after another   40 *happening* luck
41 *sorry of* upset by   42 That moves me to anger   44 That is his main
motive   45 *save* respect   46 *about* busy   *bring . . . down* overthrow it
47 Therefore he must be punished   48 *catched* captured

For his false steven.
He defames foully the Godhead,   50
And calls himself God's son of heaven.

ANNAS: I have good knowledge of that knave:
    Mary me means his mother hight,
    And Joseph his father, as God me save,
    Was kid and known well for a wright.   55

But one thing me marvels mickle over all,
    Of diverse deeds that he has done—
CAIAPHAS: With witchcraft he fares withal,
    Sir, that shall ye see full soon.

Our knights they are forth went   60
    To take him with a tray;
    By this I hold him shent,
    He can not wend away.

ANNAS: Would ye, sir, take your rest—
    This day is come on hand—   65
    And with wine slake your thirst?
    Then durst I well warrand

Ye should have tidings soon
    Of the knights that are gone,
    And how that they have done   70
    To take him by a train.

And put all thought away,
    And let your matters rest.
CAIAPHAS: I will do as ye say—
    Do get us wine of the best.   75

1 SOLDIER: My lord, here is wine that will make you to wink,
    It is liquor full delicious, my lord, and you like.

---

49 *steven* words   50 He grossly insults God's name   53 I believe his mother
was called Mary   55 *kid* recognized   *wright* carpenter   56 But one thing
surprises me above all   58 *he . . . withal* he is involved   60 *went* gone
61 *tray* stratagem   62 *shent* doomed   63 *wend* slip   65 *come . . .
hand* almost over   67 *durst* dare   *warrand* promise   71 *train* trick   72 Now
relax   73 *matters* business   76 *wink* sleep

Wherefore I rede dreely a draught that ye drink,
For in this country that we know, iwis there is none slike;
Wherefore we counsel you this cup savoury for to kiss.   80

CAIAPHAS: Do on daintily, and dress me on dais,
And hendly hill on me happing,
And warn all wights to be in peace,
For I am late laid unto napping.

ANNAS: My lord, with your leave, and it like you, I pass.   85
CAIAPHAS: Adieu be unto'ee, as the manner is.

WOMAN: Sir knights, do keep this boy in band,
For I will go wit what it may mean,
Why that yon wight was him followand,
Early and late, morn and e'en.   90

He will come near, he will not let,
He is a spy, I warrant, full bold.
3 SOLDIER: It seems by his semblant he had liever be set
By the fervent fire to fleme him from cold.

WOMAN: Yea, but and ye wist as well as I   95
What wonders that this wight has wrought,
And through his master's sorcery,
Full derfly should his death be bought.

4 SOLDIER: Dame, we have him now at will
That we have long time sought,   100
If other go by us still
Therefore we have no thought.

WOMAN: It were great scorn that he should scape
Without he had reason and skill;

78 *rede dreely* earnestly advise   79 *iwis . . . slike* indeed there is none other so
good   80 *savourly* with relish   81–2 Now in a seemly manner, put me [to bed]
on the dais, and carefully lay bedclothes over me   83 *wights* people   84 For I
am about to go to sleep   85 *pass* go   86 *manner* custom   87 *in band*
tied up   89 *wight* man   *him followand* following him   90 *e'en* evening
91 He persists in approaching, he will not give up   93 *semblant* appearance   *had
liever* would prefer to   94 *fervent* warm   *fleme him* escape   95 *wist* knew
98 He would pay for it with his death most cruelly   101–2 We are not concerned
if another continues to evade us   103 *scorn* scandal   *scape* escape   104 *skill*
cause

He looks lurking, like an ape,   105
I hope I shall haste me him till.

Thou caitiff, what moves thee stand
So stable and still in thy thought?
Thou hast wrought mickle wrong in land,
And wonderful works hast thou wrought.   110

A lorel, a leader of law,
To set him and sue has thou sought.
Stand forth and thrust in yon thrave,
Thy mastery thou bring unto nought.

Wait now, he looks like a brock,   115
Were he in a band for to bait,
Or else like an owl in a stock
Full privily his prey for to wait.

PETER: Woman, thy words and thy wind thou not waste,
Of his company never ere was I kenned.   120
Thou hast thee mismarked, truly be trast,
Wherefore of thy miss thou thee amend.

WOMAN: Then gainsays thou here the saws that thou said,
How he should claim to be called God's son,
And with the works that he wrought whilst he walked,   125
Bainly at our bidding always to be bound.

PETER: I will consent to your saws, what should I say more?
For women are crabbed—that comes them of kind.
But I say as I first said, I saw him never ere,
But as a friend of your fellowship shall ye me ay find.   130

105–6 He lurks, looking like an ape; I think I will approach him   107 *caitiff*
scoundrel   *moves* makes   109 *mickle . . . land* great harm hereabouts   110 *wonderful works* extraordinary things   111 *lorel* layabout   *leader of law* [false] exponent
of the law   112 You have sought to follow and accompany him   113 *thrust
. . . thrave* join this group   114 [And] your great deeds will be shown up for
what they are   115 *brock* badger   116 As if he were tied up to be baited
117 *in a stock* on a stump   118 *privily* covertly   119 Woman, do not waste
your words and your breath   120 *ere* beforehand   *kenned* known   121 If
the truth be known, you are mistaken   122 *miss* error   *thou . . . amend* be
disabused   123 *gainsays* contradict   126 *Bainly* Willingly   *bound* loyal
128 For women are ill-tempered, it is in their nature   130 *ay* from now on

MALCUS: Hark, knights that are known in this country, as we
    ken,
How yon boy with his boast has brewed mickle bale.
He has forsaken his master before yon women,
But I shall prove to you pertly and tell you my tale.

I was present with people when press was full prest,   135
To meet with his master with main and with might,
And hurled him hardly and hastily him arrest,
And in bands full bitterly bound him sore all that night.

And of tokening of truth shall I tell you
How yon boy with a brand brayed me full near—   140
Do move of these matters amell you—
For swiftly he swapped off mine ear.

His master, with his might, healed me all whole,
That by no sign I could see no man could it wit,
And then bad him bear peace in every-ilk bale,   145
For he that strikes with a sword, with a sword shall be smit.

Let see whether grantest thou guilt:
Do speak on, and spare not to tell us,
Or full fast I shall fond thee flit,
The sooth but thou say here amell us.   150

Come off, do tite let me see now,
In saving of thyself from shame

    .   .   .   .

Yea, and also for bearing of blame.

PETER: I was never with him in work that he wrought,
In word nor in work, in will nor in deed.   155

---

131 *ken* believe   132 *boast* extravagant words   *mickle bale* great trouble
134 *prove . . . pertly* expound to you openly   135 *when . . . prest* where the crowd
was thickest   136 *main* strength   137 *hurled* hustled   *hardly* violently
arrest arrested   138 *sore* securely   140 How with a sword this wretch gave
me a close shave   141 *move* speak   *amell* amongst   142 *swapped* struck
144 *it wit* understand how it was done   145 And then he told him [Peter] to act
peaceably in every kind of difficulty   146 *smit* struck down   147 Let us see
whether you admit your guilt   149 *fond . . . flit* send you packing   150 *sooth*
truth   151 *tite* quickly   152+ *Line missing in MS*

I know no corse that ye have hither brought,
In no court of this kith, if I should right read.

MALCUS: Hear, sirs, how he says, and has forsaken
His master to this woman here twice,
And newly our law has he taken—   160
Thus hath he denied him thrice.

JESUS: Peter, Peter, thus said I ere,
When thou said thou would abide with me
In weal and woe, in sorrow and care,
Whilst I should thrice forsaken be.   165

PETER: Alas the while that I came here,
That ever I denied my Lord in quart,
The look of his fair face so clear
With full sad sorrow shears my heart.

3 SOLDIER: Sir knights, take keep of this carl and be connand,   170
Because of Sir Caiaphas, we know well his thought.
He will reward us full well, that dare I well warrand,
When he wit of our works, how well we have wrought.

4 SOLDIER: Sir, this is Caiaphas' hall here at hand,
Go we boldly with this boy that we have here brought.   175

3 SOLDIER: Nay sirs, us must stalk to that stead and full still
stand,
For it is noon of the night, if they nap aught.
Say, who is here?

1 SOLDIER: Say who is here?

3 SOLDIER: I, a friend,
Well known in this country for a knight.

2 SOLDIER: Go forth, on your ways may ye wend,   180
For we have harboured enough for tonight.

1 SOLDIER: Go aback, beausires, ye both are to blame
To bourd when our bishop is boun to his bed.

---

156 *corse* person   157 *court* meeting-place   *kith* country   *if . . . read* if I
understand rightly   160 *newly* readily   164 *weal* prosperity   166 *while*
time   167 *Lord . . . quart* living lord   169 *shears* cuts   170 *keep* care
connand alert   173 *wit . . . works* finds out what we have done   176 *stalk*
move stealthily   *stead* place   177 *noon . . . night* midnight   *if . . . aught* in
case they are asleep   181 For we have taken indoors enough people for one
night   182 *aback* away   183 *bourd* play pranks   *boun* gone

4 SOLDIER: Why sir, it were worthy to welcome us home.
　　We have gone for this warlock and we have well sped.　　185
2 SOLDIER: Why, who is that?
3 SOLDIER:　　　　　　　　The Jews' king, Jesus by name.
1 SOLDIER: Ah, ye be welcome, that dare I well wed,
　　My lord has sent for to seek him.
4 SOLDIER:　　　　　　　　Lo, see here the same.
2 SOLDIER: Abide as I bid, and be not adread.
　　My lord, my lord, my lord, here is lake, and you list.　　190
CAIAPHAS: Peace, losels! List ye be nice?
1 SOLDIER: My lord, it is well and ye wist.
CAIAPHAS: What, nemn us no more, for it is twice.

　　Thou takest none heed to the haste that we have here on hand.
　　Go frayne how our folk fare that are forth run.　　195
2 SOLDIER: My lord, your knights have caired as ye them
　　　　command,
　　And they have fallen full fair.
CAIAPHAS:　　　　　　　　Why, and is the fool found?
1 SOLDIER: Yea lord, they have brought a boy in a band bound.
CAIAPHAS: Where now Sir Annas, that is anon able to be near?
ANNAS: My lord, with your leave, me behoves to be here.　　200
CAIAPHAS: Ah, sir, come near and sit we both in fere.

ANNAS: Do, sir, bid them bring in that boy that is bound.
CAIAPHAS: Peace now, Sir Annas, be still and let him stand,
　　And let us grope if this game be gradely begun.
ANNAS: Sir, this game is begun of the best,　　205
　　Now had he no force for to flee them.
CAIAPHAS: Now, in faith, I am fain he is fast.
　　Do lead in that lad, let me see, then.

2 SOLDIER: Lo sir, we have said to our sovereign.
　　Go now and sue to himself for the same thing.　　210

185 *well sped* had good luck　　187 *wed* wager　　189 *be . . . adread* do not worry
190 *lake . . . list* sport, if you wish　　191 Silence, hooligans! Are you fools?
192 My lord, it would be as well if you knew what is afoot　　193 *nemn* call
194 *none* no　　196 *caired* been　　*command* commanded　　197 *fallen . . . fair*
had good fortune　　199 *Where* Where [is]　　*anon* quickly　　201 *in fere* together
204 *grope* enquire　　*game* matter　　*gradely* in a proper manner　　206 *force*
power　　207 *fain* glad　　*fast* captured　　208 *lad* layabout　　209 *said*
spoken　　210 *sue* proceed　　*himself* him

3 SOLDIER: My lord, to your bidding we have been buxom and
   bain;
   Lo, here is the beausire brought that ye bad bring.
4 SOLDIER: My lord, fand now to fear him.
CAIAPHAS: Now I am fain;
   And fellows, fair mote ye fall for your finding.
ANNAS: Sir, and ye trow they be true without any train,   215
   Bid them tell you the time of the taking.
CAIAPHAS: Say, fellows, how went ye so nimbly by night?
3 SOLDIER: My lord, was there no man to mar us ne mend us.
4 SOLDIER: My lord, we had lanterns and light,
   And some of his company kenned us.   220

ANNAS: But say, how did he, Judas?
3 SOLDIER: Ah, sir, full wisely and well,
   He marked us his master among all his men
   And kissed him full kindly, his comfort to keel,
   By cause of a countenance that carl for to ken.
CAIAPHAS: And thus did he his dever?
4 SOLDIER: Yea, lord, ever-ilka deal. 225
   He taught us to take him the time after ten.
ANNAS: Now, by my faith, a faint friend might he there feel!
3 SOLDIER: Sire, ye might so have said had ye him seen then.
4 SOLDIER: He set us to the same that he sold us,
   And feigned to be his friend, as a faitour,   230
   This was the tokening before that he told us.
CAIAPHAS: Now truly, this was a trant of a traitor.

ANNAS: Yah, be he traitor or true give we never tale;
   But take tent at this time, and hear what he tells.
CAIAPHAS: Now see that our household be held here whole,   235
   So that none carp in case but that in court dwells.
3 SOLDIER: Ah, lord, this brethel hath brewed much bale.

---

211 *buxom* obedient   213 *fand . . . him* seek now to put him in his place
214 *fair . . . fall* a blessing on you   215 *and* if   *trow* believe   *train* deceit
216 *time* circumstances   218 *mar . . . us* interfere with nor prevent us
220 *kenned* showed (the way)   222 *marked* picked out   223 *keel* put an end
to   224 By way of a sign to show which man he was   225 *dever* duty   *ever-*
ilka deal each and every bit   226 *taught* arranged for   227 *feel* perceive
229 *set* directed   230 *faitour* cheat   232 *trant* trick   233 *give . . .*
tale it is of no concern to us   235 *held . . . whole* kept here together   236 *carp*
speak   *in case* in [this] matter   237 *brethel* wretch   *brewed . . . bale* stirred
up a lot of trouble

CAIAPHAS: Therefore shall we speed us to speer of his spells.
    Sir Annas, take heed now, and hear him.
ANNAS: Say, lad, list thee not lout to a lord?   240
4 SOLDIER: No sir, with your leave, we shall lere him.

CAIAPHAS: Nay sir, not so, no haste;
    It is no bourd to beat beasts that are bound.
    And therefore with fairness first we will him fraist,
    And sithen further him forth as we have found.   245
    And tell us some tales, truly to traist.
ANNAS: Sir, we might as well talk till a tome tun.
    I warrant him witless, or else he is wrong wraist,
    Or else he waits to work as he was ere wone.
3 SOLDIER: His wone was to work mickle woe,   250
    And make many masteries amell us.
CAIAPHAS: And some shall he grant ere he go,
    Or must you tent him and tell us.

4 SOLDIER: My lord, to wit the wonders that he has wrought,
    For to tell you the tenth it would our tongues tire.   255
CAIAPHAS: Since the boy for his boast is into bale brought,
    We will wit, ere he wend, how his works were.
3 SOLDIER: Our Sabbath day, we say, saves he right nought,
    That he should hallow and hold full digne and full dear.
4 SOLDIER: No sir, in the same feast as we the sot sought,   260
    He salved them of sickness on many sides sere.
CAIAPHAS: What then, makes he them gradely to gang?
3 SOLDIER: Yea lord, even forth in every-ilka town
    He them leeches to life after long.
CAIAPHAS: Ah, this makes he by the mights of Mahound.   265

---

238 We shall therefore hasten to enquire into what he says   240 *list thee* are you
not inclined   *lout* bow down   241 *lere* teach   243 *bourd* sport   244 *fraist*
question   245 And then proceed with him according to what we find   246 *truly*
. . . *traist* truthfully   247 *till* . . . *tun* to an empty barrel   248 *wrong wraist*
twisted mentally   249 *waits* looks for a chance   *wone* accustomed   250 *His*
. . . *was* He was wont   251 *make* . . . *maistries* to perform many extraordinary
deeds   252 *grant* admit to   253 *tent* attend to   254 *wit* go into   257 *wit*
understand   258 *saves* . . . *nought* he does not observe at all   259 *hallow*
respect   *digne* worthy   260 *sot* fool   261 *salved* healed   *on* . . . *sere*
on every side   262 *makes* . . . *gang* does he restore them completely to health
264 He resurrects them after they have been long-dead   265 Ah, he performs
this through the power of Muhammad (M. *intended diabolically*)

4 SOLDIER: Sir, our stiff temple that made is of stone,
   That passes any palace of price for to praise,
   And it were down to the earth and to the ground gone,
   This ribald he rouses him it rathely to raise.

3 SOLDIER: Yea lord, and other wonders he works great wone,   270
   And with his loud leasing he loses our lays.

CAIAPHAS: Go loose him, and leave then, and let me alone,
   For myself shall search him and hear what he says.

ANNAS: Hark, Jesus of Jews, we will have joy
   To spill all thy sport for thy spells.   275

CAIAPHAS: Do move, fellow, of thy friends that fed thee before,
   And sithen, fellow, of thy fare further will I frayne;
   Do neven us lightly. His language is lorn!

3 SOLDIER: My lord, with your leave, him likes for to lain,
   But and he should scape scatheless it were a full scorn,   280
   For he has mustered among us full mickle of his main.

4 SOLDIER: Malcus your man, lord, that had his ear shorn,
   This harlot full hastily healed it again.

CAIAPHAS: What, and list him be nice for the nonce,
   And hear how we hast to rehete him.   285

ANNAS: Now by Belial's blood and his bones,
   I hold it best to go beat him.

CAIAPHAS: Nay sir, none haste, we shall have game ere we go.
   Boy, be not aghast if we seem gay.
   I conjure thee kindly and command thee also,   290
   By great God that is living and last shall ay,
   If thou be Christ, God's son, tell to us two.

---

266 *stiff* strong   268–9 If it were demolished and scattered on the ground, this
rascal boasts he could swiftly rebuild it   270 *great wone* in large numbers
271 *loud leasing* flagrant lies   *loses* flouts   *lays* laws   275 Because of your
words, to put an end to all your pleasurable activities   276 *friends* relatives   *fed*
. . . *before* brought you up   277 *sithen* then   *fare* business   278 *neven* tell
lightly quickly   *His . . . lorn* He has lost his power of speech   279 *him . . . lain* it
suits him not to answer   280 *scatheless* unscathed   *full* gross   281 *mustered*
displayed   *full . . . main* a great deal of his power   282 *shorn* cut off   283 *harlot*
scoundrel   284–5 What, if he chooses to act the fool in this matter, then just
watch how quickly we will rebuke him   288 *game* sport   289 *aghast* afraid
gay beautifully dressed   290 *conjure* enjoin

JESUS: Sir, thou says it thyself, and soothly I say
    That I shall go to my Father that I come fro
    And dwell with him winly in wealth alway.   295
CAIAPHAS: Why, fie on thee, faitour untrue,
    Thy Father hast thou foully defamed.
    Now needs us no notes of new,
    Himself with his saws has he shamed.

ANNAS: Now needs neither witness ne council to call,   300
    But take his saws as he sayeth in the same stead.
    He slanders the Godhead and grieves us all,
    Wherefore he is well worthy to be dead—
    And therefore, sir, say him the sooth.
CAIAPHAS: Certes, so I shall.
    Hears thou not, harlot? Ill hap on thy head!   305
    Answer here gradely to great and to small,
    And reach us out rathely some reason, I rede.
JESUS: My reasons are not to rehearse,
    Nor they that might help me are not here now.
ANNAS: Say lad, list thee make verse?   310
    Do tell on belive, let us hear now.

JESUS: Sir, if I say the sooth thou shall not assent,
    But hinder, or haste me to hang.
    I preached where people was most in present,
    And no point in privity, to old ne young.   315
    And also in your temple I told mine intent;
    Ye might have ta'en me that time for my telling,
    Well better than bring me with brands on bent,
    And thus to noy me by night, and also for nothing.
CAIAPHAS: For nothing, losel? Thou lies!   320
    Thy words and works will have a wreaking.

---

293 *soothly* truly   295 *winly . . . alway* worthily in bliss for ever   296 *fie* curse   297 *defamed* insulted   298–9 Now we need no more evidence, he has condemned himself with his own words   300 *needs* need we   301 *in . . . stead* in this very place   302 *grieves* offends   304 *Certes* Indeed   305 *Ill hap* a curse   306 *gradely* fittingly   *to . . . small* to everybody   307 And I advise you quickly to come out with something sensible   308 *rehearse* recite   310 *list thee* are you pleased to   311 *belive* quickly   313 *hinder* slander   314 *was . . . present* were most numerous   315 *no . . . privity* never secretly   316 *mine intent* my purpose   318 More appropriately than to take me with swords in the open   319 *noy* harass   321 *have . . . wreaking* be punished

JESUS: Sire, since thou with wrong so me wries,
  Go speer them that heard of my speaking.

CAIAPHAS: Ah, this traitor has teened me with tales that he has
    told.
  Yet had I never such hething of a harlot as he.   325
1 SOLDIER: What, fie on thee, beggar, who made thee so bold
  To bourd with our bishop? Thy bane shall I be.
JESUS: Sir, if my words be wrong or worse than thou would,
  A wrong witness I wot now are ye;
  And if my saws be sooth they mun be sore sold,   330
  Wherefore thou bourds too broad for to beat me.
2 SOLDIER: My lord, will ye hear? For Mahound,
  No more now for to neven that it needs.
CAIAPHAS: Go dress you and ding ye him down,
  And deaf us no more with his deeds.   335

ANNAS: Nay sir, then blemish ye prelates' estate,
  Ye owe to deem no man to death for to ding.
CAIAPHAS: Why sir? So were better than be in debate,
  Ye see the boy will not bow for our bidding.
ANNAS: Now, sir, ye must present this boy unto Sir Pilate,   340
  For he is doomsman near and next to the king,
  And let him hear all the whole, how ye him hate,
  And whether he will help him or haste him to hang.
1 SOLDIER: My lord, let men lead him by night,
  So shall ye best scape out of scorning.   345
2 SOLDIER: My lord, it is noon in the night,
  I rede ye abide till the morning.

CAIAPHAS: Beausire, thou says the best and so shall it be—
  But learn yon boy better to bend and bow.
1 SOLDIER: We shall learn yon lad, by my lewty,   350
  For to lout unto ilk lord like unto you.
CAIAPHAS: Yea, and fellows, wait that ye be ay wakand.

322 *with . . . wries* denounce me untruthfully   323 *speer* ask   324 *teened*
angered   325 Never have I been so abused by a scoundrel such as he   327 *bane*
death   329 *wrong* false   330 *sore sold* dearly paid for   331 *bourds* . . .
broad act hastily   332 *For* By   333 No more need be said   334 *Go*
and beat him thoroughly   335 *deaf* deafen   336 *blemish* dishonour   *prelates'*
estate the high priests' dignity   338 *debate* difficulty   341 *doomsman* judge
near . . . next deputy   345 *scape . . . scorning* avoid scandal   347 *rede* advise
350 *lewty* faith   352 *wait . . . wakand* make sure you remain watchful

2 SOLDIER: Yes lord, that warrant will we,
It were a full needless note to bid us nap now.

3 SOLDIER: Certes, will ye sit and soon shall ye see
How we shall play pops for the page's prow.   355

4 SOLDIER: Let see, who starts for a stool?
For I have here a hater to hide him.

1 SOLDIER: Lo, here is one full fit for a fool,
Go get it and set thee beside him.

2 SOLDIER: Nay, I shall set it myself and frush him also.   360
Lo here a shroud for a shrew, and of sheen shape.

3 SOLDIER: Play fair, in fere, and there is one and there is two;
I shall fand to fast it with a fair flap—
And there is three, and there is four.
Say now, with an evil hap,   365
Who nigheth thee now? Not one word, no!

4 SOLDIER: Do noddle on him with nieves, that he not nap.

1 SOLDIER: Nay, now to nap is no need,
Wassail! Wassail! I warrant him waking.

2 SOLDIER: Yea, and but he better bourds can bid,   370
Such buffets shall he be taking.

3 SOLDIER: Prophet, I say, to be out of debate,
Quis te percussit, man? Read, if thou may.

4 SOLDIER: Those words are in waste, what weens thou he
wot?
It seems by his working his wits were away.   375

1 SOLDIER: Now let him stand as he stood in a fool's state,
For he likes not this lake, my life dare I lay.

2 SOLDIER: Sirs, us must present this page to Sir Pilate,
But go we first to our sovereign and see what he say.

353 *note* piece of advice   *bid us nap* tell us to rest   355 *pops* a kind of buffeting
game   *page's prow* wretch's benefit   356 *starts* goes   357 *hater* piece of
cloth   *hide* blindfold   360 *frush* beat   361 *shroud* garment   *shrew* evil
person   *sheen* good   363 *fand . . . it* endeavour to lay it on   *fair flap* good
blow   366 *nigheth* approaches   367 Let us hit him with [our] fists, so that
he does not fall asleep   369 *Wassail* Festive expression, usually used in drinking
healths   370–1 Yes, unless he can offer better sport than this, he will continue
to endure such a beating   373 'Who is he that smote thee?' (Matthew 26: 68;
Luke 22: 64)   *Read* Prophesy   374 Those words are wasted; what do you
suppose he understands?   375 *working* behaviour   *were away* have gone
376 *as* as if   *fool's state* ceremony for a fool   377 *lake* game   *lay* wager

3 SOLDIER: My lord, we have bourded with this boy. 380
    And held him full hot amell us.
CAIAPHAS: Then heard ye some japes of joy?
4 SOLDIER: The devil have the word, lord, he would tell us.

ANNAS: Sir, bid belive they go and bind him again,
    So that he scape not, for that were a scorn. 385
CAIAPHAS: Do tell to Sir Pilate our plaints all plain,
    And say this lad with his leasing has our laws lorn.
    And say this same day must he be slain,
    Because of Sabbath day that shall be tomorn.
    And say that we come ourselves, for certain, 390
    And for to further this fare, fare ye before.
1 SOLDIER: My lord, with your leave, us must wend,
    Our message to make as we may.
CAIAPHAS: Sir, your fair fellowship we betake to the fiend.
    Go on now, and dance forth in the devil way. 395

380 *bourded* sported   381 *held . . . hot* made it hot for him   382 *japes of joy* amusing jests   386 *plaints . . . plain* grievances clearly   387 *leasing* lying   389 *tomorn* tomorrow   391 And that you came on ahead to expedite the matter   393 To do our errand as best we can   394 *betake* entrust   395 *dance . . . way* away with you, in the devil's name

Christ before Pilate 1:
The Dream of Pilate's Wife

The Dream of Pilate's Wife was the responsibility of the Tapiters, who worked figured clothes, and the Couchers, who made bedding and the ornamental hangings which surrounded beds. However the two locations of their play were organized, Pilate's chamber and Procula's bed would have presented an extravagant and sumptuous spectacle.

Unfortunately the play, which contains instances of the so-called York Realist's best dialogue, presents considerable textual problems, as a number of obscure lines and difficult passages show. There are two stanza types: the first, to line 157, is in a nine-line stanza of long alliterative lines, $abab_4bcbbc_3$. From line 158, there is a second nine-line stanza, $abab_4cdddc_3$. Neither form is found elsewhere in the cycle. Some other isolated lines seem to be extra-metrical.

The beginning of the play is given over to Procula's dream, apocryphally associated with Satan. From the introduction of the 'doctrine of divine duplicity' into the cycle at *The Temptation*, grows the dramatic implication that Satan is standing 'in the wings' as it were, throughout the ensuing action, gradually coming to understand the implications of the chain of events he set moving in Eden. Procula is established as an extremely vain woman, proud of her position as Pilate's wife. The playwright thus sets up the possibility of another temptation scene. It was believed that, as Satan used a woman to procure man's Fall, so he tried to use another to prevent his losing all he gained thereby. The Realist manages here to show Satan persuading Procula to do the right thing for the wrong reason. Satan himself is already morally compromised, as he is forced to attempt to instigate a good and just action in order to protect himself. After the dream sequence, however, he moves into the background as other characters take over as the immediate agents of the Passion.

Pilate is historically an ambivalent character: in one sense, as he ordered the Crucifixion, he was seen as Christ's arch-enemy; in another he was viewed for the same reason as an important agent of the Redemption. Here, at any given point, Pilate interests the audience as he is both rational and sadistic by seemingly arbitrary turns. A close examination of his responses, however, shows that the dramatist has dealt cleverly with the inherent ambiguities of the role by showing Pilate to be a sanguine and fair judge until his own position is threatened, when he abandons the reasoned stance.

Annas and Caiaphas are not given such prominence as Pilate; but, as the debate proceeds, they, with their brutal soldiers, assume a more sinister cast. The most potent presence in the play, however, must be that of Christ himself. The reader must make a particular effort to consider the effect his silent presence must have on an audience. Meditative tradition required that his torture be dragged out as long and inventively as possible, and also that he remain passively silent. Here the dramatist has him speak only when asked a direct question. His super-human power is twice suggested within the structure of the play, when, by uncanny coincidence, the report of Procula's dream arrives at the moment he is brought in to Pilate, and then when Pilate's most obsequious beadle defies his masters, feeling compelled to fall down and worship the prisoner.

PILATE: Ye cursed creatures that cruelly are crying,
  Restrain you from striving for strengh of my strakes;
  Your plaints in my presence use platly applying,
  Or else this brand in your brains soon bursts and breaks.
  This brand in his bones breaks,   5
  What brawl that with brawling me brews,
  That wretch may not wry from my wreaks,
  Nor his sleights not slyly him slakes;
  Let that traitor not trust in my truce.

  For Sir Caesar was my sire and I soothly his son,   10
  That excellent emperor exalted in height,
  Who all this wild world with wights had won,
  And my mother hight Pila that proud was of plight;
  Of Pila that proud, Atus her father he hight.
  This 'Pila' was had into 'Atus'—   15
  Now renks, read ye it right?
  For thus shortly I have showed you in sight
  How I am proudly proved 'Pilatus'.

  Lo, Pilate I am, proved a prince of great pride.
  I was put into Pontus the people to press,   20
  And sithen Caesar himself with senators by his side,
  Remit me to these realms the renks to redress.

---

2 *for* for [fear of the] *strengh* force   *strakes* strokes   3 Put forward your complaints in my presence in an orderly manner   4 *brand* sword   7–9 Whatever bully makes trouble for me with his brawling, that wretch may not avoid my vengeance, nor by cunning slyly set himself free   10 *sire* father   *soothly* truly   12 *wights* men   13 *hight* was called   *plight* bearing   15 *had into* added to   16 *renks* people   18 *proved* acknowledged   20 *press* repress   21 *sithen* after that   22 Sent me to these realms to reform the people

And yet am I granted on ground, as I guess,
To justify and judge all the Jews.
Ah, love, here lady? No less?   25
Lo sirs, my worthy wife, that she is,
So seemly, lo, certain she shews.

PROCULA: Was never judge in this Jewry of so jocund
    generation,
Nor of so joyful genealogy to gentrice enjoined
As ye, my duke doughty, deemer of damnation   30
To princes and prelates that your precepts perloined.
Who that your precepts pertly perloined,
With dread into death shall ye drive him;
By my troth, he untruly is throned
That against your behests has honed;   35
All to rags shall ye rent him and rive him.

I am dame precious Procula, of princes the prize,
Wife to Sir Pilate here, prince without peer.
All well of all womanhood I am, witty and wise,
Conceive now my countenance so comely and clear.   40
The colour of my corse is full clear
And in richesse of robes I am rayed,
There is no lord in this land, as I lere,
In faith, that hath a friendlier fere
Than ye my lord, myself though I say it.   45

PILATE: Now say it may ye safely, for I will certify the same.
PROCULA: Gracious lord, gramercy, your good word is gain.
PILATE: Yet for to comfort my corse me must kiss you madam.
PROCULA: To fulfil your foreward, my fair lord, I am fain.
PILATE: Ho, ho, fellows! Now in faith am I fain   50
    Of these lips so lovely to be lapped—
    In bed she is full buxom and bain.

24 *justify* bring to justice 27 *seemly* beautiful *shews* appears 28 *jocund generation* fortunate lineage 29 Nor connected to the worthy descent of so noble a family 30 *doughty* resolute *deemer* judge 31 *precepts purloined* commands put aside 32 *pertly* boldly 34 *untruly* falsely 35 Who has tarried in carrying out your commands 36 *rent* pull asunder *rive* tear 38 *peer* equal 39 *well* source 40 *Conceive* Perceive 41 *corse* complexion 42 *richesse* wealth *rayed* arrayed 43 *as . . . lere* I gather 44 *fere* companion 47 *gramercy* many thanks *gain* pleasing 49 *foreward* promise *fain* happy 50–2 Now indeed I am eager to be kissed by these lovely lips—[*Aside*] In bed she is most willing and eager

PROCULA: Yea sir, it needeth not to lain,
   All ladies we covet then both to be kissed and clapped.

BEADLE: My liberal lord, oh leader of laws,   55
   Oh shining show that all shames eschews,
   I beseech you, my sovereign, assent to my saws,
   As ye are gentle judger and justice of Jews.
PROCULA: Do hark how yon javel jangles of Jews.
   Why, go bet, whoreson boy, when I bid thee.   60
BEADLE: Madam, I do but that due is.
PROCULA: But if thou rest of thy reason thou rues,
   For as a cursed carl hast thou kid thee.

PILATE: Do mend you madam, and your mood be amending,
   For me seems it were sitting to see what he says.   65
PROCULA: My lord, he told never tale that to me was tending,
   But with wrenks and with wiles to wend me my ways.
BEADLE: Iwis, of your ways to be wending it longs to our laws.
PROCULA: Lo lord, this lad with his laws!
   How, think ye it profits well his preaching to praise?   70
PILATE: Yea love, he knows all our custom,
   I know well . . .

BEADLE: My seignior, will ye see now the sun in your sight,
   For his stately strengh he stems in his streams?
   Behold over your head how he hields from height   75
   And glides to the ground with his glittering gleams.
   To the ground he goes with his beams
   And the night is nighing anon.

---

53 *it . . . lain* it should not be concealed   54 *clapped* embraced   55 *leader* expounder   56 *show* spectacle   *eschews* shuns   57 *assent . . . saws* hear me speak   59 *javel* worthless fellow   *jangles* chatters   60 *go bet* go away *bid* tell   61 Madam, I do only what is appropriate   62 Unless you stop your talking you'll be sorry   63 You have shown yourself to be a worthless wretch   64 *mend* cheer   *mood* disposition   65 For it seems to me to be proper   66 *tending* complimentary   67 But [is always trying] with tricks and deceits to get me to go my way   68 Indeed for you to go your way accords with our laws   68–70 *The precise meaning here is obscure, but it appears that Pilate must dismiss his wife either because legal business has arisen, or in order to conform with a curfew. The lines are corrupt, and the last line breaks off unfinished.*   70 What good do you think it does to praise his preaching   73 *seignior* lord   *stems* diminishes   75 *hields* descends   78 *nighing* approaching

Ye may deem after no dreams,
But let my lady here, with all her light leams,   80
Wightly go wend to her wone;

For ye must sit, sir, this same night, of life and of limb.
It is not leeful for my lady by the law of this land
In doom for to dwell fro the day wax aught dim,
For she may stacker in the street but she stalworthly stand.   85

.   .   .   .

Let her take her leave while that light is.
PILATE: Now wife, then ye blithely be buskand.
PROCULA: I am here sir, hendly at hand.
PILATE: Lo, this renk has us redde as right is.

PROCULA: Your commandment to keep to cair forth I cast me.   90
My lord, with your leave, no longer I let you.
PILATE: It were a reproof to my person that privily ye passed
        me,
Or ye went from these wones ere with wine ye had wet you.
Ye shall wend forth with win when that ye have wet you.
Get drink! What does thou? Have done!   95
Come seemly, beside me, and sit you.
Look, now it is even here that I ere behete you,
Yea, say it now sadly and soon.

PROCULA: It would glad me, my lord, if ye goodly begin.
PILATE: Now I assent to your counsel so comely and clear.   100
Now, drink madam—to death all this din.
PROCULA: If it like you mine own lord, I am not to lere—
This lore I am not to lere.
PILATE: Give eft to your damsel, madam.

---

80 *leams* brightness   81 *wightly* quickly   *wend* go   *wone* dwelling-place
82 *sit* sit in judgement   83 *leeful* permissible   84 To remain at the judgement
when the daylight wanes   85 *stacker* totter   *stalworthly* strongly   85+ *Line
missing in MS*   87 *blithely* readily   *buskand* going on your way   88 *hendly*
in a seemly manner   89 *renk* man   *redde* counselled   90 *cair* go   *cast*
prepare   91 *let* hinder   92–3 It would be a disgrace to me if you left me
discreetly, and went now from this place before you had refreshed yourself with some
wine   94 *wend* go   *win* joy   95 *Have done!* expression of impatience
97 Look, what I have just promised you has already arrived   98 *say* taste   *sadly*
earnestly   *soon* straight away   99 *goodly* in seemly manner   100 *comely*
worthy   *clear* sure   101 *din* clamour   102–3 If it pleases you, my own
lord, I have no need of teaching; I need no instruction in this matter   104 *eft*
likewise   *damsel* lady-in-waiting

PROCULA: In thy hand, hold now and have here.   105
MAID: Gramercy, my lady so dear.
PILATE: Now farewell, and walk on your way.

.   .   .   .

PROCULA: Now farewell the friendliest, your foemen to fend.
PILATE: Now farewell the fairest figure that ever did food feed,
    And farewell ye damsel, indeed.   110
MAID: My lord, I commend me to your royalty.
PILATE: Fair lady, here is shall you lead.
    Sir, go with this worthy in weed,
    And what she bids you do look that buxom you be.

BOY: I am proud and prest to pass on apace,   115
    To go with this gracious, her goodly to guide.
PILATE: Take tent to my tale thou turn on no trace,
    Come tite and tell me if any tidings betide.
BOY: If any tidings my lady betide,
    I shall full soon, sir, wit you to say.   120
    This seemly shall I show by her side
    Belive, sir; no longer we bide.
PILATE: Now farewell, and walk on your way.

Now went is my wife, if it were not her will,
And she raiks to her rest as of nothing she rought.   125
Time is, I tell thee, thou tent me until;
And busk thee belive, belamy, to bed that I were brought

.   .   .   .

And look I be richly arrayed.
BEADLE: As your servant I have sadly it sought,
    And this night, sir, noy shall ye nought,   130
    I dare lay, fro ye lovely be laid.

107+ *Two lines missing in MS*   108 your enemies to assail   109 that ever ate food   112 here is [someone] to guide you   113 *worthy in weed* worthy person 114 *buxom* obedient   115 *prest* ready   *pass* proceed   116 *gracious* fair one   117 Pay attention to my command and do not deviate   118 *tite* quickly *if . . . betide* if anything happens   120 *wit you to say* inform you   122 *belive* quickly   *bide* stay   124 even though she did not want to   125 *raiks* proceeds   *rought* cared about   126 you paid attention to me   127 *busk* hasten   *belamy* good friend   127+ *Line missing in MS*   130 nothing shall annoy you   131 *lay* wager   *fro* when   *lovely* in a seemly manner

PILATE: I command thee to come near, for I will cair to my
    couch.
  Have in thy hands hendly and heave me from hyne,
  But look that thou teen me not with thy tasting, but tenderly
    me touch.
BEADLE: Ah, sir, ye weigh well.
PILATE: Yea, I have wet me with wine. 135

   .   .   .   .

  Yet hield down and lap me even here,
  For I will slyly sleep until syne.
  Look that no man nor no myron of mine
  With no noise be nighing me near.

BEADLE: Sir, what warlock you wakens with words full wild,   140
  That boy for his brawling were better be unborn.
PILATE: Yea, who chatters, him chastise, be he churl or child,
  For and he scape scatheless it were to us a great scorn—
  If scatheless he scape it were a scorn.
  What ribald that readily will roar,   145
  I shall meet with that myron tomorn
  And for his lither lewdness him learn to be lorn.
BEADLE: We! So sir, sleep ye, and say no more.

PROCULA: Now are we at home. Do help if ye may,
  For I will make me ready and raik to my rest.   150
MAID: Ye are weary madam, forwent of your way,
  Do boun you to bed, for that hold I best.
BOY: Here is a bed arrayed of the best.
PROCULA: Do hap me, and fast hence ye hie.
MAID: Madam, anon all duly is dressed.   155
BOY: With no stalking nor no strife be ye stressed.
PROCULA: Now be ye in peace, both your carping and cry.

---

133 *hyne* hence   134 *teen* anger   *tasting* handling   135 *weigh well* are heavy
135+ *Line missing in MS*   136 *lap* cover   137 *slyly* surreptitiously   *syne*
later   138 *myron* servant   139 *nighing* approaching   140 *warlock*
scoundrel   *wild* headstrong   141 That lout for his misbehaviour would
be better never to have been born   142 *churl* low-born man   *child* knight
143 If he should get away unharmed   145 *ribald* rascal   146 *tomorn* tomorrow
147 And for his wicked misconduct show him how to die   151 tired out by your
journey   152 *boun* make ready [to go]   154 Tuck me in and go away soon
155 *dressed* prepared   156 *stalking* stealthy movement   *strife* commotion
stressed disturbed   157 *in peace* quiet   *carping* talking   *cry* shouting

DEVIL: Out! Out! Harrow!   157a
  Into bale am I brought, this bargain may I ban;
  But if I work some wile, in woe must I won.
  This gentleman, Jesu, of cursedness he can;   160
  By any sign that I see this same is God's son.
  And he be slain our solace will cease,
  He will save man's soul from our sound
  And reave us the realms that are round.
  I will on stiffly in this stound   165
  Unto Sir Pilate's wife, pertly, and put me in press.

  Oh woman, be wise and ware, and won in thy wit
  There shall a gentleman, Jesu, unjustly be judged
  Before thy husband in haste, and with harlots be hit.
  And that doughty today to death thus be dighted,   170
  For his preaching, Sir Pilate and thou
  With need shall ye namely be noyed.
  Your strife and your strengh shall be stroyed,
  Your richesse shall be reft you that is rude,
  With vengeance, and that dare I avow.   175

PROCULA: Ah, I am dretched with a dream full dreadfully to
    doubt.
  Say child, rise up radly and rest for no ro,
  Thou must lance to my lord and lowly him lout,
  Commend me to his reverence, as right will I do.
BOY: Oh, what, shall I travail thus timely this tide?   180
  Madam, for the dretching of heaven,
  Such note is noisesome to neven
  And it nighs unto midnight full even.
PROCULA: Go bet, boy, I bid no longer thou bide,

157a Noises conventionally made by devils; the line is extra-metrical   158 *bale* misery
bargain state of affairs   *ban* curse   159 Unless I effect some trick, I must
dwell in misery   160 is capable of malice   162 *And* Unless   *solace* comfort
163 *sound* safe-keeping   164 *reave us* deprive us of   165 *stiffly* resolutely
stound short time   166 *pertly* skilfully   *put me in press* make the attempt
167 *ware* vigilant   *won . . . wit* grasp in your mind   169 and be beaten by
scoundrels   170 *doughty* good man   *dighted* condemned   172 You in particular must needs be afflicted   173 *strife* efforts   *stroyed* destroyed   174 You
will be deprived of all your great wealth   175 *avow* promise   176 *dretched*
tormented   *doubt* fear   177 *radly* without delay   *ro* rest   178 *lance*
spring   *lout* bow   180 *travail* work   *timely* early   *this tide* now   182 Such
a business is troublesome to mention   183 *full even* almost

And say to my sovereign this same is sooth that I send him: 185
All naked this night as I napped
With teen and with train was I trapped,
With a sweven that swiftly me swapped
Of one Jesu, the just man the Jews will undo.

She prays tent to that true man, with teen be not trapped,   190
But as a doomsman duly to be dressing,
And leally deliver that lede.
BOY: Madam, I am dressed to that deed—
But first will I nap in this need,
For he has mister of a morning sleep that midnight is missing.   195

ANNAS: Sir Caiaphas, ye ken well this caitiff we have catched
That oft-times in our temple has teached untruly.
Our meinie with might at midnight him matched
And have driven him to his deeming for his deeds unduly;
Wherefore I counsel that kindly we cair   200
Unto Sir Pilate our prince, and pray him
That he for our right will array him—
This faitour—for his falsehood to flay him;
For fro we say him the sooth he shall sit him full sore.

CAIAPHAS: Sir Annas, this sport have ye speedily espied,   205
As I am pontifical prince of all priests.
We will press to Sir Pilate, and present him with pride
With this harlot that has hewed our hearts from our breasts,
Through talking of tales untrue.
And therefore, sir knights—
SOLDIERS: Lord.   210
CAIAPHAS: Sir knights that are courteous and kind,
We charge you that churl be well chained.
Do busk you and gradely him bind,
And rug him in ropes his race till he rue.

---

185 *sooth* the truth   187 *train* guile   *trapped* ensnared   188 *sweven*
dream   *swapped* dealt a blow   190 *She* (referring to herself)   *tent* take heed
191–2 But act as a righteous judge, and in good faith set that man free   195 For
he who lacks sleep at midnight needs it in the morning   196 *ken* know   *caitiff*
wretch   198 *meinie* people   *matched* set upon   199 And have brought
him to judgement for his wicked deeds   200 in accordance with custom we go
202 *array* provide for   203 *faitour* impostor   204 it will make it worse for
him   205 *sport* good idea   206 *pontifical* high priestly   213 *gradely*
directly   214 *rug* pull violently   *race* behaviour

1 SOLDIER: Sir, your saws shall be served shortly and soon.   215
Yea, do fellow, by thy faith; let us fast this faitour full fast.

2 SOLDIER: I am doughty to this deed, deliver, have done;
Let us pull on with pride till his power be passed.

1 SOLDIER: Do have fast and hold at his hands.

2 SOLDIER: For this same is he that lightly avaunted,   220
And God's son he gradely him granted.

1 SOLDIER: He is hurled from the highness he haunted—
Lo, he stonies for us, he stares where he stands.

2 SOLDIER: Now is the brothel bound for all the boast that he
blew,
And the Last Day he let no lordings might low him.   225

ANNAS: Yea, he weened this world had been wholly his own.
As ye are doughtiest today to his deeming ye draw him,
And then shall we ken how that he can excuse him.

1 SOLDIER: Here, ye gomes, go a-room, give us gate,
We must step to yon star of estate.   230

2 SOLDIER: We must yaply wend in at this gate,
For he that comes to court, to courtesy must use him.

1 SOLDIER: Do rap on the renks that we may raise with our
rolling.
Come forth, sir coward, why cower ye behind?

BEADLE: Oh, what javels are ye that jape with gowling?   235

1 SOLDIER: Ah, good sir, be not wroth, for words are as the
wind.

BEADLE: I say, gadlings, go back with your gauds.

2 SOLDIER: Be suffering, I beseech you,
And more of this matter ye meek you.

BEADLE: Why, uncunning knaves, and I cleek you,   240
I shall fell you, by my faith, for all your false frauds.

---

215 *saws* words   *served* obeyed   216 *fast* fasten   217 *deliver* make haste
have done expression of impatience   220 *avaunted* boasted   221 And boldly
claimed that he was God's son   222 *hurled* pushed violently   *highness* exalted
position   *haunted* sought   223 he is stupified with fright by us   224 *brothel*
wretch   *blew* gave vent to   225 And he believed that at the Last Judgement
nobody could overthrow him   226 *weened* believed   229 *gomes* men   *go*
a-room stand aside   *gate* way   231 *yaply* nimbly   232 must accustom
himself   233 *rap* push sharply   *raise* ascend   *rolling* prisoner(?)   235 *jape*
. . . *gowling* play tricks and make such a noise   237 *gadlings* knaves   *gauds*
jests   238 *suffering* patient   239 *meek you* pay attention to   240 *uncunning*
ignorant   *cleek* catch   241 *fell* knock down

PILATE: Say, child, ill cheve you! What churls are so clattering?
BEADLE: My lord, uncunning knaves they cry and they call.
PILATE: Go boldly belive and those brothels be battering,
   And put them in prison upon pain that may fall.   245
   Yea, speedily speer them if any sport can they spell—
   Yea, and look what lordings they be.
BEADLE: My lord that is loveful in lee,
   I am buxom and blithe to your blee.
PILATE: And if they talk any tidings come tite and me tell.   250

BEADLE: Can ye talk any tidings, by your faith, my fellows?
1 SOLDIER: Yea sir, Sir Caiaphas and Annas are come both
      together
   To Sir Pilate of Pontus and prince of our laws;
   And they have latched a lorel that is lawless and lither.
BEADLE: My lord, my lord!
PILATE: How?   255
BEADLE: My lord, unlap you belive where ye lie.
   Sir Caiaphas to your court is carried,
   And Sir Annas, but a traitor them tarried.
   Many wights of that warlock have waried,
   They have brought him in a band his bales to buy.   260

PILATE: But are these saws certain in sooth that thou says?
BEADLE: Yea lord, the states yonder stands, for strife they are
      stunned.
PILATE: Now then am I light as a roe, and eath for to raise.
   Go bid them come in both, and the boy they have bound.
BEADLE: Sirs, my lord gives leave in for to come.   265
CAIAPHAS: Hail, prince that is peerless in price,
   Ye are leader of laws in this land,
   Your help is full hendly at hand.
ANNAS: Hail, strong in your state for to stand,
   All this doom must be dressed at your duly device.   270

242 *child* fellow   *ill . . . you* may bad luck befall you   244 *battering* beating
246 *speer* ask   *sport* pleasurable activities   *spell* say of   247 and find out who
they are   248 that loves tranquillity   249 *blee* countenance   254 *latched*
taken by force   *lorel* wretch   *lither* wicked   256 *unlap you* arise   257 *is
carried* has come   259 *waried* cursed   260 They have brought him tied in
a rope to pay for his misdeeds   262 *states* magnates   263 *roe* roe deer   *eath
. . . raise* most willing to get up   270 *duly device* lawful judgement

PILATE: Who is there, my prelates?
CAIAPHAS: Yea, lord.
PILATE: Now be ye welcome, iwis.
CAIAPHAS: Gramercy, my sovereign. But we beseech you all
    sam
  Because of waking you unwarely be not wroth with this,
  For we have brought here a lorel—he looks like a lamb.
PILATE: Come in, you both, and to the bench braid you.   275
CAIAPHAS: Nay, good sir, lower is leeful for us.
PILATE: Ah, Sir Caiaphas, be courteous ye bus.
ANNAS: Nay, good lord, it may not be thus.
PILATE: Say no more, but come sit you beside me in sorrow as I
    said you.

BOY: Hail, the seemliest segge under sun sought,   280
  Hail, the dearest duke and doughtiest in deed.
PILATE: Now bienvenue beausire, what bodeword hast thou
    brought?
  Has any languor my lady new latched in this lede?
BOY: Sir, that comely commends her you to,
  And says, all naked this night as she napped   285
  With teen and with tray was she trapped,
  With a sweven that swiftly her swapped
  Of one Jesu, the just man the Jews will undo.

  She beseeches you as her sovereign that simple to save,
  Deem him not to death for dread of vengeance.   290
PILATE: What, I hope this be he that hither harled ye have.
CAIAPHAS: Yea sir, the same and the self—but this is but a
    skaunce,
  With witchcraft this wile has he wrought.
  Some fiend of his sand has he sent
  And warned your wife ere he went.   295

---

271 *iwis* indeed   272 *sam* together   273 *unwarely* unexpectedly
275 *braid* hasten   276 *leeful* appropriate   277 *bus* must   279 *in sorrow*
humbly   280 *segge* man   *sought* found   282 *bienvenue beausire* welcome, good
man   *bodeword* message   283 *languor* sickness   *latched* caught   *lede*
place   284 *comely* fair one   286 *tray* affliction   289 *simple* innocent
man   291 *hope* believe   *harled* dragged   292 *skaunce* jest   293 *wile*
trick   294 *of his sand* as his messenger   295 *warned* instructed

PILATE: Yow! That shalk should not shamely be shent,
　This is siker in certain, and sooth should be sought.

ANNAS: Yea, through his phantom and falsehood and fiend's-
　　　craft
　He has wrought many wonder where he walked full wide,
　Wherefore, my lord, it were leeful his life were him reft.　　300
PILATE: Be ye never so breme, ye both bus abide
　But if the traitor be taught for untruth,
　And therefore sermon you no more.
　I will sikerly send himself for,
　And see what he says to thee sore.　　305
　Beadle, go bring him, for of that renk have I ruth.

BEADLE: This foreward to fulfil am I fain moved in mine heart.
　Say, Jesu, the judges and the Jews have me enjoined
　To bring thee before them even bound as thou art.
　Yon lordings to lose thee full long have they hoined,　　310
　But first shall I worship thee with wit and with will.
　This reverence I do thee forthy,
　For wights that were wiser than I,
　They worshipped thee full wholly on high
　And with solemnity sang Hosanna till.　　315

1 SOLDIER: My lord that is leader of laws in this land,
　All beadles to your bidding should be buxom and bain,
　And yet this boy here before you full boldly was bowand
　To worship this warlock—methinks we work all in vain.
2 SOLDIER: Yea, and in your presence he prayed him of peace,　320
　In kneeling on knees to this knave
　He besought him his servant to save.
CAIAPHAS: Lo, lord, such error among them they have
　It is great sorrow to see, no segge may it cease.

296 *Yow!* exclamation　*shalk* man　*shamely* unjustly　*shent* destroyed　297 *siker*
true　*and . . . sought* if the truth be known　298 *phantom* guile　299 *full*
wide in many places　301 However angry you are you must both wait　302 *But*
if Unless　*taught* exposed　303 *sermon* speak　304 I will certainly send
for him　305 *to* in answer to　*sore* urgently　306 *ruth* pity　307 *fain*
eagerly　310 *lose* destroy　*hoined* lain in wait　312 *forthy* therefore
314 *wholly* devoutly　315 *till* to [you]　318 *bowand* bowing　320 *of*
for　322 *besought* begged　324 *cease* put a stop to

It is no mensk to your manhood, that mickle is of might, 325
To forbear such forfeits that falsely are feigned,
Such spites in especial would be eschewed in your sight.
PILATE: Sirs, move you not in this matter but be mildly
    demeaned,
For yon courtesy I ken had some cause.
ANNAS: In your sight, sir, the sooth shall I say, 330
  As ye are prince take heed I you pray,
  Such a lurdan unleal, dare I lay,
  Many lords of our lands might lead from our laws.

PILATE: Say, losel, who gave thee leave so for to lout to yon lad,
  And solace him in my sight so seemly that I saw? 335
BEADLE: Ah, gracious lord, grieve you not, for good case I had.
  Ye commanded me to cair, as ye ken well and know,
  To Jerusalem on a journey, with sele;
  And then this seemly on an ass was set
  And many men mildly him met, 340
  As a God in that ground they him gret,
  Well psalming him in way with worship leal.

'Hosanna' they sang, 'the son of David',
Rich men with their robes they ran to his feet,
And poor folk fetched flowers of the frith 345
And made mirth and melody this man for to meet.
PILATE: Now good sir, by thy faith, what is 'Hosanna' to say?
BEADLE: Sir, construe it we may by language of this land as I
  leve,
  It is as much to me for to move—
  Your prelates in this place can it prove— 350
  As, 'our saviour and sovereign thou save us we pray'.

PILATE: Lo seigniors, how seems you? The sooth I you said.

---

325 *mensk* honour   *mickle* great   326 *forbear* tolerate   *forfeits* offences
feigned fabricated   327 *spites* insults   *would* ought to   328 *demeaned*
mannered   332 *lurdan* wretch   *unleal* disloyal   334 *losel* knave   *lout*
bow   *lad* fellow   335 *seemly* in such a seemly fashion   336 *grieve* . . .
not do not be angry   *case* reason   338 *with sele* fittingly   339 *seemly*
worthy one   341 *ground* place   *gret* hailed   342 Singing psalms to him
along the way with faithful worship   345 *frith* meadow   347 what does
'Hosanna' mean   348 *construe* translate   *leve* believe   349 I believe it
means   350 *prove* establish   352 *how . . . you?* what do you think?

CAIAPHAS: Yea lord, this lad is full lither, by this light.
 If his saws were searched and sadly assayed,
 Save your reverence, his reasons they reckon not with right.   355
 This caitiff thus cursedly can construe us.
BEADLE: Sirs, truly the truth I have told
 Of this wight ye have wrapped in wold.
ANNAS: I say, harlot, thy tongue should thou hold,
 And not against thy masters to move thus.   360

PILATE: Do cease of your saying and I shall examine full sore.
ANNAS: Sir, deem him to death or do him away.
PILATE: Sir, have ye said?
ANNAS: Yea, lord.
PILATE: Now go sit you with sorrow and care,
 For I will lose no lede that is leal to our lay.
 But step forth and stand up on height   365
 And busk to my bidding, thou boy,
 And for the nonce that thou neven us an 'oy'.
BEADLE: I am here at your hand to hollo a hoy,
 Do move of your master, for I shall mell it with might.

PILATE: Cry 'Oyez'.
BEADLE: Oyez.
PILATE: Yet eft, by thy faith.
BEADLE: Oyez! [*Aloud*]   370
PILATE: Yet louder, that ilk lede may lithe—
 Cry peace in this press, upon pain thereupon,
 Bid them swage of their sweying both swiftly and swith,
 And stint of their striving and stand still as a stone.
 Call Jesu the gentle of Jacob, the Jew.   375
 Come prest and appear,
 To the bar draw near,
 To thy judgement here,
 To be deemed for thy deeds undue.

---

354 If his words were closely examined and seriously tested   355 reasoning does not conform with what is right   356 *cursedly* misleadingly   *construe* expound   358 *wrapped in wold* placed under arrest   361 *full sore* most carefully   364 *lay* law   365 *height* high   367 And to the purpose speak out an 'Oyez' (literally 'Hear ye!')   368 to cry out a shout   369 Tell me what you wish [me to say] and I shall shout it out loudly   371 Even louder, so that everyone can hear   372 *press* assembly   373 *swage of* abate   *sweying* noise   *swith* quickly   374 *stint of* break off from   *striving* commotion 376 *prest* quickly   379 *undue* illegal

1 SOLDIER: We, hark how this harlot he hields out of harre,   380
    This lotterel list not my lord to lout.
2 SOLDIER: Say, beggar, why brawlest thou? Go boun thee to
    the bar.
1 SOLDIER: Step on thy standing so stern and so stout.
2 SOLDIER: Step on thy standing so still.
1 SOLDIER: Sir coward, to court must ye cair—   385
2 SOLDIER: A lesson to learn of our lore.
1 SOLDIER: Flit forth, foul might thou fare.
2 SOLDIER: Say, warlock, thou wantest of thy will.

BOY: Oh Jesus ungentle, thy joy is in japes,
    Thou cannot be courteous, thou caitiff I call thee,   390
    No ruth were it to rug thee and rive thee in ropes,
    Why falls thou not flat here, foul fall thee,
    For fear of my father so free?
    Thou wot not his wisdom, iwis,
    All thine help in his hand that it is,   395
    How soon he might save thee from this.
    Obey him, brothel, I bid thee.

PILATE: Now Jesu, thou art welcome iwis, as I ween,
    Be not abashed but boldly boun thee to the bar;
    What seignior will sue for thee sore I have seen.   400
    To work on this warlock, his wit is in were.
    Come prest, of a pain, and appear,
    And sir prelates, your points be proving.
    What cause can ye cast of accusing?
    This matter ye mark to be moving,   405
    And hendly in haste let us hear.

CAIAPHAS: Sir Pilate of Pontus and prince of great price,
    We trust ye will trow our tales they be true,

---

380 *We* expression of indignation   *harlot* hooligan   *hields . . . harre* behaves in a
disorderly manner   381 This scoundrel does not care to bow to my lord
382 *boun thee* betake yourself   383 *standing* place of standing in a court
386 *lore* teachings   387 Move forward, [and] may things go badly for you
388 Say, traitor, you've lost your wits   389 *ungentle* unmannerly   391 *rive*
gash   392 *foul . . . thee* a curse on you   393 *free* liberal   399 *abashed*
afraid   400 I have seen the elders who are intent upon proceeding against you
401 his wits are confused   402 *of a pain* under threat of punishment   404 *cast*
put forward   405 *mark* undertake

To death for to deem him with duly device.
For cursedness yon knave has in case, if ye knew,   410
In heart would ye hate him in hie.
For if it ne were so
We meant not to misdo;
Trust, sir, shall ye thereto,
We had not him taken to thee.   415

PILATE: Sir, your tales would I trow but they touch none intent.
What cause, can ye find now the freke for to fell?
ANNAS: Our Sabbath he saves not, but sadly assent
To work full unwisely, this wot I right well,

.   .   .   .

He works when he will, well I wot,   420
And therefore in heart we him hate.
It sits you, to strengh your estate,
Yon losel to lose for his lay.

PILATE: Ilka lede to lose for his lay is not leal.
Your laws are leeful, but to your laws longs it   425
This faitour to feeze well with flaps full fele,
And woe may ye work him by law, for he wrongs it.
Therefore take him unto you full tite,
And like as your laws will you lead
Ye deem him to death for his deed.   430
CAIAPHAS: Nay, nay sir, that doom must us dread,

.   .   .   .

It longs not to us no lede for to lose.
PILATE: What would ye I did then? The devil mote your draw!
Full few are his friends but fele are his foes.
His life for to lose there longs no law,   435

---

410 *cursedness* [the] evil   *has in case* is devising   411 *in hie* swiftly   413 *misdo* offend   415 We would not have brought him to you   416 *touch . . . intent* are not to the point   418 *saves* observes   *sadly assent* is solemnly willing 419+ *Line missing in MS*   422 It befits you, to strengthen your position 423 *lay* manner of living   424 To kill every man because of the way he lives is not lawful   425 *longs* belongs   426 To settle the business of this deceiver with numerous blows   429 And if the interpretation of your laws demands it 431 we must not proceed to that judgement   431+ *Line missing in MS*   432 We are not permitted to put any man to death   433 May the devil fetch you   434 *fele* many   435 *longs* is appropriate

Nor no cause can I kindly contrive
Why that he should lose thus his life.
ANNAS: Ah, good sir, it raiks full rife
In steads where he has stirred mickle strife
Of ledes that are leal to your leve.   440

CAIAPHAS: Sir, halt men and hurt he healed in haste,
The deaf and the dumb he delivered from dole
By witchcraft, I warrant—his wits shall waste—
For the ferlies that he fareth with, lo how they follow yon fool,
Our folk so thus he frays in fere.   445
ANNAS: The dead he raises anon—
This Lazarus that low lay alone,
He grant him his gates for to gone,
And pertly thus proved he his power.

PILATE: Now good sirs, I say, what would ye seem?   450
CAIAPHAS: Sir, to death for to do him or do him adawe.
PILATE: Yea, for he does well his death for to deem?
Go lake you sir, lightly; where learned ye such law?
This touches no treason, I tell you.
Ye prelates that proved are for price,   455
Ye should be both witty and wise
And ledge our law where it lies,
Our matters ye move thus amell you.

ANNAS: Misplease not your person, ye prince without peer,
It touches to treason, this tale I shall tell: 460
Yon briber, full bainly he bad to forbear
The tribute to the emperor, thus would he compel
Our people thus his points to apply.
CAIAPHAS: The people he says he shall save,
And Christ gars he call him, yon knave,   465

---

436 *kindly contrive* naturally fabricate   438 it [trouble] goes on everywhere
439 *steads* places   440 *leve* trust   441 *halt* lame   442 *delivered from*
dole released from misery   444 *ferlies* marvels   *fareth with* achieves   445 *frays*
in fere frightens altogether   448 He allowed him to go his way   450 What
would you have   451 *do him adawe* have him put to death   453 *lake* play the
fool   457 And expound our law as it stands   458 *amell* amongst   459 Do
not be displeased   461 *briber* strolling vagrant   *bainly* readily   *forbear*
withhold   462 *tribute* tax   463 *points . . . apply* act upon his teachings
465 *gars* makes them to

And says he will the high kingdom have—
Look whether he deserve to die.

PILATE: To die he deserves if he do thus indeed,
    But I will see myself what he says.
    Speak, Jesu, and spend now thy space for to speed.   470
    These lordings they ledge thee thou list not leve on our lays,
    They accuse thee cruelly and keen;
    And therefore as a chieftain I charge thee,
    If thou be Christ, that thou tell me,
    And God's son thou grudge not to grant thee,   475
    For this is the matter that I mean.

JESUS: Thou sayest so thyself. I am soothly the same
    Here woning in world to work all my will.
    My Father is faithful to fell all thy fame;
    Without trespass or teen am I taken thee till.   480
PILATE: Lo bishops, why blame ye this boy?
    Me seems that it is sooth that he says.
    Ye move all the malice ye may
    With your wrenches and wiles to writhe him away,
    Unjustly to judge him from joy.   485

CAIAPHAS: Not so sir, if his saying is full soothly sooth,
    It brings our bernes in bale for to bind.
ANNAS: Sir, doubtless we deem as due of the death,
    This fool that ye favour—great faults can we find
    This day for to deem him to die.   490
PILATE: Say losel, thou lies, by this light!
    Nay, thou ribald, thou reckons unright.
CAIAPHAS: Advise you, sir, with main and with might,
    And wreak not your wrath now forthy.

---

470 and use your time now to profit yourself   471 allege that you do not care to abide by our laws   473 *chieftain* paragon   475 And you do not scruple to claim that you are God's son   479 *fell* make an end to   480 *trespass* offence *taken . . . till* brought to you   484 *wrenches* crooked tricks   *writhe him away* destroy him   486–7 his saying is indeed true, he would confine our children in misery. (Meaning unclear; perhaps, 'Certainly not, sir, if what he says is really true, it enslaves our people in misery.')   488 as deserving to die   492 No, you rascal, you presume to advise wrongly   493 Consider, sir, with all your powers, 494 *wreak* avenge

PILATE: Me likes not this language so largely for to lithe.   495
CAIAPHAS: Ah, mercy lord, meekly, no malice we meant.
PILATE: Now done is it doubtless, bold be and blithe,
   Talk on that traitor and tell your intent.
   Yon segge is subtle, ye say;
   Good sirs, where learned he such lore?   500
CAIAPHAS: In faith, we cannot find where.
PILATE: Yes, his father with some ferlies gan fare
   And has lered this lad of his lay.

ANNAS: Nay, nay sir, we wist that he was but a wright,
   No subtlety he showed that any segge saw.   505
PILATE: Then mean ye of malice to mar him of might,
   Of cursedness convict no cause can ye know.
   Me marvels ye malign amiss.
CAIAPHAS: Sir, from Galilee hither and how
   The greatest against him gan go,   510
   Yon warlock to waken of woe,
   And of this work bear witness, iwis.

PILATE: Why, and has he gone in Galilee, yon gadling ungain?
ANNAS: Yea lord, there was he born, yon brethel, and bred.
PILATE: Now, without faging, my friends, in faith I am fain,   515
   For now shall our strife full sternly be stead.
   Sir Herod is king there ye ken,
   His power is proved full prest
   To rid him or reave him of rest.
   And therefore, to go with yon guest   520
   Ye mark us out of the manliest men.

CAIAPHAS: As wit and wisdom your will shall be wrought,
   Here are kemps full keen to the king for to cair.

---

495 *largely* unrestrainedly   *lithe* hear   497 Now it has completely subsided (i.e. his anger)   502–3 Yes, his father delved into some strange things, and has taught this fellow his practices   504 *wist* knew   *wright* carpenter   506–8 Then you intend out of malice to destroy him by force, [since] you can discover no reason to find [him] guilty of evil deeds. I am surprised you make false accusations mistakenly. 509 hither and thither   510 *The greatest* Great numbers [of people]   *against* towards   *gan* did   511 *waken of woe* incite to evil   513 *ungain* troublesome   514 *brethel* wretch   515 *faging* deceiving [you]   516 *sternly* firmly   *stead* settled   518–19 His power is readily acknowledged [as sufficient] to free him or deprive him of peace   520 *guest* wicked man   521 *mark . . . out* select   *of* some of   523 *kemps* strong warriors

PILATE: Now seigniors, I say you, since sooth shall be sought,
    But if he shortly be sent it may sit us full sore.   525
    And therefore, sir knights—
SOLDIERS: Lord.
PILATE: Sir knights that are cruel and keen,
    That warlock ye warrok and wrest,
    And look that he bremely be brast

    .   .   .   .

    Do take on that traitor you between.   530

    To Herod in haste with that harlot ye hie,
    Commend me full meekly unto his most might.
    Say the doom of this boy, to deem him to die,
    Is done upon him duly, to dress or to dight,
    Or life for to leave at his list.   535
    Say aught I may do him indeed,
    His own am I worthily in weed.
1 SOLDIER: My lord, we shall spring on a-speed.
    Come hence with this traitor full trist.

PILATE: Beausires, I bid you ye be not too bold,   540
    But take tent for our tribute full truly to treat.
2 SOLDIER: My lord, we shall hie this behest for to hold,
    And work it full wisely in will and in wit.
PILATE: So, sirs, me seems it is sitting.
1 SOLDIER: Mahound, sirs, he mensk you with might—   545
2 SOLDIER: And save you, sir, seemly in sight.
PILATE: Now in the wild vengeance ye walk with that wight,
    And freshly ye found to be flitting.

525 *But if* Unless   *shortly* quickly   it may make it worse for us   528 *warrok* bind   *wrest* twist   529 *bremely* fiercely   *brast* beaten up   529+ *Line missing in MS*   534 *done* bestowed   *dress* ordain   *dight* undertake   535 *Or life* Or his life   *leave* spare   *list* liking   536–7 Say if there is anything I can do for him, I am at his disposal in every respect   538 *a-speed* apace   539 *full trist* most flagrant   541 *tent* care   *treat* negotiate   547 *in . . . wild* with a   548 *freshly* briskly   *found* hasten

THE LITSTERS

Christ before Herod

The play is based upon St Luke's account of Christ's appearance before
Herod (Luke 23). Its most striking dramatic features lie not in the development of character, but in the playwright's audacious extension of two features
of the narrative, as speech and clothing become cohesive motifs in one of the
cycle's longer plays. It has generally been attributed to the York Realist.

Herod, as in the gospel account, is particularly eager to meet Christ because of the latter's reputation, which is here, by means of reductive vocabulary, transformed into that of an itinerant conjuror. The king is presented as a
figure of anarchic appetite for diversion, so that when Christ fails to provide
him with sport, Herod determines to have it at his expense. The audience's
expectations of the sadistic persecutor of Christians of popular hagiography
are not disappointed: Herod, with the potential of the alliterative line at his
disposal, swears, threatens, and eventually shouts his way through the entire
episode. The chief effect of the traditional bluster, however, lies not in the
simple virtuosity of its vocabulary, even when that makes sorties into 'court
French', but in its contrast with the potent silence of its victim. Undoubtedly
the silent Christ dominates the scene. The traditional silence of Christ throughout the Passion sequence derives from Luke's account of this occasion and is
generally extended by dramatists because of its obvious impact. Although the
idea here is not the dramatist's own, his extension of the scene to over four
hundred long lines turns that silence to immense theatrical effect, so that it is
not only Herod who is 'deafened' by it. In this way Christ assumes a presence
upon which the effect of speech would be bathetic.

Christ's intransigence prompts Herod and his sons to punish him in a
traditionally degrading manner, and one appropriate to the guild responsible
for the play, as they were dyers in the cloth trade. The dressing of the man
who refuses to perform as court-fool in a fool's gown has considerable ironic
potential. The traditional fool's coat at this date, however, is motley, whereas
the gospel account requires white, 'veste alba'. Any difficulty posed by this is
again turned to serve broad dramatic contrast. Herod and his sons discuss the
possibility that Christ is frightened into silence by the court's finery, er-
roneously considering this to be the mark of the divine. The audience will
recognize the sumptuous tawdriness of the court presented before their eyes
as one of the common marks of misplaced pride. Hence in Christ's white
fool's gown, though contemporary nonsense as such, they are presented with
a visual contrast of simplicity and purity which in turn enhances his silent
grandeur. In this manner the scene is made to cohere dramatically through
these cleverly manipulated oppositions.

The text of the play is in a poor state of preservation and presents serious problems of metrical irregularity, probably the result of careless transmission. The commonest stanza form throughout, from which some of the others may have been adapted, is the fourteener, $ababab ab_4 cdcccd_3$, which employs the long alliterative line. There are in addition fourteen cross-rhyming quatrains, with either three or four stresses per line; but there are numerous other variants.

KING: Peace, ye brothels and brawls in this broadness
    embraced,
And frekes that are friendly your freckness to frayne,
Your tongues from treating of trifles be trased,
Or this brand that is bright shall burst in your brain.
Plead for no places but plat you to this plain,   5
And draw to no droving but dress you to dread,
With dashes.
Travail not as traitors that trust in train,
Or by the blood that Mahound bled, with his blade shall ye
    bleed.
Thus shall I britten all your bones on brede,   10
Yea, and lush all your limbs with lashes.

Dragons that are dreadful shall dark in their dens
In wrath when we writhe, or in wrothness are wapped.
Against giants ungentle have we joined with engines,
And swans that are swimming to our sweetness shall be
    swapped,   15
And jagged down their jollyness, our gentrice engendering.
Whoso reprove our estate we shall chop them in chains,
All renks that are reigning to us shall be revering.

1–2 Silence, you wretches and hooligans contained in this wide space, and you men who are friendly, [in order] to learn how you should behave in a manly fashion 3 *treating* speaking   *trifles* idle gossip   *be trased* restrain   4 *brand* sword 5–7 Do not vie for position, but fall down on this ground and do not make a disturbance, but behave respectfully, [for fear of] blows   8 *Travail* Strive   *train* deceit   9 *Mahound* Muhammad (intended diabolically)   10 *britten* hack to pieces   *on brede* all over   11 *lush* strike   12 *dark* lurk   13 *wrothness . . . wapped* are consumed with anger   14 *ungentle* violent   *joined with engines* joined battle with weapons of war   15 *to . . . sweetness* at our pleasure   *swapped* smitten   16 And hacked down [in] their joy, to the enhancement of our noble qualities   17 *reprove* should challenge   *chop* clap   18 *renks* men   *reigning* flourishing, alive   *revering* respectful

Therefore I bid you cease ere any bale be,
That no brothel be so bold boast for to blow.   20
And ye that love your lives, listen to me
As a lord that is learned to lead you by law.
And ye that are of my men and of my meinie,
Since we are come from our kith as ye well know,
And semble all here sam in this city,   25
It sits us in sadness to set all our saw.

1 DUKE: My lord, we shall take keep to your call,
And stir to no stead but ye steven us,
No grievance too great ne too small.

KING: Yea, but look that no faults befall.   30

2 DUKE: Leally, my lord, so we shall,
Ye need not no more for to neven us.

1 DUKE: Monseigneur, demean you to mensk in mind what I
          mean
And boun to your bedward, for so hold I best,
For all the commons of this court are avoided clean,   35
And ilka renk, as reason asks, are gone to their rest—
Wherefore I counsel, my lord, ye command you a drink.

KING: Now certes, I assent as thou says.
See ilka wye is went on his ways
Lightly, without any delays.   40
Give us wine winly and let us go wink,
And see that no dirdum be done.

Then the King drinks

1 DUKE: My lord, unlace you to lie,
Here shall none come for to cry.

---

19 *ere . . . be* before there is any trouble   20 *brothel* wretch   *boast . . . blow* to
give vent to boasting   23 *meinie* household   24 *kith* native land   25 *semble*
assemble   *sam* together   26 It behoves us soberly to express all our views
27 *take keep* pay attention   28 *stir* go   *stead* place   *steven* command   29 No
trouble is too great or too small [for us to attend to it]   30 *faults befall* mistakes
occur   31 *Leally* Loyally   32 You have no more need to tell us   33–4 My
lord, condescend to pay attention to what I say, and get ready for bed, for I consider
that best   35 *commons* common people   *are . . . clean* have all gone   36 *ilka*
every   as is reasonable   37 *command you* demand for yourself   38 *certes*
indeed   39 *wye* man   40 *Lightly* Quickly   41 *winly* pleasantly   *wink*
sleep   42 *dirdum* noise   *done* made   43 *unlace* loosen (clothes)

KING: Now speedily look that thou spy   45
    That no noise be nighing this noon.

1 DUKE: My lord, your bed is new made, you needs not for to
    bide it.
KING: Yea, but as thou loves me heartily, lay me down softly,
    For thou wot full well that I am full tenderly hided.
1 DUKE: How lie ye, my good lord?
KING: Right well, by this light,   50
    All wholly at my desire.
    Wherefore I pray Sir Satan our sire,
    And Lucifer most lovely of lyre,
    He save you all, sirs, and give you good night.

1 SOLDIER: Sir knight, ye wot we are warned to wend   55
    To wit of this warlock what is the king's will.
2 SOLDIER: Sir, here is Herod's hall even here at our hand,
    And all our intent tite shall we tell him until.
1 SOLDIER: Who is here?
1 DUKE: Who is there?
1 SOLDIER: Sir, we are knights kenned,
    Are come to your counsel this carl for to kill.   60
1 DUKE: Sirs, but your message may mirths amend,
    Stalk forth by yon streets or stand stone still.
2 SOLDIER: Yes, certes sir, of mirths we mean,
    The king shall have matters to mell him.
    We bring here a boy us between,   65
    Wherefore to have worship we ween.
1 DUKE: Well sirs, so that it turn to no teen,
    Tent him and we shall go tell him.

    My lord, yonder is a boy bound that brought is in blame,
    Haste you in hie, they hove at your gate.   70

45 *spy* see   46 *nighing* hereabouts   *noon* midnight   47 *bide* await
49 *wot* know   *I . . . hided* I have a most sensitive skin   51 Entirely as I should
wish   53 *lyre* face   55 *warned to wend* instructed to go   56 To find
out what is the king's desire concerning this traitor   58 *intent* purpose   *tite*
immediately   *him until* to him   59 *kenned* [well-] known   60 *Are* [Who]
are   *carl* fellow   61 unless your errand portends good sport   62 *Stalk
forth* Walk stealthily away   63 *of . . . mean* we have good news   64 *mell*
concern   65 *boy* wretch   66 As a result of which we believe we shall be
honoured   67 given that it does not turn into trouble   68 Attend to him
(Jesus), and we shall go and inform him (Herod)   69 *blame* censure   70 *in
hie* swiftly   *hove* wait

KING: What, and shall I rise now, in the devil's name,
    To stightle among strangers in stalls of estate?
    But have here my hand, hold now,
    And see that my slop be well sitting.
1 DUKE: My lord, with a good will I wield you,   75
    No wrong will I wit at my witting.

    But my lord, we can tell you of uncouth tidand.
KING: Yea, but look ye tell us no tales but true.
2 DUKE: My lord, they bring you yonder a boy bound in a band
    That bodes either bourding or bales to brew.   80
KING: Then get we some harrow full hastily at hand.
1 DUKE: My lord, there is some note that is needful to neven
    you of new.
KING: Why, hopes thou they haste him to hang?
2 DUKE: We wot not their will nor their weening,
    But bodeword full blithely they bring.   85
KING: Now, do then, and let us see of their saying.
2 DUKE: Lo sirs, ye shall carp with the king,
    And tell to him manly your meaning.

1 SOLDIER: Lord, wealth and worship be with you alway.
KING: What would you?
2 SOLDIER: A word, lord, and your wills were.   90
KING: Well, say on then.
1 SOLDIER: My lord, we fare fools to flay
    That to you would forfeit.
KING: We, fair fall you therefore.
1 SOLDIER: My lord, fro ye hear what we say
    It will heave up your hearts.
KING: Yea, but say what hind have ye there?
2 SOLDIER: A present from Pilate, lord, the prince of our lay.   95
KING: Peace in my presence, and name him no more.

---

72 *stightle* concern myself   *stalls of estate* court   74 *slop* gown   *well sitting* hanging well   75 *wield* attend to   76 I will not permit myself to be conscious of any shortcoming   77 *uncouth tidand* strange news   79 *band* rope   80 *bodes* portends   *bourding* sport   *bales* trouble   81 *harrow* commotion   82 *note* news   *neven* mention [to]   83 *hopes* believes   84 *weening* intention   85 *bodeword* a message   86 *do then* proceed   87 *carp* speak   88 *manly* courteously   *meaning* purpose   90 What do you want?   *and . . . were* if you would permit it   91 *fare* make it our business   *flay* punish   92 *forfeit* cause offence   Good, may you prosper for that   93 *fro* when   94 *hind* fellow   95 *lay* law

1 SOLDIER: My lord, he will worship you fain.
KING: I conceive ye are full foes of him.
2 SOLDIER: My lord, he would mensk you with main,
    And therefore he sends you this swain.   100
KING: Go tite with that gadling again,
    And say him a borrowed bean set I not by him.

1 DUKE: Ah, my lord, with your leave, they have fared far,
    And for to fraist of your fare was no folly.
2 DUKE: My lord, and this gadling go thus it will grieve war,   105
    For he gars grow on this ground great villainy.
KING: Why, means thou that that miting should my mights mar?
DUKE: Nay lord, but he makes on this mould mickle mastery.
KING: Go in, and let us see of the saws nar,
    And but if they be to our bourding, they both shall aby.   110
2 SOLDIER: My lord, we were worthy to blame
    To bring you any message of miss.
KING: Why then, can you neven us his name?
1 SOLDIER: Sir, Christ have we called him at home.
KING: Oh, this is the ilk self and the same—   115
    Now sirs, ye be welcome iwis.

And in faith I am fain he is fun,
His ferlies to frayne and to feel;
Now these games were gradely begun.
2 SOLDIER: Lord, leally that likes us well.   120

KING: Yea, but dare ye hight heartily that harlot is he?
1 SOLDIER: My lord, take heed and in haste ye shall hear how.
KING: Yea, but what means that this message was made unto
    me?

97 he will willingly worship you   99 *mensk* honour   *with main* highly
100 *swain* fellow   101–2 Return immediately with that lout, and tell him I
wouldn't give a borrowed bean for him   103 *fared* travelled   104 *fraist* . . .
fare find out your opinion   105 *and* if   *war* worse   106 For he causes
great evil to increase in this land   107 Why, do you mean that this nonentity
could impair my power?   108 he performs in this place many high-handed deeds
109–10 let us examine these claims more closely, and unless what they say pleases us,
they shall both pay for it   111 *to* of   112 *message of miss* untoward news
113 *neven* tell   115 *ilk* very   116 *iwis* indeed   117 *fun* found
118 *ferlies* miracles   *frayne* enquire into   *feel* examine   119 *gradely* properly
120 Lord, truly we are well pleased by this   121 *hight heartily* promise faithfully
harlot scoundrel   123 *what* . . . *that* why is it

2 SOLDIER: My lord, for it touches to treason, I trow.
1 SOLDIER: My lord, he is culpable kenned in our country   125
   Of many perilous points, as Pilate proves now.
2 SOLDIER: My lord, when Pilate heard he had gone through
     Galilee
   He learned us that that lordship longed to you,
   And ere he wist what your wills were,
   No further would he speak for to spill him.   130
KING: Then knows he that our mights are the more?
1 SOLDIER: Yea, certes sir, so say we there.
KING: Now certes, and our friendship therefore
   We grant him, and no grievance we will him.

   And sirs, ye are welcome, iwis, as ye well owe,   135
   And for to wend at your will I you warrand,
   For I have covet kindly that comely to know,
   For men carp that the carl should be cunnand.
2 SOLDIER: My lord, would he say you sooth of his saw,
   Ye saw never slike selcouth, by sea nor by sand.   140
KING: Now go aback both and let the boy blow,
   For I hope we get some harre hastily at hand.
1 SOLDIER: Jerusalem and the Jews may have joy
   And heal in their heart for to hear him.
KING: Say, bienvenue in bon foi,   145
   Ne please you à parler à moi?
2 SOLDIER: Nay, my lord, he can of no bourding, this boy.
KING: No sir? With thy leave we shall lere him.

1 SON: My lord, see these knights that know and are keen,
   How they come to your court without any call.   150

---

124 *trow* believe   125 *culpable kenned* known to be blameworthy   126 *perilous points* dangerous matters   128 *learned* informed   *lordship* province   *longed* belonged   130 *spill* destroy   131 Then does he acknowledge that our power is the greater   134 *no . . . him* hold nothing against him   135 *owe* ought [to be]   136 I give you authority to go as you please   137 *covet* longed for *kindly* naturally   *comely* gracious person   138 *cunnand* clever   139 were he to tell you the truth of his sayings   140 *slike selcouth* such wonders   141 *blow* breathe   142 *harre* important matter   144 *heal* consolation   145–6 Say, welcome in good faith, does it not please you to speak with me? (Herod and others occasionally speak in a mixture of French and English, but not always intelligibly; see lines 239–41, 267–8.)   147 *he . . . bourding* he has no small talk   148 *lere* teach   149 *keen* ready for action

KING: Yea son, and muster great masteries—what may this
    bemean?
1 DUKE: My lord, for your mights are more than their all
    They seek you as sovereign, and certes that is seen.
KING: Now certes, since ye say so, assay him I shall,
    For I am fainer of that freke than other fifteen,   155
    Yea, and him that first found, fair might him fall.
1 SOLDIER: Lord, leally we lere you no lie,
    This life that he leads will lose him.
KING: Well sirs, draw you adrigh,
    And beausires, bring ye him nigh,   160
    For if all that his sleights be sly,
    Yet ere he pass we shall appose him.

    Oh, my heart hops for joy
    To see now this prophet appear.
    We shall have good game with this boy—   165
    Take heed, for in haste ye shall hear.

    I leve we shall laugh and have liking
    To see how this lidderon here he ledges our laws.
2 DUKE: Hark, cousin, thou comes to carp with a king,
    Take tent and be cunning, and carp as thou knows.   170
1 DUKE: Yea, and look that thou be not a sot of thy saying,
    But sadly and soon thou set all thy saws.
KING: Him seems full boudish, that boy that they bring.
2 DUKE: My lord, and of his bourding great boasting men
    blows.
KING: Why, therefore have I sought him to see.   175
    Look, beausires, ye be to our bodes boun.
1 DUKE: Kneel down here to the king on thy knee.
2 DUKE: Nay, needlings it will not be.

---

151 *muster* display   *masteries* deeds   *bemean* mean   152 *for* because   *their
all* all theirs   153 *seen* evident   154 *assay* put to the test   155 *fainer*
more desirous   *than . . . fifteen* than of fifteen others   156 *found* found [him]   a
blessing on him   158 *lose* ruin   159 *draw you adrigh* stand aside   161 *if all*
even though   *sleights* tricks   162 *pass* should go   *appose* interrogate   167 *leve*
believe   *liking* pleasure   168 To see how this rascal here expounds our laws
170 *tent* care   *cunning* wise   171 *sot* fool   *of* in   172 But soberly
and promptly set forth all your words   173 *boudish* sullen   174 *bourding*
idle talk   *blows* give vent to   176 *beausires* my good men   *bodes* commands
boun obedient   178 *needlings* of necessity

KING: Lo sirs, he meeks him no more unto me
　　Than it were to a man of their own town.   180

1 DUKE: We! Go, laumere, and learn thee to lout
　　Ere they more blame thee to-bring.
KING: Nay, dreadless without any doubt
　　He knows not the course of a king.

　　And here be in our bail, bourd ere we blin—   185
　　Say first at the beginning withal, where was thou born?
　　Do fellow, for thy faith, let us fall in.
　　First of thy ferlies, who fed thee before?
　　What, deigns thou not? Lo sirs, he deafens us with din.
　　Say, where led ye this lidderon? His language is lorn.   190
1 SOLDIER: My lord, his marvels to more and to min
　　Or musters among us both midday and morn.
2 SOLDIER: My lord, it were too fele
　　Of wonders, he worketh them so wightly.
1 SOLDIER: We, man, mumbling may nothing avail,   195
　　Go to the king and tell him from top unto tail.
KING: Do bring us that boy unto bail,
　　For leally we leave him not lightly.

1 DUKE: This mop means that he may mark men to their meed;
　　He makes many masteries and marvels among.   200
2 DUKE: Five thousand folk fair gan he feed
　　With five loaves and two fishes to fang.
KING: How fele folk says thou he fed?
2 DUKE: Five thousand, lord, that came to his call.
KING: Yea, boy? How mickle bread he them bid?   205
1 DUKE: But five loaves dare I well wed.

179 *he meeks him* he defers   181 *We* expression of indignation   *laumere* fool
lout bow   182 *thee to-bring* heap upon you   183 *dreadless* undoubtedly
184 *course of* procedure regarding   185 Since [you] are here in our custody,
give us some sport before we leave off   186 *withal* in any case   187 *fall in*
begin   188 *fed* raised   *before* in the first place   190 Where have you
been with this idiot? He has lost his power of speech   191 *min* less   192 *Or
musters* Now are evident   193–4 My lord, the number of his miracles is over-
whelming, he performs them so freely   196 *top . . . tail* beginning to end
197–8 Keep that fellow in close arrest, for truly, we will not readily leave [off question-
ing] him   199 This fool says he can ordain each man's reward (i.e. at the last
judgement)   201 *gan* did   203 *fele* many   205 How much bread
did he give them?   206 *wed* wager

KING: Now by the blood that Mahound bled,
What, this was a wonder at all.

2 DUKE: Now lord, two fishes blessed he eft
And gave them, and there none was forgotten. 210
1 DUKE: Yea lord, and twelve lapful there left
Of relief when all men had eaten.

KING: Of such another mangery no man mean may.
2 DUKE: My lord, thus his masteries muster his might.
KING: But say, sirs, are these saws sooth that they say? 215
2 SOLDIER: Yea lord, and more selcouth were showed to our
    sight.
One Lazar, a lad that in our land lay,
Lay locked under lair from leam and from light,
And his sister come raking in rueful array.
And lord, for their roaring he raised him full right, 220
And from his grave gart him gang
Ever forth, without any evil.
KING: We, such leasings last too long.
1 SOLDIER: Why lord, ween ye these words be wrong?
This same lad lives us among. 225
KING: Why, these hope I be deeds of the devil.

Why should ye haste him to hang
That sought not newly your noys?
2 SOLDIER: My lord, for he calls him a king
And claims to be a king of Jews. 230

KING: But say, is he king in his kith where he comes from?
1 SOLDIER: Nay lord, but he calls him a king his cares to keel.
KING: Then is it little wonder if that he be woe,
For to be waried with wrong since he works well;

---

208 Well, this certainly was a marvel   209 *eft* likewise   211 *lapful* baskets
full   *left* remained   212 *relief* left-overs   213 No man could possibly
speak of another banquet such as that   214 But my lord, his gread deeds are
what show his power   215 *sooth* true   216 *selcouth* amazing   217 *lay*
was   218 *lair* earth   *leam* brightness   219 *raking* hurrying   *in rueful
array* in a distraught state   220 *for* because of   *roaring* wailing   221 *gart*
made   *gang* go   223 *leasings* tall stories   224 *ween* believe   228 Who
provoked your anger only recently   232 *his . . . keel* make things easy for himself
233 *woe* downcast   234 *waried* cursed   *works well* does good deeds

But he shall sit by myself since ye say so. 235
Come near, king, into court. Say, can ye not kneel?
We shall have gauds full good and games ere we go.
How likes thou? Well lord? Say. What, devil, never a deal?
I fault in my reverant inutile moi,
I am of favour, lo, fairer by far. 240
Kyte oute yugilment. Uta! Oy! Oy!
By any wit that I wot it will wax war.

Saevitia perimet
Such losels and lurdans as thou, lo,
Respicias timet. 245
What the devil and his dam shall I now do?

Do carp on, carl, for I can thee cure.
Say, may thou not hear me? Hey, man, art thou wood?
Now tell me faithfully before how thou fore.
Forth, friend. By my faith, thou art a fond food. 250
1 DUKE: My lord, it astonies him, your steven is so store
Him had liever have stand stone still there he stood.
KING: And whether the boy be abashed of Herod's big blore
That were a bourd of the best, by Mahound's blood.
2 DUKE: My lord, I trow your falchion him flays 255
And lets him.
KING: Now leally I leve thee,
And therefore shall I wave it away
And softly with a sceptre assay.
Now sir, be pert I thee pray,
For none of my grooms shall grieve thee. 260

---

237 *gauds* sport   238 *How . . . thou?* How does this suit you?   *never a deal* not
a word   239 *I . . . reverent* I am not being honoured   [the rest of the line is
not intelligible]   240 *favour* appearance   241 [Either nonsense or corrupt]
242 For anything I can see, things will get worse   243 'Savage violence may
kill'   244 *losels* louts   *lurdans* hooligans   245 'Let him fear and be wary'
246 *dam* mate   247 *cure* help   248 *wood* mad   249 *fore* fared
250 *Forth* Come along   *fond food* mad creature   251 *astonies* stuns   *steven*
voice   *store* loud   252 *Him . . . have* He would prefer to   253 *whether*
should   *abashed* afraid   *blore* bluster   255 *falchion* big sword   *flays* frightens
256 *lets* hinders   259 *pert* open (of speaking)   260 *grooms* servants   *grieve*
harm

Si loqueris tibi laus,
Pariter quoque prospera dantur;
Si loqueris tibi fraus,
Fel, fex et bella parantur.
My men, ye go mensk him with main,   265
And look how that it would seem.
1 DUKE: Dewcus fayff sir and sovereign.
2 DUKE: Sir udins amangadire demain.
KING: Go, answer them gradely again.
What, devil, whether dote we or dream?   270

1 SOLDIER: Nay, we get not one word, dare I well wed,
For he is wrest of his wit or will of his wone.
KING: Ye say he lacked your laws as ye that lad led?
2 SOLDIER: Yea lord, and made many gauds as we have gone.
KING: Now since he comes as a knave and as a knave clad,   275
Whereto call ye him a king?
1 DUKE:'   Nay lord, he is none,
But an harlot is he.
KING: ·   What, devil, I am hard stead,
A man might as well stir a stock as a stone.
1 SON: My lord, this faitour so foully is afraid,
He looked never of lord so longly alone.   280
KING: No son, the ribald sees us so richly arrayed
He weens we be angels every-ilkone.
2 DUKE: My lord, I hold him aghast of your gay gear.
KING: Great lords ought to be gay.
Here shall no man do to thee dere,   285
And therefore yet nemn in mine ear—
For by great God, and thou gar me swear,
Thou had never dole ere this day.

261–4 'If you speak well of yourself, you will accordingly be treated well; but if you acquit yourself badly, bitterness, filth, and violence will ensue.'   267–8 [Partly nonsense or corrupt]   269 *gradely* politely   270 *whether . . . dream?* do we either dote or dream?   272 *wrest* driven out   or at a loss   273 *lacked* contravened   *as . . . led* when he was with you   274 *made . . . gauds* played many tricks   276 *Whereto* Why   277 *stead* pressed   278 *stir* [try to] arouse   *stock* tree-stump   279 *foully* abjectly   280 He never looked at a lord alone for such a long time   281 *arrayed* dressed   282 *every-ilkone* each and every one of us   283 I believe he is frightened by your fine clothes   285 *dere* harm   286 *nemn* speak   287 *gar me* cause me to   288 You never knew misery before today

Do carp on tite, carl, of thy kin.
1 DUKE: Nay, needlings he nevens you with none.   290
KING: That shall he buy ere he blin—
2 DUKE: Ah, leave, lord.
KING: Let me alone.

1 DUKE: Now good lord, and ye may, move you no more,
It is not fair to fight with a fond food,
But go to your counsel and comfort you there.   295
KING: Thou says sooth. We shall see if so will be good,
For certes our sorrows are sad.
2 SON: What a devil ails him?
My lord, I can gar you be glad,
For in time our master is mad.   300
He lurks, lo, and looks like a lad,
He is wood, lord, or else his wit fails him.

3 SON: My lord, ye have moved you as mickle as ye may,
For ye might mensk him no more were he Mahound;
And since it seems to be so, let us now assay.   305
KING: Look, beausires, ye be to our bodes bound.
1 DUKE: My lord, how should he doubt us? He dreads not your
      deray.
KING: Now do forth, the devil might him drown!
And since he frames falsehood and makes foul fray,
Roar on him rudely, and look ye not round.   310

1 SON: My lord, I shall enforce myself since ye say so.
Fellow, be not afeared nor feign not therefore,
But tell us now some trifles between us two,
And none of our men shall meddle them more.
And therefore by reason array thee,   315
Do tell us some point for thy prow.

---

290 *nevens . . . none* says nothing to you   291 *buy* pay for   *blin* go   292 *leave leave* leave off   293 do not become more vexed, if you can help it   295 *counsel* advisers   300 *in time* opportunely   *our master* i.e. Jesus, ironically   301 *lurks* skulks about   303 *moved you* put yourself out   305 And this being the case   307 *doubt* fear   *deray* clamour   309 *frames* concocts   *foul fray* terrible difficulty   310 Shout at him rudely and be sure you don't whisper   311 *enforce* endeavour   312 do not be frightened or hesitant because of this   314 *meddle . . . more* concern themselves any more [with you]   315 *array thee* co-operate   316 *prow* profit

Hears thou not what I say thee?
Thou mumbling miting, I may thee
Help, and turn thee from teen, as I trow.

2 SON: Look up lad, lightly, and lout to my lord here,   320
For from bale unto bliss he may now thee borrow.
Carp on, knave, cantly, and cast thee to cord here,
And say me now somewhat, thou saintrel, with sorrow.
Why stands thou as still as a stone here?
Spare not, but speak in this place here,   325
Thou gadling, it may gain thee some grace here.
3 SON: My lord, this faitour is so feared in your face here,
None answer in this need he nevens you with none here.

Do, beausire, for Belial's blood and his bones,
Say somewhat—or it will wax war.   330
1 SON: Nay, we get not one word in these wones.
2 SON: Do cry we all on him at once.
SONS: Oyez! Oyez! Oyez!
KING: Oh, ye make a foul noise for the nonce.
3 SON: Needling my lord, it is never the nar.

1 SON: My lord, all your mooting amends not a mite,   335
To meddle with a madman is marvel to me.
Command your knights to clothe him in white
And let him cair as he came to your country.
KING: Lo sirs, we lead you no longer a lite,
My son has said sadly how that it should be—   340
But such a point for a page is too perfect.
1 DUKE: My lord, fools that are fond they fall such a fee.
KING: What, in white garments to go,
Thus gaily gird in a gown?
2 DUKE: Nay lord, but as a fool forced him fro.   345

---

319 *turn . . . teen* deflect you from trouble   320 *lightly* cheerfully   321 *borrow*
save   322 *cantly* boldly   come to some agreement here   323 *saintrel*
little saint   326 *gadling* knave   327 *faitour* deceiver   *in* of   328 In
this predicament he makes no answer at all to you here   330 *somewhat* something
wax war grow worse   331 *in these wones* in this place   333 *Oyez* Hear ye
nonce purpose   334 [We] must needs, my lord, but are no nearer [getting
any reply]   335 all your disputation [with him] does not improve matters at all
338 *cair* go   339 We will detain you no longer   341 But such a thing
is too elaborate for a knave   342 such a reward falls to fools who are mad
344 *gird* clothed   345 *forced him fro* out of his wits (?)

KING: How say ye sirs, should it be so?
SONS: Yea, lord.
KING:　　　　　We, then is there no more,
　　But boldly bid them be boun.

　　Sir knights, we cast to gar you be glad,
　　Our counsel have warned us wisely and well.　　　　　350
　　White clothes we say fall for a fond lad,
　　And all his folly, in faith, fully we feel.

1 DUKE: We will with a good will for his weeds wend,
　　For we wot well enough what weeds he shall wear.
2 DUKE: Lo, here is an haterell here at your hend,　　　　355
　　All fashioned therefore fools to fere.

1 SOLDIER: Lo here a jupon of joy,
　　All such should be good for a boy.
1 DUKE: He shall be rayed like a roy,
　　And shall be found in his folly.　　　　　360
2 DUKE: We, thank them, evil mote thou thee.
1 SOLDIER: Nay, we get not a word, well I warrant.
2 SOLDIER: Man, muster some marvel to me.
1 DUKE: What, ween ye he be wiser than we?
　　Leave we, and let the king see　　　　　365
　　How it is forced and farand.

　　My lord, look if ye be paid,
　　For we have got him his gear.
KING: Why, and is this ribald arrayed?
　　My blessing, beausires, ye bear.　　　　　370

　　Go, gar cry in my court and gradely gar write
　　All the deeds that we have done in this same degree.
　　And who finds him grieved let him tell tite,
　　And if we find no default him falls to go free.

---

349 *cast* endeavour　　　351 *fall for* are appropriate to　　　352 *feel* perceive
353 *weeds* clothes　　　355 *haterell* garment　　*hend* hands　　　356 *fere* befit
357 *jupon* tunic　　　359 *rayed* dressed　　*roy* king (of fools)　　　360 *found* displayed　　　361 *evil . . . thee* a curse on you　　　365 *Leave we* Let us leave off
366 How he has been treated and is faring　　　367 *paid* satisfied　　　371 *gar
cry* proclaim　　*gradely . . . write* have suitably set down　　　372 *same degree* matter
373 *finds . . . grieved* is dissatisfied　　　374 *him falls* it is his (Jesus's) lot

1 DUKE: Oyez! If any wight with this wretch any worse wot—   375
    Works bear witness who so works wrong—
    Busk boldly to the bar his bales to abate,
    For my lord, by my lewty, will not be dealing long.
  `My lord, here appears none to appair his estate.
KING: Well then, falls him go free.   380
    Sir knights, then graith you goodly to gang,
    And repair with your present and say to Pilate
    We grant him our friendship all fully to fang.
1 SOLDIER: My lord, with your leave this way shall we lere,
    Us likes no longer here to abide.   385
2 SOLDIER: My lord, and he worth aught in war,
    We come again with good cheer.
KING: Nay, beausires, ye find us not here,
    Our leave will we take at this tide

    And rathely array us to rest,   390
    For such notes have noyed us ere now.
1 DUKE: Yea, certes lord, so hold I best,
    For this gadling ungoodly has grieved you.
2 DUKE: Look ye bear word as ye wot,
    How well we have quit us this while.   395
1 SOLDIER: We, wise men will deem it we dote
    But if we make end of our note.
KING: Wend forth, the devil in thy throat,
    We find no default him to file.

    Wherefore should we flay him or fleme him   400
    We find not in rolls of record;
    And since that he is dumb, for to deem him,
    Were this a good law for a lord?

375–7 Hear ye! If any man knows anything worse of this wretch—and (a man's) deeds
bear witness when he behaves wrongly—let him hasten to the bar and put an end to his
(i.e. the plaintiff's) grievances   378 *lewty* faith   *dealing* sitting in judgement
379 *appair* harm   *estate* standing   381 *graith you* prepare   *goodly* in a seemly
fashion   382 *repair* return   383 *fang* have   384 *this . . . lere* we
shall take our way   386 *worth . . . war* starts to behave worse   389 *tide*
time   390 *rathely* quickly   391 For such matters have already vexed us
393 *ungodly* wicked   395 *quit us* acquitted ourselves   396 *deem it* consider that
dote are foolish   · 397 Unless we finish our business [properly]   399 *file*
convict   400 *fleme* condemn   401 *rolls of record* rolls of parchment recording
the laws   402 *deem* judge

Nay losels, unleally ye learned all too late,
Go lere thus lordings of your land such lessons to lere.   405
Repair with your present and say to Pilate
We grant him our power all plain to appear,
And also our grievance forgive we algate
And we grant him our grace with good cheer.
As touching this brothel, that brawls or debate,   410
Bid him work as he will, and work not in were.
Go tell him this message from me.
And lead forth that miting, evil mote he thee.

1 SOLDIER: My lord, with your leave, let him be,
For all too long led him have we.   415

2 SOLDIER: What, ye sirs, my lord, will ye see?

KING: What, fellows? Take ye no tent what I tell you
And bid you? That yeoman ye yeme.

2 SOLDIER: My lord, we shall wage him an ill way.

KING: Nay, beausires, be not so breme.   420
Fare softly, for so will it seem.

1 SOLDIER: Now since we shall do as ye deem,
Adieu, sir.

KING: Dance on, in the devil's way.

---

404 *unleally* disloyally   405 *lere* teach   *lere* learn   407 *all . . . appear*
without scruple   410 *touching* concerning   *that . . . debate* should he wrangle or
dispute   411 *and . . . were* but not act suspiciously   416 *will . . . see?*
surely you will attend to this?   418 *yeoman* underling   *yeme* deal with
419 we shall reward him in an unpleasant manner   420 *breme* impatient
421 *Fare softly* Behave gently   *seem* appear seemly

THE TILEMAKERS

Christ before Pilate 2: The Judgement

The play of Christ's second appearance before Pilate, and the judgement upon him, is attributed to the York Realist (see the Headnote to the *Conspiracy*), and is cast in a characteristically ambitious alliterative stanza, $abab_4bcbc_3d_1ccd_3$. As in the preceding trial scenes, Christ is largely silent, and the dramatic life of the play is generated by the cut and thrust of the disputes amongst his adversaries, culminating in a scourging scene of fearful bestiality.

For his ordering of the events and for certain verbal details the dramatist drew on a vernacular narrative poem of the time, the *Gospel of Nicodemus*. It supplied him, for example, with the germ of the extended apocryphal episode in which the banners held by the soldiers spontaneously bow down to Christ as he enters. The differing reactions of Pilate and the High Priests to this incident are subtly handled. Annas and Caiaphas hasten to assert that Christ has put a spell on the soldiers—he is repeatedly referred to as a 'warlock' in the Passion sequence—but Pilate either affects to be or is genuinely frightened by the miracle, and tries to use it as an opportunity to send Christ away without more ado.

Another narrative source, the *Northern Passion*, probably suggested how the relationship between Pilate and the High Priests might be more fully realized on stage. The punctilious verbosity of Annas and Caiaphas makes little impression on Pilate until they assert, as in the poem, that he has claimed the kingship and is a threat to imperial power (line 329). Pilate has no reply to this allegation against his own authority but to order the scourging, after which the judgement upon Christ is inevitable.

When the soldiers have beaten him, they array Christ as what they elsewhere call a 'fool-king', a figure of popular medieval entertainment, whose brief 'reign' might precede his execution, and was accompanied by violent indignities similar to those inflicted on Christ in the Gospel accounts. After the crowning with thorns, the dramatist causes the soldiers to speak parodies of the 'Hail' lyrics with which Christ had been greeted earlier in the cycle, by his parents in the *Nativity*, by the Three Kings, and at the *Entry into Jerusalem*.

PILATE: Lordings that are limit to the lore of my liance,
    Ye shapely shalks and sheen for to show,

1–2 People who are bound to the doctrine of my allegiance, you fine and handsome men in my sight

I charge you as your chieftain that ye chat for no chance,
But look to your lord here, and lere at my law—
As a duke I may damn you and draw.   5
Many bernes bold are about me,
And what knight or knave I may know
That list not as a lord for to lout me,
I shall lere him
In the devil's name, that dastard, to doubt me—   10
Yea, who works any works without me,
I shall charge him in chains to chare him.

Therefore ye lusty ledes within this length lapped,
Do stint of your stalking, and of stoutness be stalling.
What traitor his tongue with tales has trapped,   15
That fiend for his flattering full foul shall be falling.
What broll over-brathly is brawling,
Or unsoftly will say in these sales,
That caitiff thus carping and calling
As a boy shall be brought into bales.   20
Therefore,
Talk not nor treat not of tales,
For that gome that grins or gales,
I myself shall him hurt full sore.

ANNAS: Ye shall sit him full sore, what segge will assay you;   25
If he like not your lordship, that lad, shall ye lere him,
As a peerless prince, full prestly to pay you,
Or as a dearworth duke with dints shall ye dere him.
CAIAPHAS: Yea, in faith ye have force for to fear him,
Through your manhood and might is he marred.   30

---

3 *charge* command   *for . . . chance* under no circumstances   4 *lere* learn
5 *draw* punish   6 *bernes* knights   7 *know* discover   8 *list not* does
not wish   *lout* reverence   9 *lere* teach   10 *dastard* wretch   *doubt* fear
11 Yes, he who does any deeds without my consent   12 *charge* clap   *chare*
punish   13–14 Therefore, you bold men enclosed in this space, cease walking
about, and put a stop to your movement   15 *trapped* loaded   16 *full . . .*
falling will be falling into great misfortune   17 The wretch who is squabbling
too noisily   18 *unsoftly* loudly   *say* talk   *sales* halls   19 *caitiff* scoundrel
carping talking   *calling* shouting   20 *boy* miscreant   *brought . . . bales* punished
severely   22 *treat* discourse   23 *gome* man   *grins* grimaces   *gales*
complains   25 Whatever man provokes you, you will make it the worse for him
26 *lordship* authority   *lad* rascal   27 *prestly* quickly   *pay* please
28 *dearworth* worthy   *dints* blows   *dere* injure   29 *force* power   *fear*
intimidate   30 *marred* destroyed

No chivalrous chieftain may cheer him
Fro that churl with charge ye have charred.

.　　.　　.　　.　　.　　.　　.　　.　　.

In pining pain is he parred.
ANNAS: Yea, and with scathe of skelps ill scarred,
　From time that your teen he have tasted.　　　　　　35

PILATE: Now certes, as me seems, whoso sadly has sought you,
　Your praising is profitable, ye prelates of peace.
　Gramercy your good word, and ungain shall it nought you,
　That ye will say the sooth, and for no segge cease.
CAIAPHAS: Else were it pity we appeared in this press—　　40
　But conceive how your knights are coming.
ANNAS: Yea, my lord, that leve ye no lease,
　I can tell you, you tides some tiding
　Full sad.
PILATE: See, they bring yon broll in a band.　　　　　　45
　We shall hear now hastily at hand
　What unhap before Herod he had.

1 SOLDIER: Hail, loveliest lord that ever law led yet,
　Hail, seemliest under silk on everilka side,
　Hail, stateliest on steed in strength that is stead yet,　　50
　Hail, liberal, hail, lusty, to lords allied.
PILATE: Welcome, what tidings this tide?
　Let no language lightly now let you.
1 SOLDIER: Sir Herod, sir, it is not to hide,
　As his good friend gradely he gret you　　　　　　55
　Forever.
　In what manner that ever he met you,

---

31 *cheer* console　　　32 When you have chastised that scoundrel with a punishment
32+ *Line missing in MS*　　33 He is flayed by tormenting pain　　34 Yes,
and badly scarred by injuries caused by blows　　35 *teen* wrath　　36–7 Now
indeed, it seems to me, that to anyone who has seriously heard you out, your words of
praise are just, you peace-loving prelates　　38 *Gramercy* Many thanks for　　*and*
. . . *you* it will not be unprofitable to you　　39 *sooth* truth　　*and* . . . *cease* and
not hesitate for any man's sake　　40 *press* assembly　　41 *conceive* see　　42 *leve*
believe　　*lease* lie　　43 *you tides* you are due　　44 *sad* serious　　45 *broll*
wretch　　*band* rope　　47 *unhap* misfortune　　48 *led* expounded　　49 *everilka*
each and every　　50 *in* . . . *yet* that is yet established in power　　51 *lusty*
bold one　　52 *this tide* [at] this time　　53 Let no florid speech hinder you
unnecessarily　　54 *it* . . . *hide* it should not be concealed　　55 *gradely*
courteously　　*gret* greeted　　57 *what manner* whatever circumstances

By himself full soon will he set you,
And says that ye shall not dissever.

PILATE: I thank him full throly; and sir, I say him the same—   60
But what marvellous matters did this myron there mell?
1 SOLDIER: For all the lord's language, his lips, sir, were lame;
For any speerings in that space no speech would he spell,
But dumb as a door gan he dwell.
Thus no fault in him gan he find,   65
For his deeds to deem him to quell,
Nor in bands him brathly to bind;
And thus
He sent him to yourself, and assigned
That we, your knights, should be cleanly inclined,   70
And tite with him to you to truss.

PILATE: Sirs, harken, hear ye not what we have upon hand?
Lo how these knights carp that to the king caired.
Sir Herod, they say, no fault in me found,
He fast me to his friendship, so friendly he fared.   75
Moreover, sirs, he spake—and nought spared—
Full gently to Jesu, this Jew,
And sithen to these knights declared
How faults in him found he but few
To die.   80
He tasted him, I tell you, for true,
For to dere him he deemed undue,
And sirs, ye soothly say I.

CAIAPHAS: Sir Pilate our prince, we prelates now pray you,
Since Herod fraisted no further this faitour to flay,   85
Receive in your sale these saws that I say you:
Let bring him to bar and at his beard shall we bay.

---

59 *dissever* part   60 *throly* sincerely   61 *myron* layabout   *mell* speak of
62 *language* encouraging words   63 *speerings . . . space* enquiries at that time
spell speak   64 *gan* did   *dwell* remain   66 *deem . . . quell* judge him worthy
of death   67 *brathly* painfully   70 *be cleanly inclined* behave courteously
71 *tite* quickly   *truss* go   73 *carp* speak   *caired* went   75 *fast* bound
he fared was he   76 *nought* nothing   78 *sithen* then   80 Worthy of
death   81 *tasted* tried and found   82 *undue* inappropriate   83 *soothly*
truly   85 *fraisted* sought   *faitour* deceiver   *flay* punish   86 *sale* hall
saws words   87 *Let bring* Let him be brought

196   *The Tilemakers*

ANNAS: Yea, for and he wend thus by wiles away,
    I wot well he work will us wonder.
    Our meinie he mars that he may,   90
    With his sayings he sets them in sunder,
    With sin;
    With his blore he breeds mickle blunder.
    Whilst ye have him now, hold him under—
    We shall wary him away if he win.   95

CAIAPHAS: Sir, no time is to tarry this traitor to taste.
    Against Sir Caesar himself he segges, and says
    All the wights in this world work in waste
    That take him any tribute—thus his teaching outrays.
    Yet further he feigns slike affrays,   100
    And says that himself is God's son.
    And sir, our law ledges and lays,
    In what faitour falsehood is found,
    Should be slain.
PILATE: For no shame him to shend will we shun.   105
ANNAS: Sir, witness of these wones may be won,
    That will tell this without any train.

CAIAPHAS: I can reckon a rabble of renks full right,
    Of pert men in press, from this place ere I pass,
    That will witness, I warrant, the words of this wight,   110
    How wickedly wrought that this wretch has:
    Simon, Jairus and Judas,
    Dathan and Gamaliel,
    Naphtali, Levi and Lucas,
    And Amys these matters can mell   115
    Together.
    These tales for true can they tell

88 *wend* escape   *wiles* trickery   89–90 I am certain he will do us mischief. He subverts our people where he can   91 *sunder* disarray   93 *blore* extravagant words   *mickle blunder* great disturbance   95 *wary* curse   *win* escape 96 Sir, let there be no delay now in examining this traitor   97 *segges* speaks 98 *wights* men   *work . . . waste* waste their time   99 *take* give   *outrays* goes beyond the limit   100 *feigns . . . affrays* contrives such outrages   102 *ledges . . . lays* affirms and specifies   104 He should be put to death   105 If he is not guilty, we (I) refuse to condemn him (?)   106 *wones* things   *won* found 107 *train* deceit   108 I can summon up a crowd of worthy men   109 *Of . . . press* Sharp fellows under any circumstances   *ere* before

Of this faitour that false is and fell,
And in ledging of laws full lither.

PILATE: Yah, tush for your tales, they touch not intent.   120
  These witnesses I warrant that to witness ye wage,
  Some hatred in their hearts against him have hent,
  And purpose by this process to put down this page.
CAIAPHAS: Sir, in faith, us falleth not to fage,
  They are trist men and true that we tell you.   125
PILATE: Your swearing, sirs, swiftly ye swage,
  And no more in these matters ye mell you
  I charge.
ANNAS: Sir, despise not this speech that we spell you.
PILATE: If ye feign like frauds I shall fell you,   130
  For me likes not your language so large.

CAIAPHAS: Our language is too large, but your lordship relieve
  us.
  Yet we both beseech you, let bring him to bar.
  What points that we put forth, let your presence appreve us—
  Ye shall hear how this harlot hields out of harre.   135
PILATE: Yea, but be wise, witty, and ware.
ANNAS: Yes, sir, dread you not for nothing we doubt him.
PILATE: Fetch him, he is not right far—
  Do, beadle, busk thee about him.
BEADLE: I am fain,   140
  My lord, for to lead him or lout him.
  Uncloth him, clap him and clout him,
  If ye bid me, I am buxom and bain.

---

118 *fell* wicked   119 And exceedingly deceitful in expounding the laws
120 *touch . . . intent* are not to the point   121 *to . . . wage* you bribe them to
testify   122 *have hent* they have conceived   123 *purpose* intend   *page*
wretch   124 *us . . . fage* it is not in us to deceive   125 *trist* honest
126 *swage* cease   127 *ye mell you* concern yourselves   130–1 If you contrive such deceits I shall punish you, for I do not care for your unrestrained allegations
132 *large* extravagant   *but . . . us* but, all the same, your lordship, help us
134 May you commend the points that we shall make—you will hear how this wretch
behaves in a disorderly fashion   136 *witty* thoughtful   *ware* vigilant   137 *dread*
. . . him do not think we have no reason to suspect him   138 *right far* far away
139 *busk . . . him* set about fetching him   140 *fain* willing   142 *clap* beat
143 *buxom* obedient   *bain* eager

Knights, ye are commanded with this caitiff to cair,
And bring him to bar, and so my lord bad.   145
1 SOLDIER: Is this thy message?
BEADLE: Yea, sir.
1 SOLDIER: Then move thee no more,
For we are light for to leap and lead forth this lad.
2 SOLDIER: Do step forth; in strife art thou stad,
I uphold full evil has thee happed.
1 SOLDIER: O man, thy mind is full mad,   150
In our clutches to be clouted and clapped
And closed.
2 SOLDIER: Thou art lashed, lushed and lapped.
1 SOLDIER: Yea, routed, rushed and rapped;
Thus thy name with noy shall be noised.   155

2 SOLDIER: Lo this segge here, my sovereign, that ye for sent.
PILATE: Well, stir not from that stead, but stand still there.
But he shape some shrewdness, with shame is he shent,
And I will fraist, in faith, to frayne of his fare.
CAIAPHAS: We! Out! Stand may I not, so I stare.   160
ANNAS: Yea, harrow off this traitor, with teen.
PILATE: Say, renks, what ruth gars you roar?
Ye are wood or witless, I ween.
What ails you?
CAIAPHAS: Out! Slike a sight shoulde be seen.   165
ANNAS: Yea, alas, conquered are we clean.
PILATE: We! Are ye fond, or your force fails you?

CAIAPHAS: Ah, sir, saw ye not this sight, how that these shafts
shook,
And these banners to this brothel they bowed all on brede?

---

144 *cair* move   145 *bad* commanded   146 *move thee* say   147 *light* glad
leap move quickly   148 *in . . . stad* you are in serious trouble   149 I
contend that great misfortune has befallen you   152 *closed* held   153 *lushed*
beaten   *lapped* hemmed in   154 *routed* thrashed   *rushed* dragged violently
155 *with . . . noised* shall be spoken with vexation   156 *segge* man   157 *stead*
place   158 If he does not perform some wicked trick, he will be shamefully
condemned   159 *fraist* endeavour   *frayne* enquire into   *fare* behaviour
160 *We! Out!* expressions of dismay   I may not stand up, I am so astounded
161 *harrow* drag   *teen* violence   162 Say, men, what affliction causes you to
cry out?   163 *wood* mad   *ween* believe   165 You would not believe such
a sight   166 *clean* completely   167 *fond* mad   *force* strength   168 *shafts*
spears   169 *brothel* rascal   *all . . . brede* on every side

ANNAS: Yea, these cursed knights by craft let them crook,   170
   To worship this warlock unworthy in weed.
PILATE: Was it duly done thus indeed?
CAIAPHAS: Yea, yea, sir, ourselves we it saw.
PILATE: We! Spit on them, ill mote they speed!
   Say, dastards, the devil mote ye draw,   175
   How dare ye
   These banners on brede that here blow
   Let lout to this lurdan so low?
   O, faitours, with falsehood how fare ye?

2 SOLDIER: We beseech you and these seigniors beside you sir
     sit,   180
   With none of our governance to be grievous and grill,
   For it lay not in our lot these lances to let,
   And this work that we have wrought, it was not our will.
PILATE: Thou lies—hearest thou, lurdan?—full ill.
   Well thou wot if thou witness it would.   185
4 SOLDIER: Sir, our strength might not stable them still,
   They hielded for aught we could hold,
   Our unwitting.
5 SOLDIER: For all our force, in faith, did they fold,
   As this warlock worship they would—   190
   And us seemed, forsooth, it unsitting.

CAIAPHAS: Ah, unfriendly faitours, full false is your fable,
   This segge with his subtlety to his set hath you seized.
6 SOLDIER: Ye may say what you seems, sir, but these
     standards to stable
   What freke him enforces full foul shall he be feezed.   195
ANNAS: By the devil's nose, ye are doggedly diseased—
   Ah, hen-hearts, ill hap mote you hent.

170 *craft* cunning   *crook* bow down   171 *unworthy . . . weed* utterly disreputable
174 *ill . . . speed* a curse on them   175 *mote* may   178 Allow to bow to this
wretched knave   179 What kind of deceit are you involved in?   180 *seigniors*
worthy men   *sit* [who] sit   181 *governance* behaviour   *grievous and grill* angry
and furious   182 *lot* power   *let* prevent [from bowing down]   184 *full
ill* most wickedly   185 You know it perfectly well, if you would but admit it
186 *stable* keep   187–8 They bowed down for anything we could do, we did not
realize what was happening   189 *fold* bow   191 And it seemed to us,
truly, unbecoming   192 *fable* tale   193 *to . . . seized* has seduced you to his
party   194–5 You may say how things appear to you, sir, but whatever man
attempts to hold these banners steady, he will be most rudely discomfited   196 *doggedly diseased* accursedly afflicted   197 *ill . . . hent* a curse on you

PILATE: For a whap so he whined and wheezed,
   And yet no lash to the lurdan was lent.
   Foul fall you!   200
2 SOLDIER: Sir, iwis, no wiles we have went.
PILATE: Shamefully you sat to be shent;
   Here cumbered caitiffs I call you.

4 SOLDIER: Since you likes not, my lord, our language to leve,
   Let bring the biggest men that abide in this land,   205
   Properly in your presence their poustie to prove;
   Behold that they hield not from they have them in hand.
PILATE: Now ye are fearedest that ever I found;
   Fie on your faint hearts, in fere.
   Stir thee, no longer thou stand,   210
   Thou beadle, this bodeword thou bear
   Through this town,
   The wightest men unto were,
   And the strongest these standards to steer,
   Hither blithely bid them be boun.   215

BEADLE: My sovereign, full soon shall be served your saw,
   I shall bring to these banners right big men and strong.
   A company of cavels in this country I know,
   That great are and grill, to these gomes will I gang.
   Say, ye ledes both lusty and long,   220
   Ye must pass to Sir Pilate apace.
1 SOLDIER: If we work not his will it were wrong,
   We are ready to run on a race
   And rake.
BEADLE: Then tarry not, but trine on a trace,   225
   And follow me fast to his face.
2 SOLDIER: Do lead us, us likes well this lake.

198–200 He groaned and complained as if struck, but nobody attempted to hit the
rascal. A curse on you   201 *iwis* truly   *went* attempted   202 *you sat* you
allowed yourselves   *shent* overcome   203 *cumbered caitiffs* faint-hearted wretches
204 *language* words   206 *Properly* In person   *poustie* strength   207 Make sure
that they do not bow once they are holding them [the banners]   208 *fearedest*
most faint-hearted   209 *Fie* A curse   *in fere* the lot of you   211 *bodeword*
message   213 To warn the boldest men   214 *steer* handle   215 Bid
them come here eagerly   216 *full . . . saw* your command will swiftly be carried
out   218 *cavels* brawny fellows   219 *grill* bold   *gang* go   220 *ledes*
men   *long* tall   221 *pass* go   *apace* quickly   223 *run . . . race* make
haste   224 *rake* proceed   225 *trine . . . trace* step along swiftly   227 *us
. . . lake* we are pleased with this business

BEADLE: Lord, here are the biggest bernes that bield in this
    burgh,
    Most stately and strong, if with strength they be strained.
    Leve me, sir, I lie not, to look this land through,   230
    They are mightiest men with manhood demeaned.
PILATE: Wot thou well, or else has thou weened?
BEADLE: Sir, I wot well, without words more.
CAIAPHAS: In thy tale be not tainted nor teened.
BEADLE: We! Nay, sir, why should I be so?   235
PILATE: Well then,
    We shall fraist, ere they found us far fro,
    To what game they begin for to go.
    Sir Caiaphas, declare them ye can.

CAIAPHAS: Ye lusty ledes, now lith to my lore,   240
    Shape you to these shafts that so sheenly here shine.
    If yon banners bow the brede of an hair,
    Platly ye be put to perpetual pine.
1 SOLDIER: I shall hold this as even as a line.
ANNAS: Whoso shakes, with shames he shends.   245
2 SOLDIER: Ay, certain I say as for mine,
    When it settles, or sadly descends
    Where I stand—
    When it wrings, or wrong it wends,
    Other bursts, barks, or bends—   250
    Hardly let hack off mine hand.

PILATE: Sirs, wait to these wights, that no wiles be wrought;
    They are burly and broad, their boast have they blown.
ANNAS: To neven of that now, sir, it needs right nought,
    For who cursedly him quits, he soon shall be known.   255

---

228 *bield* live   *burgh* town   229 *stately* fierce   *strained* assailed   230 *to . . . through* if you were to look everywhere in this country [you would find]   231 *demeaned* endowed   232 Are you sure, or do you merely think so?   234 *tainted* suspect   *teened* inaccurate   237–8 We shall find out, before they leave us, what they are made of   239 *declare* instruct   240 *lith* listen   *lore* instructions   241 *Shape . . . to* Take hold of   *sheenly* brightly   242 *brede* breadth   243 *Platly* Directly   *be* [will] be   *pine* torment   245 Whoever wavers, disgraces himself   247 *settles* sinks   *sadly* perceptibly   249 *wrings* deviates   *or . . . wends* or moves out of place   250 *Other* Or   *bursts* shatters   *barks* splinters   251 Let my hand be cut off forthwith   252 *wait* attend   254 There is no need to mention that at the moment, sir   255 *cursedly . . . quits* performs badly

CAIAPHAS: Yea, that dastard to death shall be drawn;
  Whoso faults, he foully shall fall.
PILATE: Now, knights, since the cocks have crown,
  Have him hence with haste from this hall
  His ways.   260
  Do stiffly step on this stall,
  Make a cry, and cantly thou call,
  Even like as Sir Annas thee says.

ANNAS: Oyez! Jesu, thou Jew of gentle Jacob's kin,
  Thou netherest of Nazareth, now nevened is thy name.   265
  All creatures thee accuse. We command thee come in
  And answer to thine enemies. Defend now thy fame.

And the Beadle shall recite after Annas 'Let Jesus be judged'.

CAIAPHAS: We! Out! We are shent all for shame,
  This is wrasted all wrong, as I ween.
ANNAS: For all their boast, yon boys are to blame.   270
PILATE: Such a sight was never yet seen.
  Come sit.
  My comfort was caught from me clean—
  I upstrit, I me might not abstain
  To worship him in work and in wit.   275

CAIAPHAS: Thereof marvelled we mickle what moved you in
    mind,
  In reverence of this ribald so rudely to rise.
PILATE: I was past all my power, though I pained me and pined,
  I wrought not as I would in no manner of wise.
  But sirs, my speech well aspise: 280
  Wightly his ways let him wend,
  Thus my doom will duly devise,

257 *faults* fails   *he . . . fall* it will be the worse for him   260 On his way
261 *stiffly* boldly   *stall* rostrum   262 *cantly* loudly   264 *Oyez* Hear
ye   265 *netherest* lowest   *nevened* called   267 *fame* reputation   268 *shent
. . . shame* all utterly disgraced   269 Everything seems to have gone wrong
273–5 I was completely overcome—I rose up, I could not prevent myself from wor-
shipping him in thought and deed   276 *mickle* greatly   *moved . . . mind* upset
you   277 *ribald* scoundrel   *rudely* suddenly   278–9 It was beyond my
control, though I struggled and wrestled with myself; I could not do as I wished in any
respect   280 *aspise* attend to   281 *Wightly* Quickly   282 That is my
lawful judgement

For I am feared him, in faith, to offend
  In sights.
ANNAS: Then our law were laught to an end,   285
  To his tales if ye truly attend—
  He enchanted and charmed our knights.

CAIAPHAS: By his sorcery, sir—yourself the sooth saw—
  He charmed our chevaliers and with mischief enchanted.
  To reverence him royally we rose all on row;   290
  Doubtless we endure not of this dastard be daunted.
PILATE: Why, what harms has this hathel here haunted?
  I ken to convict him no cause.
ANNAS: To all gomes he God's son him granted,
  And list not to leve on our laws.   295
PILATE: Say man,
  Conceives thou not what cumberous clause
  That these clergy accusing thee knows?
  Speak, and excuse thee if thou can.

JESUS: Every man has a mouth that made is on mould,   300
  In weal and in woe to wield at his will;
  If he govern it goodly like as God would,
  For his spiritual speech him thar not to spill.
  And what gome so govern it ill,
  Full unhendly and ill shall he hap;   305
  Of ilk tale thou talks us until
  Thou account shall, thou can not escape.
PILATE: Sirs mine,
  Ye fon, in faith, all the frap,
  For in this lede no lease can I lap,   310
  Nor no point to put him to pine.

283 *feared* frightened   284 Publicly   285 *laught* brought   287 *charmed*
put spells on   291 Surely we will not stand to be intimidated by this wretch?
292 *harms* evils   *hathel* man   *haunted* practised   293 *ken* know   294 *him
granted* claimed himself to be   295 *list . . . on* would not respect   297–8 Do
you not see what a serious allegation these clergy who are accusing you bring forward?
300 *mould* earth   301 *weal* prosperity   302 *goodly* righteously   303 He
need never die, on account of his holy words   304 *govern . . . ill* uses it badly
305 He will have very great misfortune   306 For everything that you say to me
308–9 Truly, my good men, you are mad, all of you   310 *lease* deceit   *lap*
find   311 *point* reason

CAIAPHAS: Without cause, sir, we come not this carl to accuse
     him,
     And that will we ye wit as well is worthy.
PILATE: Now I record well the right ye will no rather refuse
     him
     Till he be driven to this death and deemed to die;   315
     But take him unto you forthy,
     And like as your law will you lere,
     Deem ye his body to aby.
ANNAS: O, Sir Pilate, without any peer,
     Do way.   320
     Ye wot well, without any were,
     Us falls not, nor our fellows in fere,
     To slay no man—yourself the sooth say.

PILATE: Why should I deem to death, then, without deserving
     in deed?
     But I have heard all wholly why in hearts ye him hate.   325
     He is faultless, in faith, and so God mote me speed,
     I grant him my good will to gang on his gate.
CAIAPHAS: Not so, sir, for well ye it wot,
     To be king, he claimeth, with crown,
     And whoso stoutly will step to that state   330
     Ye should deem, sir, to be dinged down
     And dead.
PILATE: Sir, truly that touched to treason,
     And ere I remove, he rue shall that reason,
     And ere I stalk or stir from this stead.   335

     Sir knights that are comely, take this caitiff in keeping,
     Skelp him with scourges and with scathes him scorn.

312 *carl* fellow   313 And that we would wish you rightfully to understand
314–15 Now I see very clearly that you will never release him until he is doomed to
die and under sentence of death   316 *forthy* therefore   317 *like* accordingly
318 Sentence him to pay the penalty   320 Say no more [of that]   321 *wot*
know   *were* doubt   322–3 It is inappropriate for us or for our people to put
anybody to death—you have truly said so yourself   324 *without . . . deed* without
[his having done] anything to deserve it   326 *and . . . speed* so help me God
327 *gate* way   330 *stoutly . . . state* will boldly lay claim to that dignity
331 *dinged* struck   332 And put to death   333 *touched* appertained
334 *remove* go   *rue* repent   *reason* claim   335 *stalk* walk   336 *comely*
well built   337 *Skelp* Whip   *scathes* blows

Wraist and wring him too, for woe till he be weeping,
And then bring him before us as he was before.

1 SOLDIER: He may ban the time he was born; 340
Soon shall he be served as ye said us.

ANNAS: Do wap off his weeds that are worn.

2 SOLDIER: All ready, sir, we have arrayed us.
Have done,
To this broll let us busk us and braid us, 345
As Sir Pilate has properly prayed us.

3 SOLDIER: We shall set to him sadly and soon.

4 SOLDIER: Let us get off his gear, God give him ill grace.

1 SOLDIER: They are tit off tite—lo, take there his trashes.

3 SOLDIER: Now knit him in this cord.

2 SOLDIER: I am cant in this case. 350

4 SOLDIER: He is bound fast—now beat on with bitter brashes.

1 SOLDIER: Go on, leap, harry, lordings, with lashes,
And enforce we—this faitour—to flay him.

2 SOLDIER: Let us drive to him derfly, with dashes.
All red with our routs we array him, 355
And rent him.

3 SOLDIER: For my part, I am prest for to pay him.

4 SOLDIER: Yea, send him sorrow, assay him.

1 SOLDIER: Take him, that I have tome for to tent him.

2 SOLDIER: Swing to his swire, till swiftly he sweat. 360

3 SOLDIER: Sweat may this swain for sweight of our swaps.

4 SOLDIER: Rush on this ribald and him rathely rehete.

1 SOLDIER: Rehete him, I rede you, with routs and raps.

2 SOLDIER: For all our noy, this niggard, he naps.

3 SOLDIER: We shall waken him with wind of our whips. 365

4 SOLDIER: Now fling to this flatterer with flaps.

338 *Wraist* Twist   340 *ban* curse   341 *said* commanded   342 *wap* rip
343 *arrayed us* prepared ourselves   344 Enough   345 *busk . . . us* hasten
and apply ourselves   346 *properly . . . us* personally instructed us   347 *sadly*
earnestly   349 *tit* snatched   *trashes* rags   350 *knit* bind   *cant* eager
case matter   351 *brashes* blows   352 *harry* beat [him]   353 *enforce*
we let us endeavour   354 *drive to* thrust upon   *derfly* cruelly   *dashes* blows
355 *routs* blows   *array* make   356 *rent* tear   357 *prest* eager   358 *assay*
try   359 *tome* time   *tent* attend to   360 Whip his neck, so that he sweats
freely   361 *swain* fellow   *sweight* weight   *swaps* blows   362 *rathely*
rehete fiercely attack   363 *rede* counsel   364 *noy* attentions   *niggard* lout
366 *fling to* flail at   *flaps* blows

1 SOLDIER: I shall heartily hit on his hips
And haunch.

2 SOLDIER: From our skelps not scatheless he skips.

3 SOLDIER: Yet him list not lift up his lips 370
And pray us to have pity on his paunch.

4 SOLDIER: To have pity of his paunch he proffers no prayer.

1 SOLDIER: Lord, how likes you this lake and this lore that we
lere you?

2 SOLDIER: Lo, I pull at his pilch, I am a proud player.

3 SOLDIER: Thus your cloak shall we clout to cleanse you and
clear you. 375

4 SOLDIER: I am strong in strife for to stir you.

1 SOLDIER: Thus with chops this churl shall we chasty.

2 SOLDIER: I trow with this trace we shall tire you.

3 SOLDIER: All thine untrue teachings thus taste I,
Thou tarand. 380

4 SOLDIER: I hope I be hardy and hasty.

1 SOLDIER: I wot well my weapon not waste I.

2 SOLDIER: He swoons or swelts, I swarrand.

3 SOLDIER: Let us loose him lightly—do lay on your hands.

4 SOLDIER: Yea, for and he die for this deed, undone are we
all. 385

1 SOLDIER: Now unbound is this broll and unbraced his bands.

2 SOLDIER: O, fool, how fares thou now? Foul mote thee fall!

3 SOLDIER: Now because he our king gan him call,
We will kindly him crown with a briar.

4 SOLDIER: Yea, but first this purpure and pall 390
And this worthy weed shall he wear,
For scorn.

1 SOLDIER: I am proud at this point to appear.

2 SOLDIER: Let us clothe him in these clothes full clear,
As a lord that his lordship has lorn. 395

369 He does not escape unscathed from our blows   370 *him list* he will
373 *lake* game   374 *pilch* garment   376 *stir* rouse   377 *chops* blows
chasty punish   378 *trace* course of action   379 *taste* try   380 *tarand*
(apparently = *tarandre*) a creature supposed to have the chameleon-like power of
changing colour   381 *hope* believe   *hardly* tough   *hasty* fierce   383 *swelts*
is overcome (with pain)   *swarrand* tell you   384 *lightly* quickly   385 *and*
if   386 *unbraced* untied   387 *Foul . . . fall* A curse on you   389 *kindly*
accordingly   390 *purpure . . . pall* royal garment and robe   391 *weed* piece
of clothing   394 *clear* fine   395 *lorn* lost

3 SOLDIER: Long ere thou meet slike a meinie as thou met
   with his morn!
4 SOLDIER: Do set him in this seat as a seemly in sales.
1 SOLDIER: Now thring to him throly with this thick thorn.
2 SOLDIER: Lo, it hields to his head that the harness out hales.
3 SOLDIER: Thus we teach him to temper his tales—   400
   His brain begins for to bleed.
4 SOLDIER: Yea, his blunder has him brought to these bales.
   Now reach him and raught him in a reed
   So round,
   For his sceptre it serves indeed.   405
1 SOLDIER: Yea, it is good enough in this need.
   Let us goodly him greet on this ground.

Ave, royal roy and *rex judeorum*,
Hail, comely king that no kingdom has kenned.
Hail, undoughty duke, thy deeds are dumb,   410
Hail, man unmighty thy meinie to mend.
3 SOLDIER: Hail, lord without land for to lend,
   Hail king, hail, knave uncunnand.
4 SOLDIER: Hail, freke without force thee to fend,
   Hail, strong, that may not well stand   415
   To strive.
1 SOLDIER: We, harlot, heave up thy hand,
   And us all that thee worship are workand,
   Thank us, or ill mote thou thrive.

2 SOLDIER: So let lead him belive and leng here no longer.   420
   To Sir Pilate our prince our pride will we praise.
3 SOLDIER: Yea, he may sing, ere he sleep, of sorrow and
   anger,
   For many derf deeds he has done in his days.

396 It will be a long time before you meet such another crowd as you met this morning
397 *seemly . . . sales* great man at court   398 *thring . . . throly* thrust upon him
fiercely   399 Look, it goes on to his head in such a way as to cause his brains to
pour out   400 *temper* moderate   402 *blunder* trouble-making   *bales* misfortune   403 Now stretch out and present him with a stick   407 *goodly* in
a seemly fashion   *on . . . ground* here   408 *Ave* Hail   *roy* king   *rex judeorum*
king of the Jews   409 *kenned* known   410 *undoughty* feeble   *dumb* useless
411 Hail, man too weak to support your followers   413 *uncunnand* foolish
414 *freke* man   *fend* defend   415 *strong* strong man   416 *strive* fight
417 *We* cry of derision   *harlot* miscreant   418–19 And thank all of us who
are reverencing you, or may you be cursed   420 *belive* quickly   *leng* remain
423 *derf* wicked

4 SOLDIER: Now wightly let wend on our ways,
    Let us truss us, no time is to tarry.   425
1 SOLDIER: My lord, will you listen our lays?
    Here this boy is ye bade us go bary
    With bats.
2 SOLDIER: We are cumbered his *corpus* for to carry,
    Many wights on him wonder and wary—   430
    Lo, his flesh all beflapped, that fat is.

PILATE: Well, bring him before us as he blushes all blo;
    I suppose of his saying he will cease evermore.
    Sirs, behold upon height and *ecce homo*,
    Thus bound and beaten and brought you before.   435
    Me seems that it sues him full sore;
    For his guilt on this ground is he grieved.
    If you like for to listen my lore

    .   .   .   .

    In race

    .   .   .   .

[PILATE:] For properly by this process will I prove   440
    I had no force from this fellowship this freke for to fend.
BEADLE: Here is all, sir, that ye for send.
    Will ye wash while the water is hot?

    Then he washes his hands

PILATE: Now this Barabas's bands ye unbend,
    With grace let him gang on his gate   445
    Where he will.

---

424 *wightly* briskly   425 Let us hasten, this is no time to loiter   426 *listen*
. . . *lays* hear how we have proceeded   427 *bary* beat   428 *bats* blows
429 *cumbered* burdened   *corpus* body   431 *beflapped* bruised   432 *blo*
livid   433 *saying* talk   434 *ecce homo* 'Behold, the man' (John 19: 5)   436 It
appears that he has been treated harshly   437 *grieved* hurt   439+ *A leaf is
missing from the MS here, and about 50 lines are lost. The incidents which are lacking
probably included the call by the Jews to crucify Jesus, Pilate's offer that Jesus be the prisoner
customarily released at the Passover, and the decision to release Barabas instead. The text
resumes with the scene of Pilate washing his hands of the matter*: 'And Pilate seeing that he
nothing prevailed, but rather tumult was toward, taking water, he washed his hands
before the people . . .' (Matthew 27: 24).   441 I had no power to preserve this
man from these people   444 *unbend* untie

BARABAS: Ye worthy men that I here wot,
  God increase all your comely estate,
  For the grace ye have grant me until.

PILATE: Here the judgement of Jesu, all Jews in this stead: 450
  Crucify him on a cross and on Calvary him kill.
  I damn him today to die this same death,
  Therefore hang him on height upon that high hill.
  And on either side him I will
  That a harlot ye hang in this haste— 455
  Methinks it both reason and skill
  Amidst, since his malice is most,
  Ye hang him;
  Then him torment, some teen for to taste.
  More words I will not now waste, 460
  But blin not to death till ye bring him.

CAIAPHAS: Sir, us seems in our sight that ye sadly have said.
  Now knights that are cunning, with this caitiff ye cair,
  The life of this losel in your list is it laid.
1 SOLDIER: Let us alone, my lord, and lere us no lore. 465
  Sirs, set to him sadly and sore,
  All in cords his corse umbecast.
2 SOLDIER: Let us bind him in bands all bare.
3 SOLDIER: Here is one, full long will it last.
4 SOLDIER: Lay on hand here. 470
5 SOLDIER: I pull till my power is passed.
  Now fast is he, fellows, full fast;
  Let us stir us, we may not long stand here.

ANNAS: Draw him fast, hence deliver you, have done.
  Go, do see him to death without longer delay, 475

---

447 *wot* perceive   448 *comely estate* worthy status   449 *grant . . . until* granted me   454 *will* command   455 *harlot* thief   456 *reason . . . skill* reasonable and fitting   457 *Amidst* In the middle   459 *some . . . taste* so that he will feel some pain   461 *blin* rest   462 *us . . . sight* it appears very clearly to us   *sadly . . . said* you have made a well-considered judgement   463 *cunning* wise   *cair* go   464 You are now responsible for the life of this wretch   465 *lere . . . lore* give no more instructions   466 *sadly . . . sore* diligently and urgently   467 *his . . . umbecast* bind his body   472 *fast* bound   *fast* tightly   474 *deliver you* hasten   *have done* expression of impatience

For dead bus him be, needling, by noon.
All mirth bus us move tomorn that we may,
It is soothly our great Sabbath day—
No dead bodies unburied shall be.

6 SOLDIER: We see well the sooth ye us say.   480
We shall trail him tite to his tree,
Thus talking.

4 SOLDIER: Farewell, now wightly wend we.

PILATE: Now, certes, ye are a manly meinie,
Forth in the wild waniand be walking.   485

476–7 He must needs be dead by noon. Tomorrow we must celebrate to the full
481 *trail* drag   *tree* cross   484 *manly meinie* fine body of men   485 *waniand*
waning (of the moon) [i.e. an evil hour]

THE PINNERS

The Crucifixion

The York dramatist's treatment of the Crucifixion is one of innumerable reflections of a distinct shift in medieval sensibility. Largely through the influence of meditative literature, the event came to be viewed less as Christ's triumph over death, and more as the passive endurance of torture for the love and redemption of mankind. Extended and affective contemplation on the most gruesome aspects of the scene in mystical and penitential treatises, through the visual arts, and in the witnessing of plays, became a popular cult. The instruments of the Passion, including the tools of their trade so ostentatiously displayed by the soldiers in the York play, were systematically treated in literature and art as the 'Arma Christi': they figure again in Christ's speech in the *Last Judgement* play. The additional torment of stretching Christ's limbs to fit a cross on which the holes had been bored in the wrong places derives from the 'Legend of the Rood'. This supposed history of the wood of the cross, tracing it back to a seed from the fruit of the Tree of Life placed in Adam's mouth on his death-bed, recounted that the cross constantly changed shape in an attempt to prevent its being abused. In the play, the soldiers attribute this variously to bad workmanship and to spells cast by Christ, whom they believe to be a sorcerer.

As the actor playing Christ spends a large part of the play lying silently on the platform of the wagon, the sight-lines afforded to most of the audience mean that the focus of attention falls chiefly on the soldiers, who are not shown to be aware of their victim in any subjective sense. Hence, although they describe for the audience every gruesome detail of what they are doing, it is in detached terms, as a job executed by craftsmen forced to work under difficult conditions. This leads to the development of an interesting relationship between soldiers and audience, one approaching identification rather than alienation, which the playwright goes on to exploit.

Christ speaks twice in the play, on the first occasion offering himself as a sacrificial victim to the Father, a speech which preserves the balance between Christ as human victim and divine protagonist. This, combined with his voluntary lying down on the cross, is a muted reminder that the Crucifixion is also a triumphal event. In order to create the correct emotional balance in the episode, the dramatist draws on a well-established vernacular tradition of Crucifixion lyrics, and on the liturgy of Holy Week. In the great speech from the cross, the dramatist turns the tables on the audience in a most striking manner. As the cross rises and drops upright into the mortice, the full force of the soldiers' workmanship becomes apparent, and the audience realize that in their laughter at the awkward efforts of four local workmen, they have been seduced into condoning the Crucifixion. The tenor of Christ's address to, 'all men that walk by way or street', combined with this visual impact, makes it plain that, for the playwright, the Crucifixion is an act in which all men at all times are necessarily implicated.

1 SOLDIER: Sir knights, take heed hither in hie,
This deed on dreigh we may not draw.
Ye wot yourselves as well as I
How lords and leaders of our law
Have given doom that this dote shall die.   5

2 SOLDIER: Sir, all their counsel well we know.
Since we are come to Calvary
Let ilk man help now as him owe.

3 SOLDIER: We are all ready, lo,
That foreward to fulfil.   10

4 SOLDIER: Let hear how we shall do,
And go we tite theretill.

1 SOLDIER: It may not help here for to hone
If we shall any worship win.

2 SOLDIER: He must be dead needlings by noon.   15

3 SOLDIER: Then is good time that we begin.

4 SOLDIER: Let ding him down, then is he done—
He shall not dere us with his din.

1 SOLDIER: He shall be set and learned soon,
With care to him and all his kin.   20

2 SOLDIER: The foulest death of all
Shall he die for his deeds.

3 SOLDIER: That means cross him we shall.

4 SOLDIER: Behold, so right he redes.

1 SOLDIER: Then to this work us must take heed,   25
So that our working be not wrong.

2 SOLDIER: None other note to neven is need,
But let us haste him for to hang.

1 *in hie* in haste   2 We may not draw this task out too long   3 *wot* know
4 *leaders* upholders   5 *doom* judgement   *dote* fool   8 Let each man help
now as he ought to   10 *foreward* undertaking   11 *Let hear* Let us see
12 *tite* quickly   *theretill* to it   13 *hone* tarry   14 *worship* esteem
15 *needlings* of necessity   17 Let him be struck down, then [may he] be dealt
with   18 *dere* harm   *din* clamour   19 *set* secured   *learned* taught (a
lesson)   20 *care* woe   23 *cross* crucify   24 Indeed he advises us well
25 we must pay attention   27 There is no need to mention any other matter

3 SOLDIER: And I have gone for gear good speed,
   Both hammers and nails large and long.   30
4 SOLDIER: Then may we boldly do this deed.
   Come on, let kill this traitor strong.
1 SOLDIER: Fair might ye fall in fere
   That has wrought on this wise.
2 SOLDIER: Us needs not for to lere   35
   Such faitours to chastise.

3 SOLDIER: Since ilka thing is right arrayed,
   The wiselier now work may we.
4 SOLDIER: The cross on ground is goodly graid
   And bored even as it ought to be.   40
1 SOLDIER: Look that the lad on length be laid
   And made me then unto this tree.
2 SOLDIER: For all his fare he shall be flayed,
   That on assay soon shall ye see.
3 SOLDIER: Come forth, thou cursed knave,   45
   Thy comfort soon shall keel.
4 SOLDIER: Thine hire here shall thou have.
1 SOLDIER: Walk on—now work we well.

JESUS: Almighty God, my Father free,
   Let these matters be made in mind: 50
   Thou bade that I should buxom be,
   For Adam's plight for to be pined.
   Here to death I oblige me,
   For that sin for to save mankind,
   And sovereignly beseech I thee   55
   That they for me may favour find.
   And from the fiend them fend,
   So that their souls be safe
   In wealth without end—
   I keep nought else to crave.   60

29 *good speed* speedily   32 *let kill* let us kill   *traitor strong* flagrant traitor
33–4 May you all have good luck who have acted in this way   35 We don't
need to be taught   36 *faitours* deceivers   37 *ilka* every   *right arrayed*
well prepared   39 *goodly graid* well prepared   40 *bored* bored with holes
41 *lad* wretch   42 And then fastened to this cross   43 *fare* practices
flayed punished   44 That [claim] you will soon see put to the test   46 *keel* cool
(i.e. vanish)   47 *hire* reward   49 *free* gracious   50 *made in mind* particularly
called to mind   51 *bade* commanded   *buxom* willing   52 *pined* tormented
53 *oblige me* pledge myself   55 *sovereignly* above all   56 *for* because of   57 *fend*
defend   59 *wealth* joy   60 I have no care to ask for anything else

1 SOLDIER: We, hark sir knights, for Mahound's blood,
  Of Adam's kind is all his thought.
2 SOLDIER: The warlock waxes war than wood;
  This doleful death ne dreadeth he nought.
3 SOLDIER: Thou should have mind, with main and mood,   65
  Of wicked works that thou hast wrought.
4 SOLDIER: I hope that he had been as good
  Have ceased of saws that he upsought.
1 SOLDIER: Tho saws shall rue him sore,
  For all his sauntering, soon.   70
2 SOLDIER: Ill speed them that him spare
  Till he to death be done.

3 SOLDIER: Have done belive, boy, and make thee boun,
  And bend thy back unto this tree.
4 SOLDIER: Behold, himself has laid him down   75
  In length and breadth as he should be.
1 SOLDIER: This traitor here tainted of treason,
  Go fast and fetter him then ye three;
  And since he claimeth kingdom with crown,
  Even as a king here hang shall he.   80
2 SOLDIER: Now, certes, I shall not fine
  Ere his right hand be fast.
3 SOLDIER: The left hand then is mine—
  Let see who bears him best.

4 SOLDIER: His limbs on length then shall I lead,   85
  And even unto the bore them bring.
1 SOLDIER: Unto his head I shall take heed,
  And with mine hand help him to hang.
2 SOLDIER: Now since we four shall do this deed
  And meddle with this unthrifty thing,   90
  Let no man spare for special speed
  Till that we have made ending.

61 *We* exclamation of contempt   *for Mahound's* by Muhammad's (diabolical oath)
62 *kind* offspring   63 The sorcerer grows worse than mad   64 He has
no fear of this terrible death   65 You should try to think very hard   67–8 I
believe he would have done well to have stopped saying the things that he thought up
69 He will greatly regret those words   70 *sauntering* babbling   71 *Ill speed them*
Bad luck to those   73 *belive* quickly   *boy* wretch   *boun* ready   77 *tainted*
convicted   81 *certes* indeed   *fine* stop   82 *Ere* Before   84 *bears*
him acquits himself   85 *on length* outstretched   *lead* hold   90 *unthrifty*
unprofitable   91 *spare for* refrain from [using]   *special* the utmost

3 SOLDIER: This foreward may not fail;
  Now are we right arrayed.
4 SOLDIER: This boy here in our bail   95
  Shall bide full bitter braid.

1 SOLDIER: Sir knights, say, how work we now?
2 SOLDIER: Yes, certes, I hope I hold this hand,
  And to the bore I have it brought
  Full buxomly without band.   100
1 SOLDIER: Strike on then hard, for him thee bought.
2 SOLDIER: Yes, here is a stub will stiffly stand,
  Through bones and sinews it shall be sought—
  This work is well, I will warrand.
1 SOLDIER: Say sir, how do we there?   105
  This bargain may not blin.
3 SOLDIER: It fails a foot and more,
  The sinews are so gone in.

4 SOLDIER: I hope that mark amiss be bored.
2 SOLDIER: Then must he bide in bitter bale.   110
3 SOLDIER: In faith, it was over-scantily scored,
  That makes it foully for to fail.
1 SOLDIER: Why carp ye so? Fast on a cord
  And tug him to, by top and tail.
3 SOLDIER: Yah, thou commands lightly as a lord;   115
  Come help to haul, with ill hail.
1 SOLDIER: Now certes that shall I do—
  Full snelly as a snail.
3 SOLDIER: And I shall tache him to,
  Full nimbly with a nail.   120

  This work will hold, that dare I hete,
  For now are fest fast both his hend.

93 This deed must be assuredly done   95 *bail* custody   96 Shall undergo
very dreadful torment   98 *hope* think   100 *buxomly* obediently   *without
band* without using a rope   101 for he who redeemed you (usually refers to
Christ)   102 *stub* short thick nail   *stiffly* stoutly   103 *sought* applied
104 *warrand* guarantee   106 This business is not at an end   107 It (the
bore) is more than a foot out   108 *gone in* shrunken   109 I believe the
spot which was marked has been bored in the wrong place (i.e. and not where it was
marked)   110 *bide* endure   *bale* pain   111 *over-scantily scored* inaccurately
drilled   112 That is why it is such a bad piece of work   113 *carp* speak   *Fast
Fasten*   114 And pull him [to the bores], by his head and feet   115 *lightly*
effortlessly   116 *with ill hail* curse you   118 *snelly* swiftly (an aside)   119 *tache*
fasten   *to* to [the cross]   121 *hete* promise   122 *hend* hands

4 SOLDIER: Go we all four then to his feet,
So shall our space be speedily spend.

2 SOLDIER: Let see what bourd his bale might beet,   125
Thereto my back now would I bend.

4 SOLDIER: Oh, this work is all unmeet—
This boring must all be amend.

1 SOLDIER: Ah, peace man, for Mahound,
Let no man wot that wonder,   130
A rope shall rug him down
If all his sinews go asunder.

2 SOLDIER: That cord full kindly can I knit,
The comfort of this carl to keel.

1 SOLDIER: Fast on then fast, that all be fit,   135
It is no force how fell he feel.

2 SOLDIER: Lug on ye both a little yet.

3 SOLDIER: I shall not cease, as I have sele.

4 SOLDIER: And I shall fond him for to hit.

2 SOLDIER: Oh, hale!

4 SOLDIER: Whoa, now, I hold it well.   140

1 SOLDIER: Have done, drive in that nail,
So that no fault be found.

4 SOLDIER: This working would not fail
If four bulls here were bound.

1 SOLDIER: These cords have evil increased his pains,   145
Ere he were to the borings brought.

2 SOLDIER: Yea, asunder are both sinews and veins
On ilka side, so have we sought.

3 SOLDIER: Now all his gauds nothing him gains,
His sauntering shall with bale be bought.   150

4 SOLDIER: I will go say to our sovereigns
Of all these works how we have wrought.

1 SOLDIER: Nay sirs, another thing
Falls first to you and me,

124 So we shall usefully pass our time   125 *bourd* jest   *beet* lighten
127 *unmeet* out of place   128 *amend* altered   130 *wonder* strange thing
(i.e. a piece of magic)   131 *rug* tug   132 *If* Even if   133 *kindly*
fittingly   *knit* fasten   134 *carl* wretch   135 *Fast* Bind   *fit* ready
136 *no force* no matter   *fell* terrible (i.e. how much pain)   138 as I have joy
139 *fond* attempt   140 *hale* haul   141 *Have done* Stop   145 *evil*
severely   148 *so . . . sought* as far as we can see   149–50 Now all his
tricks are of no avail, he will pay for his babbling with pain   154 *Falls* Is allotted

They bade we should him hang   155
On high, that men might see.

2 SOLDIER: We wot well so their words were,
But sir, that deed will do us dere.

1 SOLDIER: It may not mend for to moot more,
This harlot must be hanged here.   160

2 SOLDIER: The mortice is made fit therefore.

3 SOLDIER: Fast on your fingers then, in fere.

4 SOLDIER: I ween it will never come there—
We four raise it not right to-year.

1 SOLDIER: Say man, why carps thou so?   165
Thy lifting was but light.

2 SOLDIER: He means there must be more
To heave him up on height.

3 SOLDIER: Now certes, I hope it shall not need
To call to us more company.   170
Methink we four should do this deed
And bear him to yon hill on high.

1 SOLDIER: It must be done, without dread.
No more, but look ye be ready,
And this part shall I lift and lead;   175
On length he shall no longer lie.
Therefore now make you boun,
Let bear him to yon hill.

4 SOLDIER: Then will I bear here down,
And tent his toes until.   180

2 SOLDIER: We two shall see to either side,
For else this work will wry all wrong.

3 SOLDIER: We are ready.

4 SOLDIER: Good sirs, abide,
And let me first his feet up fang.

2 SOLDIER: Why tent ye so to tales this tide?   185

1 SOLDIER: Lift up!

157 *so* what   159 It won't do any good to argue any more   160 *harlot*
scoundrel   162 *in fere* all together   163 *ween* believe   164 The four
of us will not raise it upright this year   166 *light* weak   173 *dread* doubt
174 Say no more, but make sure you're ready   179 *here down* this end
180 And attend to his toes   182 *wry* go   183 *abide* wait   184 *up*
fang catch up   185 Why are you paying such attention to talk just now (i.e.
instead of working)

4 SOLDIER: Let see!
2 SOLDIER: Oh, lift along.
3 SOLDIER: From all this harm he should him hide
And he were God.
4 SOLDIER: The devil him hang!
1 SOLDIER: For-great harm have I hent,
My shoulder is in sunder.   190
2 SOLDIER: And certes, I am near shent,
So long have I borne under.

3 SOLDIER: This cross and I in two must twin,
Else breaks my back in sunder soon.
4 SOLDIER: Lay down again and leave your din,   195
This deed for us will never be done.
1 SOLDIER: Assay, sirs, let see if any gin
May help him up without hone,
For here should wight men worship win,
And not with gauds all day to gone.   200
2 SOLDIER: More wighter men than we
Full few I hope ye find.
3 SOLDIER: This bargain will not be,
For certes, me wants wind.

4 SOLDIER: So will of work never we were—   205
I hope this carl some cautels cast.
2 SOLDIER: My burden sat me wonder sore,
Unto the hill I might not last.
1 SOLDIER: Lift up, and soon he shall be there,
Therefore fast on your fingers fast.   210
3 SOLDIER: Oh, lift!
1 SOLDIER: We, lo!
4 SOLDIER: A little more.
2 SOLDIER: Hold then!
1 SOLDIER: How now?
2 SOLDIER: The worst is past.

186 *along* from end to end   187 *him hide* protect himself   188 *And* If
189 *For-great* Excessive   *hent* suffered   190 *in sunder* out of joint   191 *shent*
exhausted   192 *borne under* held up from underneath   193 *twin* part
194 *sunder* half   196 *for* by   197 *gin* device   198 *hone* delay   199 *wight*
robust   200 And not spend the whole day in jests   203 This job will
never be done   204 *me wants wind* I am out of breath   205 *will of* at a loss
in [our]   206 I believe this wretch has cast some spells   207 afflicted me
most grievously

3 SOLDIER: He weighs a wicked weight.
2 SOLDIER: So may we all four say,
    Ere he was heaved on height   215
    And raised in this array.

4 SOLDIER: He made us stand as any stones,
    So boistous was he for to bear.
1 SOLDIER: Now raise him nimbly for the nonce
    And set him by this mortice here,   220
    And let him fall in all at once,
    For certes, that pain shall have no peer.
3 SOLDIER: Heave up!
4 SOLDIER: Let down, so all his bones
    Are asunder now on sides sere.
1 SOLDIER: This falling was more fell   225
    Than all the harms he had.
    Now may a man well tell
    The least lith of this lad.

3 SOLDIER: Methinketh this cross will not abide
    Ne stand still in this mortice yet.   230
4 SOLDIER: At the first time was it made over-wide;
    That makes it wave, thou may well wit.
1 SOLDIER: It shall be set on ilka side
    So that it shall no further flit.
    Good wedges shall we take this tide   235
    And fast the foot, then is all fit.
2 SOLDIER: Here are wedges arrayed
    For that, both great and small.
3 SOLDIER: Where are our hammers laid
    That we should work withal?   240

4 SOLDIER: We have them even here at our hand.
2 SOLDIER: Give me this wedge, I shall it in drive.
4 SOLDIER: Here is another yet ordained.
3 SOLDIER: Do take it me hither belive.

216 *array* fashion   217 He brought us to a standstill   218 *boistous* awkward
219 *for the nonce* (rhyming tag)   222 *peer* equal   224 *on sides sere* in many
places   225 *fell* terrible   227 *tell* count   228 *least lith* smallest part
of the body   229 *abide* remain firm   230 *Ne* Nor   232 *wave* move about
wit understand   233 *set* fixed   *ilka* each   234 *flit* move   235 *this
tide* at this time   236 *foot* base of cross   237 *arrayed* ready   240 *withal*
with   243 *ordained* ready   244 Bring it here to me quickly

1 SOLDIER: Lay on then fast.
2 SOLDIER: Yes, I warrand.   245
  I thring them sam, so mote I thrive.
  Now will this cross full stably stand,
  All if he rave they will not rive.
1 SOLDIER: Say sir, how likes you now,
  This work that we have wrought?   250
4 SOLDIER: We pray you say us how
  Ye feel, or faint ye aught.

JESUS: All men that walk by way or street,
  Take tent ye shall no travail tine.
  Behold mine head, mine hands, and my feet,   255
  And fully feel now, ere ye fine,
  If any mourning may be meet,
  Or mischief measured unto mine.
  My father, that all bales may beet,
  Forgive these men that do me pine.   260
  What they work, wot they not;
  Therefore, my father, I crave,
  Let never their sins be sought,
  But see their souls to save.

1 SOLDIER: We, hark, he jangles like a jay.   265
2 SOLDIER: Methink he patters like a pie.
3 SOLDIER: He has been doing all this day,
  And made great moving of mercy.
4 SOLDIER: Is this the same that gan us say
  That he was God's son almighty?   270
1 SOLDIER: Therefore he feels full fell affray,
  And deemed this day for to die.
2 SOLDIER: *Vath, qui destruis templum!*
3 SOLDIER: His saws were so, certain.
4 SOLDIER: And sirs, he said to some   275
  He might raise it again.

246 I'll thrust them in together, so may I prosper   247 *stably* firmly   248 *All
if* Even if   *rive* split   252 or whether you feel faint at all   254 Take heed
that you miss none of my suffering   256 *fine* pass   257 *meet* equal   258 *mischief* misfortune   259 who may relieve all torments   260 *do . . . pine* torment me
261 They know not what they do   263 *sought* visited upon them   264 *see*
see that   266 *pie* magpie   268 *moving of* reference to   269 *gan* did
271 Because of that he suffered this very cruel assault   272 *deemed* was judged
273 'Ah, thou who destroyest the temple' (Mark 14: 58, John 2: 19)   274 *saws* words

1 SOLDIER: To muster that he had no might,
   For all the cautels that he could cast.
   All if he were in word so wight,
   For all his force now is he fast.   280
   As Pilate deemed is done and dight,
   Therefore I rede that we go rest.
2 SOLDIER: This race mun be rehearsed right,
   Through the world both east and west.
3 SOLDIER: Yea, let him hang there still   285
   And make mows on the moon.
4 SOLDIER: Then may we wend at will.
1 SOLDIER: Nay, good sirs, not so soon.

   For certes us needs another note:
   This kirtle would I of you crave.   290
2 SOLDIER: Nay, nay, sir, we will look by lot
   Which of us four falls it to have.
3 SOLDIER: I rede we draw cut for this coat—
   Lo, see how soon—all sides to save.
4 SOLDIER: The short cut shall win, that well ye wot,   295
   Whether it fall to knight or knave.
1 SOLDIER: Fellows, ye tharf not flite,
   For this mantle is mine.
2 SOLDIER: Go we then hence tite,
   This travail here we tine.   300

277 *muster* manifest   278 *cautels* spells   279 Even though his words were
so bold   281 *dight* dealt with   282 *rede* advise   283 These events
must be properly reported   286 *make mows on* pull faces at   289 we have
other business   290 *kirtle* garment   291 *look . . . lot* draw lots   292 *falls
. . . have* shall have it   293 *cut* straws   294 *all . . . save* so everybody shall
be content   297 *tharf not flite* need not wrangle   300 We are wasting effort
here

THE BUTCHERS

The Death of Christ

The *Death of Christ* is from the point of view of its dramatic art one of the most remarkable and ambitious plays in the cycle. Though it rarely moves outside the framework of events provided by the Gospels, some of the dramatic techniques employed tend repeatedly to suspend the narrative or temporal dimension in order to create profound meditative moments outside time. The places where the action pauses for Christ and the Virgin to utter their lyrical lamentations are clear examples of this tendency, and stand out like arias amidst the demotic recitative of the Jews. The dramaturgy of the play is also contrived in such a way as to evoke the traditional iconography of the scene. The actors are called upon to compose themselves in a series of slowly changing tableaux whose elements are all vividly familiar to the audience from representations of the scene in the visual arts: the three crosses, the jeering of the Jews, John embracing the Virgin, the two thieves, the boy with the sponge, the piercing of Christ's side, the faithful Centurion, the Deposition. In depicting the climactic moment of the Passion, and of the cycle as a whole, the dramatist reaches towards those emotional registers in the audience normally approached only through music and painting.

Some of the raw materials from which the dramatist was working are identifiable. Two of Christ's speeches from the cross are addressed directly to the audience, and draw ultimately on the liturgy of Holy Week via the medium of vernacular penitential lyric poetry. The affective power of these speeches was undoubtedly considerable. As a contemporary put it, the audiences who saw the suffering of Christ were often 'moved to compassion and devotion, weeping bitter tears'. The Virgin's speeches of sorrow, so felicitously blended in the texture of the verse with the words of her son, provided a powerful directive to the audience's feelings. In the Gospels she suffers in silence, but her lamentation in the play has strong liturgical affiliations in the form of the Latin hymn known as the *planctus Mariae*, which also had its counterpart in the vernacular lyrics of the period. An elaboration on the Gospel accounts is the role of the blind knight Longinus. Upon piercing Christ's side, blood runs down the spear and restores his sight. This episode, which demonstrates Christ's divinity at the moment of his apparent defeat, is derived from the apocryphal *Gospel of Nicodemus*, which the dramatist evidently knew in a Middle English verse translation.

The play is written in a complicated but musical twelve-line stanza, ababbcbc$_3$d$_1$eee$_2$d$_3$, with functional rather than ornamental alliteration. Its attribution to the York Realist (see the Headnote to the *Conspiracy*) is not altogether convincing. The verse relies more for its effects on the repetition of certain conventional but evocative words and expressions (e.g. *rood . . . ragged . . . rent*; *death . . . dolefully . . . dight*), rather than on the wider and more recondite kind of vocabulary usually employed by the Realist. The three-stress alliterative line of the *Death* may also be contrasted with the four-stress form normally favoured by the Realist for the *frons* of his stanzas.

The York Butchers occupied the neighbourhood of the ancient street now known as the Shambles, where there were numerous slaughter-houses.

PILATE: Cease, seigniors, and see what I say,
 Take tent to my talking entire.
 Devoid all this din here this day,
 And fall to my friendship in fere.
 Sir Pilate, a prince without peer,   5
 My name is, full namely to neven,
 And doomsman full dearworth and dear
 Of gentlest Jewry full even
 Am I.
 Who makes oppression,   10
 Or does transgression,
 By my discretion
 Shall be deemed duly to die.

 To die shall I deem them indeed,
 Tho rebels that rule them unright.   15
 Who that to yon hill will take heed
 May see there the sooth in his sight,
 How doleful to death they are dight
 That list not our laws for to lere.
 Lo, thus by my main and my might   20
 Tho churls shall I chastise and chare,
 By law.
 Ilk felon false
 Shall hang by the halse.
 Transgressors als   25
 On the cross shall be knit for to gnaw.

1 *seigniors* worthy men   2 Pay close attention to what I say   3 *Devoid* Put an end to   4 And all of you, show friendship towards me   6 *full . . . neven* to state it most precisely   7 *doomsman* judge   *dearworth* worthy   8 *full even* indeed   10 *makes* causes   13 *deemed* judged   15 Those rebels who behave themselves in a disorderly manner   17 *sooth* truth   18 *doleful* cruelly   *dight* put   19 *list not* do not care   *lere* learn   20 *main* strength 21 *Tho churls* Those wretches   *chare* punish   23 *Ilk* Every   24 *halse* neck   25 *als* also   26 *knit* nailed   *gnaw* grind their teeth

To gnaw shall I knit them on cross,
To shend them with shame shall I shape.
Their lives for to leese is no loss,
Such tyrants with teen for to trap.   30
Thus leally the law I unlap,
And punish them piteously.
Of Jesu I hold it unhap
That he on yon hill hang so high
For guilt.   35
His blood to spill
Took ye you till,
Thus was your will,
Full spitously to speed he were spilt.

CAIAPHAS: To spill him we spoke in a speed,   40
For falsehood he followed in fay.
With frauds our folk gan he feed
And laboured to lere them his lay.

ANNAS: Sir Pilate, of peace we you pray—
Our law was full like to be lorn,   45
He saved not our dear Sabbath day,
And that—for to scape it—were a scorn,
By law.

PILATE: Sirs, before your sight,
With all my might   50
I examined him right,
And cause none in him could I know.

CAIAPHAS: Ye know well the cause, sir, in case;
It touched treason untrue.
The tribute to take or to trace   55
Forbade he, our bale for to brew.

28 *shend* destroy   *shape* endeavour   29 *leese* destroy   30 Violently to
ensnare such outlaws   31 *leally* faithfully   *unlap* expound   32 *piteously*
unmercifully   33 *hold . . . unhap* consider it unfortunate   37 You took upon
yourselves   39 To expedite his death most maliciously   40 *spill* destroy   *in
a speed* in haste   41 *fay* faith   42 *gan* did   43 *lere* teach   *lay* doctrine
44 we urge you pursue this no further   45 *full . . . lorn* in danger of being
overthrown   46 *saved* observed   47 *scape* ignore   *scorn* scandal   51 *right*
carefully   52 And I could discover in him no reason [why he should be con-
demned]   53 *case* [this] case   54 *touched* concerned   55–6 To stir
up trouble for us, he forbade the collecting or seeking out of tribute-money

ANNAS: Of japes yet jangled yon Jew,
 And cursedly he called him a king.
 To deem him to death it is due,
 For treason it touches, that thing,   60
 Indeed.
CAIAPHAS: Yet principal,
 And worst of all,
 He gart him call
 God's son—that foul mote him speed.   65

PILATE: He speeds for to spill in space,
 So wonderly wrought is your will.
 His blood shall your bodies embrace,
 For that have ye taken you till.
ANNAS: That foreward full fain to fulfil   70
 Indeed shall we dress us bedene.
 Yon losel him likes full ill,
 For turned are his trants all to teen,
 I trow.
CAIAPHAS: He called him king,   75
 Ill joy him wring.
 Yea, let him hang
 Full madly on the moon for to mow.

ANNAS: To mow on the moon has he meant.
 We! Fie on thee, faitour, in fay!   80
 Who, trows thou, to thy tales took tent?
 Thou saggard, thyself gan thou say,
 The temple destroy thee today,
 By the third day were done ilka deal
 To raise it thou should thee array.   85
 Lo, how was thy falsehood to feel,

---

57 *japes* preposterous things   *jangled* spoke   64 He caused himself to be called
65 *that . . . speed* a curse on him   66–7 He will die in a short time, your
will having been so promptly performed   68 *your . . . embrace* be on your head
69 *taken . . . till* undertaken   70 *foreward* promise   *fain* eagerly   71 *dress
us* endeavour   *bedene* forthwith   72 Yonder wretch is in a miserable condition
73 *trants* tricks   *teen* trouble   74 *trow* think   76 Sorrow torment him
78 *mow* pull faces   79 It is appropriate that he should pull faces at the moon
80 *We* expression of contempt   *Fie* A curse   *faitour* deceiver   81 *tent* heed
82 *saggard* sagging one (?)   *thyself . . . say* you said yourself   83–5 [If] you
were to destroy the temple today, by the time three days were fully passed, you would
yourself endeavour to raise it again   86 *how* so   *to feel* manifest

Foul fall thee.
For thy presumption
Thou hast thy warison.
Do fast come down,   90
And a comely king shall I call thee.

CAIAPHAS: I call thee a coward to ken,
That marvels and miracles made.
Thou mustered among many men,
But, brothel, thou bourded too broad.   95
Thou saved them from sorrows, they said—
To save now thyself let us see.
God's son if thou gradely be graid,
Deliver thee down of that tree
Anon.   100
If thou be found
To be God's son,
We shall be bound
To trow on thee truly, ilkone.

ANNAS: Sir Pilate, your pleasance we pray,   105
Take tent to our talking this tide,
And wipe ye yon writing away,
It is not best it abide.
It sits you to set it aside
And set that he said in his saw,   110
As he that was prent full of pride:
'Jews' king am I', comely to know,
Full plain.
PILATE: *Quod scripsi, scripsi.*
Yon same wrote I;   115
I bide thereby,
What gadling will grutch thereagain.

87 A curse on you   89 *warison* reward   91 *comely* worthy   92 I call
you a blatant coward   94 *mustered* showed [your tricks]   95 But, wretch,
you spoke unwisely   98 *thou . . . graid* you truly are   100 Immediately
104 Truly to believe in thee, every one of us   105 *pleasance* indulgence   106 *tide*
time   108 *abide* remain   109 *sits* behoves   110 *set that* put what
saw teachings   111 *he* one   *prent* stained   114 'What I have written, I
have written' (John 19: 22)   116 I abide by that   117 Whatever scoundrel
complains about it

JESUS: Thou man that of miss here has meant,
   To me tent entirely thou take.
   On rood am I ragged and rent,   120
   Thou sinful soul, for thy sake:
   For thy miss amends will I make.
   My back for to bend here I bide,
   This teen for thy trespass I take.
   Who could thee more kindness have kid   125
   Than I?
   Thus for thy good
   I shed my blood.
   Man, mend thy mood,
   For full bitter thy bliss mun I buy.   130

MARY: Alas for my sweet son, I say,
   That dolefully to death thus is dight.
   Alas, for full lovely he lay
   In my womb, this worthily wight.
   Alas that I should see this sight   135
   Of my son so seemly to see.
   Alas, that this blossom so bright
   Untruly is tugged to this tree.
   Alas,
   My lord, my lief,   140
   With full great grief
   Hangs as a thief.
   Alas, he did never trespass.

JESUS: Thou woman, do way of thy weeping,
   For me may thou nothing amend.   145
   My Father's will to be working,
   For mankind my body I bend.
MARY: Alas, that thou likes not to lend,
   How shall I but weep for thy woe?
   To care now my comfort is kenned.   150

118 *Thou man* here who is a sinner   120 *rood* cross   *ragged* torn   *rent* gashed
122 *miss* misdeeds   124 *teen* suffering   *trespass* offences   125 *kid* shown
129 *mend . . . mood* mend your ways   130 *bitter* bitterly   *mun* must   132 *dolefully* grievously   *dight* put   134 *worthily wight* beloved man   136 *seemly* fair   138 *Untruly* Unnaturally   *tugged* nailed   140 *lief* dear   144 *do way* cease   145 You can do nothing to help me   146 *working* fulfilling
147 *bend* stretch out   148 *thou . . . lend* you do not wish to stay [with us]   150 My comfort is now shown to be sorrow

Alas, why should we twin thus in two
Forever?
JESUS: Woman, instead of me,
Lo, John thy son shall be.
John, see to thy mother free,   155
For my sake do thou thy dever.

MARY: Alas, son, for sorrow and site,
That me were closed in clay.
A sword of sorrow me smite,
To death I were done this day.   160
JOHN: Ah, mother, so shall ye not say.
I pray you, be peace in this press,
For with all the might that I may
Your comfort I cast to increase,
Indeed.   165
Your son am I,
Lo, here ready;
And now forthy
I pray you hence for to speed.

MARY: My steven for to stead or to steer,   170
How should I, such sorrow to see,
My son that is dearworthy and dear
Thus doleful a death for to die?
JOHN: Ah, dear mother, blin of this blee,
Your mourning it may not amend.   175
MARY CLEOPHAS: Ah, Mary, take trist unto thee,
For succour to thee will he send
This tide.
JOHN: Fair mother, fast
Hence let us cast.   180
MARY: Till he be passed
Will I busk here bainly to bide.

151 *twin* part   155 *free* worthy   156 *dever* duty   157 *site* grief   158 I
wish I were buried in the earth   160 [So that] I might be put to death today
161 *so . . . say* do not say so   162 *peace* quiet   *press* crowd   164 *cast*
endeavour   168 *forthy* therefore   169 *speed* hasten   170 *steven* voice
stead steady   *steer* control   172 *dearworthy* beloved   173 *Thus doleful* Such
a cruel   174 *blin* put an end to   *blee* behaviour   176 *trist* hope   177 *succour*
comfort   180 *cast* go   181 *passed* dead   182 *busk* seek   *bainly*
meekly

JESUS: With bitterful bale have I bought,
   Thus, man, all thy miss for to mend.
   On me for to look let thou nought,   185
   How bainly my body I bend.
   No wight in this world would have wend
   What sorrow I suffer for thy sake.
   Man, cast thee my kindness be kenned;
   True tent unto me that thou take,   190
   And trest.
   For foxes their dens have they,
   Birds have their nests to pay,
   But the son of man this day
   Has nought his head on for to rest.   195

1 THIEF: If thou be God's son so free,
   Why hangs thou thus on this hill?
   To save now thyself let us see,
   And us two, that speed for to spill.

2 THIEF: Man, stint of thy steven and be still,   200
   For doubtless thy God dreads thou nought.
   Full well are we worthy theretill,
   Unwisely wrong have we wrought,
   Iwis.
   None ill did he   205
   Thus for to die.
   Lord, have mind of me
   When thou art come to thy bliss.

JESUS: Forsooth, son, to thee shall I say,
   Since thou from thy folly will fall,   210
   With me shall thou dwell now this day
   In Paradise, place principal.
   Eli, Eli!
   My God, my God full free,
   Lama sabacthani?   215
   Whereto forsook thou me

183 *bitterful bale* intense suffering   *bought* paid [the penalty]   185 *let . . . nought* never cease   186 *bainly* willingly   187 *would . . . wend* could imagine   189 *cast thee* endeavour [that]   *kenned* made known   191 *trest* trust   193 *to pay* at their liking   200 *stint* cease   *steven* noise   202 We fully deserve it (i.e. crucifixion)   204 Indeed   205 *None ill* No evil   207 *have . . . of* remember   210 *fall* desist   212 *place principal* best of all places   213–15 'My God, my God, why hast thou forsaken me?' (Matthew 27: 46)   216 *Whereto* Why

In care?
And I did never ill
This deed for to go till,
But be it at thy will.   220
Ah, me thirsts sore.

BOY: A drink shall I dress thee, indeed,
A draught that is full daintily dight.
Full fast shall I spring for to speed,
I hope I shall hold that I have hight.   225
CAIAPHAS: Sir Pilate, that most is of might,
Hark, 'Elias' now heard I him cry.
He weens that that worthily wight
In haste for to help him in hie
In his need.   230
PILATE: If he do so
He shall have woe.
ANNAS: He were our foe
If he dress him to do us that deed.

BOY: That deed for to dress if he do,   235
In certes he shall rue it full sore.
Nevertheless, if he like it not, lo,
Full soon may he cover that care.
Now, sweet sir, your will if it were,
A draught here of drink have I dressed;   240
To speed for no spence that ye spare,
But boldly ye bib it for the best.
Forwhy
Eisell and gall
Is menged withal,   245
Drink it ye shall—
Your lips, I hold them full dry.

219 *go till* endure   221 I am very thirsty   222 *dress* prepare   223 *daintily
dight* carefully mixed   225 Indeed I shall do as I have said   228 *weens*
thinks   *worthily wight* good man   229 [Comes] in haste   *in hie* forthwith
234 *dress him* seeks   *do us* perform   235 *dress* undertake   236 *In certes*
For certain   *rue* repent   238 *cover* be relieved of   241 To expedite matters,
do not be sparing on account of the expense   242 *bib* drink   243 Because
244 *Eisell* Vinegar   245 Are mingled therein   247 *hold* consider

JESUS: Thy drink it shall do me no dere,
    Wit thou well, thereof will I none.
    Now Father, that formed all in fere,   250
    To thy most might make I my moan:
    Thy will have I wrought in this wone,
    Thus ragged and rent on this rood,
    Thus dolefully to death have they done.
    Forgive them, by grace that is good,   255
    They ne wot not what it was.
    My Father, hear my boon,
    For now all thing is done.
    My spirit to thee right soon
    Commend I, *in manus tuas*.   260

MARY: Now dear son, Jesus so gent,
    Since my heart is heavy as lead,
    One word would I wit ere thou went.
    Alas, now my dear son is dead,
    Full ruefully reft is my rede.   265
    Alas for my darling so dear.
JOHN: Ah, mother, ye hold up your head,
    And sigh not with sorrows so sere
    I pray.
MARY CLEOPHAS: It does her pine   270
    To see him tine.
    Lead we her hyne,
    This mourning help her ne may.

CAIAPHAS: Sir Pilate, perceive, I you pray,
    Our customs to keep well ye can.   275
    Tomorn is our dear Sabbath day,
    Of mirth must us move ilka man.
    Yon warlocks now wax full wan,
    And needs must they buried be.
    Deliver their death, sir, and then   280

248 *dere* harm   249 Understand clearly, I will take none of it   250 *in fere* thoughout   252 *wone* place   254 *done* put [me]   256 They did not know what they were doing   257 *boon* request   260 'into thy hands' (Luke 23: 46)   261 *gent* worthy   263 *wit* hear   *ere* before   265 *ruefully* cruelly *reft* removed   *rede* support   268 *sere* manifold   270 *pine* pain   271 *tine* die   272 *hyne* hence   273 cannot help her   276 *Tomorn* Tomorrow 277 Every man should rejoice   278 *wax* grow   *wan* pale   280 *Deliver* Hasten

Shall we sue to our said solemnity
Indeed.
PILATE: It shall be done
In words fone.
Sir knights, go soon,   285
To yon harlots you hendly take heed.

Tho caitiffs thou kill with thy knife—
Deliver, have done they were dead.
SOLDIER: My lord, I shall length so their life
That those brothels shall never bite bread.   290
PILATE: Sir Longinus, step forth in this stead;
This spear, lo, have hold in thy hand.
To Jesus thou rake forth, I rede,
And stead not, but stiffly thou stand
A stound.   295
In Jesu's side
Shove it this tide.
No longer bide,
But gradely thou go to the ground.

LONGINUS: O maker unmade, full of might,   300
O Jesu so gentle and gent
That suddenly has sent me my sight,
Lord, lofing to thee be it lent.
On rood art thou ragged and rent,
Mankind for to mend of his miss.   305
Full spitously spilt is and spent
Thy blood, Lord, to bring us to bliss
Full free.
Ah, mercy, my succour,
Mercy, my treasure,   310
Mercy, my saviour,
Thy mercy be marked in me.

281 *sue* proceed   *solemnity* feast   284 *fone* few   286 *harlots* criminals
hendly fittingly   288 Hasten, dispatch them quickly   289 *length* prolong
290 *brothels* wretches   291 *stead* place   293 *rake* go   *rede* counsel
294 *stead* hesitate   *stiffly* boldly   *stand* stand forth   295 *stound* while
299 *gradely* in a seemly manner   *ground* place   300 *unmade* eternal   303 *lofing*
praise   *lent* given   306 *spent* let   308 Most serene   312 *marked*
observed

CENTURION: Oh, wonderful worker, iwis,
    This weather is waxen full wan.
    True token I trow that it is   315
    That mercy is meant unto man.
    Full clearly conceive thus I can
    No cause in this corse would they know,
    Yet dolefully they deemed him then
    To lose thus his life by their law,   320
    No right.
    Truly I say,
    God's son verray
    Was he this day,
    That dolefully to death thus is dight.   325

JOSEPH: That lord leal, ay-lasting in land,
    Sir Pilate, full prest in this press,
    He save thee by sea and by sand,
    And all that is dearworth on dais.
PILATE: Joseph, this is leally, no less,   330
    To me art thou welcome, iwis.
    Do say me the sooth ere thou cease,
    Thy worthily will, what it is,
    Anon.
JOSEPH: To thee I pray,   335
    Give me in hie
    Jesu's body,
    In gree it for to grave all alone.

PILATE: Joseph, sir, I grant thee that guest,
    I grutch not to graith him in grave.   340
    Deliver, have done he were dressed,
    And sue, sir, our Sabbath to save.
JOSEPH: With hands and heart that I have,
    I thank thee, in faith, for my friend.
    God keep thee thy comfort to crave,   345
    For wightly my way will I wend

314 *waxen* become   *wan* dark   315 *token* sign   318 They knew of no cause in this man [to condemn him]   320 *lose* end   321 Unjustly   323 *verray* truly 326 *leal* true   *ay-lasting* eternal   327 *full . . . press* most bold in this gathering (complimentary expression)   329 *that . . . dais* other worthy persons with you 330 *leally* loyal, loyally spoken   333 *worthily* worthy   334 *Anon* Forthwith   336 *in hie* quickly   338 *gree* seemly manner *grave* bury   339 *guest* wicked man   340–1 I do not object to having him buried. Hasten, deal with him quickly   342 *save* observe   345 God grant you the comfort you pray for   346 *wightly* quickly *wend* go

In hie.
To do that deed,
He be my speed
That arms gan spread,   350
Mankind by his blood for to buy.

NICODEMUS: Well met, sir. In mind gan I move
For Jesu, that judged was ungent.
Ye laboured for licence and leave
To bury his body on bent?   355
JOSEPH: Full mildly that matter I meant,
And that for to do will I dress.
NICODEMUS: Both sam I would that we went,
And let not for more ne for less;
Forwhy   360
Our friend was he,
Faithful and free.
JOSEPH: Therefore go we
To bury that body in hye.

All mankind may mark in his mind   365
To see here this sorrowful sight.
No falseness in him could they find,
That dolefully to death thus is dight.
NICODEMUS: He was a full worthy wight,
Now blemished, and bolned with blood.   370
JOSEPH: Yea, for that he mustered his might,
Full falsely they felled that food,
I ween.
Both back and side
Have wounds wide,   375
Forthy this tide
Take we him down us between.

NICODEMUS: Between us take we him down,
And lay him on length on this land.

347 *hie* haste   351 *buy* ransom   352 *In . . . move* My mind was moved
353 *ungent* unjustly   354 *licence* permission   355 *on bent* afield   356 *meant*
spoke of   358 *sam* together   359 And hesitated under no circumstances
360 Because   365 *may . . . mind* should ponder deeply   370 *blemished*
fatally wounded   *bolned* swollen   372 *felled* destroyed   *food* person   373 *ween*
believe

JOSEPH: This reverent and rich of renown,   380
    Let us hold him and halse him with hand.
    A grave have I gart here be ordained
    That never was in note, it is new.
NICODEMUS: To this corse it is comely accordand,
    To dress him with deeds full due   385
    This stound.
JOSEPH: A sudary,
    Lo here, have I.
    Wind him, forthy,
    And soon shall we grave him in ground.   390

NICODEMUS: In ground let us grave him and go;
    Do lively let us lay him alone.
    Now, saviour of me and of mo,
    Thou keep us in cleanness ilkone.
JOSEPH: To thy mercy now make I my moan: 395
    As saviour by sea and by sand,
    Thou guide me, that my grief be all gone,
    With leal life to leng in this land,
    And ease.
NICODEMUS: Sere ointments here have I   400
    Brought for this fair body.
    I annoint thee, forthy,
    With myrrh and aloes.

JOSEPH: This deed it is done ilka deal,
    And wrought is this work well, iwis.   405
    To thee, king, on knees here I kneel,
    That bainly thou bield me in bliss.
NICODEMUS: He hight me full hendly to be his,
    A night when I nighed him full near.
    Have mind, Lord, and mend me of miss,   410
    For done are our deeds full dear
    This tide.

380 *reverent* holy one   381 *halse* embrace   382 *gart . . . ordained* caused to be made here   383 *note* use   384–6 It is fitting and appropriate to him that we now dress his body in a proper manner   387 *sudary* shroud   392 *lively* quickly   393 *mo* others   394 Keep each one of us pure   398 *leal* righteous   *leng* dwell   400 *Sere* Various   404 *ilka deal* in every respect   407 *bield* place   408 He promised me most graciously that I should be one of his [people]   409 *nighed* approached   410 Remember me, Lord, and forgive my sins

JOSEPH: This Lord so good,
  That shed his blood,
  He mend your mood,   415
  And busk on his bliss for to bide.

415–16 May he give you joy, and hasten to bring you to his felicity

THE SADDLERS

The Harrowing of Hell

The *Harrowing of Hell* is based upon legendary narratives associated from early times with the Gospels, notably the *Gospel of Nicodemus*, purportedly an eye-witness account of Christ's defeat of Satan in hell. The York dramatist seems to have known a Middle English verse rendering of this text, and used it in composing the play. He also drew on the liturgical associations of the event: the quotations from Psalm 24, traditionally attributed to Christ in this context, were also sung on Holy Saturday in the medieval Church. The play is cast in the same twelve-line stanza as *Moses and Pharaoh*, with which it has not only close figural links, but also a number of verbal and stylistic resemblances: the same dramatist probably wrote both. As is also the case with *Moses and Pharaoh*, another copy of the *Harrowing* appears in the Towneley manuscript, and both were therefore probably also in Wakefield's repertoire.

The *Harrowing* brings to a climax the conflict between God and the devil for possession of the souls of mankind. This is implicit in many episodes in the cycle, and is openly treated in the *Fall of Man*, the *Temptation*, and the *Dream of Pilate's Wife*. Though the *Raising of Lazarus* has gone some way to establishing Christ's credentials with some of the lesser devils (see lines 169–76), Satan still·fails to grasp Christ's true nature. However, he is presented as a formidable· debater, and his disputation with Christ over the justice of the Redemption renders the entire episode less fantastic and more immediate, especially in Christ's admission of his willingness to combat guile with guile. The hard-headed nature of the debate contrasts tonally with the more emotional passages involving the patriarchs and prophets, from their anxious expectation of reunion with God to their serene joy as their ordeal is brought to an end. The theme of their release is intimately connected with the imagery of the episode, that of an intense light piercing the darkness, which is derived from the prophecy of Isaiah (lines 53–4). In this and other respects the play has more than a passing resemblance to the climactic Harrowing of Hell scene in *Piers Plowman* (B-Text, Passus XVIII). For example, the dramatist does not appear to have called for special effects to demonstrate the power of the Godhead, and the devil is subjugated by Christ's verbal might, an effective dramatic realization of Langland's memorable line 'And with that breath, Hell broke, with all Belial's bars'. Though the siege of the barred hell-mouth must have been visually spectacular, the dramatist's approach to the subject was primarily restrained and cerebral, with little in the way of squibs and scatology of the kind associated with the devils and hell in popular tradition.

JESUS: Man on mould, be meek to me,
    And have thy maker in thy mind,
    And think how I have tholed for thee,
    With peerless pains for to be pined.
    The foreward of my father free   5
    Have I fulfilled, as folk may find,
    Therefore about now will I be
    That I have bought for to unbind.
    The fiend them won with train
    Through fruit of earthly food;   10
    I have them got again
    Through buying with my blood.

    And so I shall that stead restore
    From which the fiend fell for sin,
    There shall mankind won evermore   15
    In bliss that shall never blin.
    All that in world my workmen were,
    Out of their woe I will them win,
    And some sign shall I send before
    Of grace, to gar their games begin.   20
    A light I will they have
    To show them I shall come soon.
    My body bides in grave
    Till all these deeds be done.

    My Father ordained on this wise   25
    After his will that I should wend,
    For to fulfil the prophecies,
    And as I spoke my solace to spend.
    My friends that in me faith affies,
    Now from their foes I shall them fend,   30
    And on the third day right uprise,
    And so to heaven I shall ascend.

---

1 *mould* earth   *meek* obedient   3 *tholed* endured   4 *peerless* unequalled
pined made to suffer   5 *foreward* covenant   *free* gracious   7 *about* busy
8 To release those whom I have redeemed   9 *train* guile   13 *stead* place
15 *won* live   16 *blin* cease   18 *win* rescue   20 *gar* make   *games*
rejoicings   23 *bides* stays   25 *ordained* decreed   *on* in   *wise* way
26 *wend* go   28 And to dispense my comfort according to my word   29 *faith*
affies put trust   30 *fend* defend   31 *right uprise* rise upright

Sithen shall I come again
To deem both good and ill
To endless joy or pain; 35
Thus is my father's will.

Then they shall sing.

ADAM: My brethren, harken to me here,
Swilk hope of heal never ere we had;
Four thousand and six hundred year
Have we been here in this stead. 40
Now see I sign of solace sere,
A glorious gleam to make us glad,
Wherefore I hope our help is near
And soon shall cease our sorrows sad.
EVE: Adam, my husband hend, 45
This means solace certain.
Such light gan on us lend
In Paradise full plain.

ISAIAH: Adam, we shall well understand—
I, Isaiah, as God me kenned, 50
I preached in Naphtali, that land,
And Zebulun, even until end.
I spoke of folk in murk walkand
And said a light should on them lend.
This lered I while I was livand, 55
Now see I God this same hath send.
This light comes all of Christ,
That died to save us now.
Thus is my point published—
But Simeon, what says thou? 60

SIMEON: This, my tale of ferlies fele,
For in the temple his friends me fand.
I had delight with him to deal
And halsed him homely with my hand.

33 *Sithen* Afterwards   34 *deem* judge   37 *harken* listen   38 *Swilk* Such   *heal* consolation   *ere* before   41 *solace sere* special joy   43 *hope* believe   45 *hend* worthy   47 *gan* did   *lend* descend   48 *full plain* quite openly   50 *kenned* directed   53 *murk* darkness   *walkand* walking   55 *lered* taught   *livand* alive   56 *send* sent   59 *published* shown   61 *ferlies fele* many marvels   62 *fand* found   64 *halsed* embraced   *homely* affectionately

I said, 'Lord, let thy servant leal   65
Pass now in peace to life lastand,
For now myself has seen thy heal
Me list no longer to live in land.'
This light thou hast purveyed
To folks that live in lede,   70
The same that I them said
I see fulfilled indeed.

JOHN THE BAPTIST: As voice crying to folk I kenned
        The ways of Christ as I well can.
I baptised him with both my hend   75
Even in the flood of flume Jordan.
The Holy Ghost from heaven descend
As a white dove down on him then;
The Father's voice, my mirth to mend,
Was made to me even as man: 80
'This is my Son,' he said,
'In whom me pays full well.'
His light is on us laid,
He comes our cares to keel.

MOSES: Of that same light learning have I: 85
        To me, Moses, he mustered his might,
And also unto another, Eli,
Where we were on an hill on height.
White as snow was his body,
And his face like to the sun to sight;   90
No man on mould was so mighty
Gradely to look against that light.
That same light see I now
Shining on us certain,
Wherefore truly I trow   95
We shall soon pass from pain.

RIBALD: Help, Beelzebub, to bind these boys—
        Such harrow was never ere heard in hell.

65 *leal* loyal   66 *lastand* (ever)lasting   68 I have no further desire to live
69 *purveyed* provided   70 *lede* place   73 *kenned* made known   74 as
well as I knew how   75 *hend* hands   76 *flume* [the] River   77 *descend*
descended   79 to cheer me   82 *me pays* I am pleased   84 *keel* relieve
86 *mustered* manifested   88 *height* high   90 *to sight* in appearance
92 *Gradely* Properly   *against* at   95 *trow* trust   97 *boys* fellows
98 *harrow* uproar

BEELZEBUB: Why roars thou so, Ribald? Thou roys—
    What is betid, can thou aught tell?   100
RIBALD: What, hears thou not this ugly noise?
    These lurdans that in Limbo dwell,
    They make meaning of many joys
    And musters great mirth them amell.
BEELZEBUB: Mirth? Nay, nay, that point is past,   105
    More heal shall they never have.
RIBALD: They cry on Christ full fast,
    And say he shall them save.

BEELZEBUB: Yea, if he save them not, we shall,
    For they are speared in special space.   110
    While I am prince and principal
    Shall they never pass out of this place.
    Call up Astoreth and Anaball
    To give their counsel in this case,
    Baal-Berith and Belial,   115
    To mar them that swilk masteries makes.
    Say to Satan our sire,
    And bid them bring also
    Lucifer, lovely of lyre.
RIBALD: All ready, lord, I go.   120

JESUS: *Atollite portas, principes,*
    Open up, ye princes of pains sere,
    Et elevamini eternales,
    Your endless gates that ye have here.
SATAN: What page is there that makes press   125
    And calls him king of us in fere?
DAVID: I lered living, without lease,
    He is a king of virtues clear,
    A lord mickle of might
    And strong in ilka stour,   130

99 *roys* talk nonsense   100 What has happened, have you anything to say?
102 *lurdans* wretches   103 *meaning* mention   104 *amell* among
105 *point* question   107 *full fast* most earnestly   109 *save* pun: (1) redeem
(2) keep   110 *speared* locked   116 To obstruct those who perform such
high-handed deeds   119 *lyre* face   121, 123 'Lift up your heads, O ye
gates; and be ye lift up, ye everlasting doors' (Psalm 24: 7)   122 *sere* various
124 *endless* eternal   125 *page* knave   *press* commotion   126 *in fere*
altogether   127 Whilst I was alive I taught for certain [that]   128 *clear* for
sure   129 *mickle* great   130 *ilka stour* every conflict

In battles fierce to fight
And worthy to win honour.

SATAN: Honour? In the devil's way! For what deed?
　　All earthly men to me are thrall.
　　The lad that thou calls lord in lede   135
　　Had never yet harbour, house, nor hall.
RIBALD: Hark Beelzebub, I have great dread,
　　For hideously I heard him call.
BELIAL: We, spear our gates, all ill may thou speed,
　　And set forth watches on the wall—   140
　　And if he call or cry
　　To make us more debate,
　　Lay on him then hardily
　　And gar him gang his gate.

SATAN: Tell me what boys dare be so bold   145
　　For dread to make so mickle deray.
RIBALD: It is the Jew that Judas sold
　　For to be dead this other day.
SATAN: Oh, this tale in time is told,
　　This traitor traverses us alway.   150
　　He shall be here full hard in hold,
　　Look that he pass not, I thee pray.
BEELZEBUB: Nay, nay, he will not wend
　　Away ere I be ware,
　　He shapes him for to shend   155
　　All hell ere he go far.

SATAN: Nay, faitour, thereof shall he fail,
　　For all his fare I him defy.
　　I know his trants from top to tail,
　　He lives with gauds and with guilery.   160
　　Thereby he brought out of our bail
　　Now late Lazarus of Bethany;

134 *thrall* in subjection   136 *harbour* lodging   139 *We* interjection   *spear*
fasten *all . . . speed*   curse you   140 *watches* look-outs   142 *debate* dispute
143 Beat him then fiercely   144 *gar* make   *gang his gate* go his way   146 *deray*
clamour   148 To be killed the other day   149 *in time* opportunely
150 *traverses* crosses *alway* continually   151 *in hold* held in   152 Make
sure that he does not leave   153 *wend* go   154 *ware* aware   155 He
plans to destroy   157 *faitour* liar   *thereof* in that   158 *fare* commotion
159 *trants* strategems   160 *gauds* tricks   *guilery* deceit   161 *bail* captivity
162 *Now late* Just recently

Therefore I gave to the Jews counsel
That they should always gar him die.
I entered in Judas   165
That foreward to fulfil,
Therefore his hire he has
Always to won here still.

BEELZEBUB: Sir Satan, since we hear thee say
That thou and the Jews were sam assent,   170
And wot he won Lazarus away
That to us was ta'en for to tent,
Trow thou that thou mar him may,
To muster mights what he has meant?
If he now deprive us of our prey,   175
We will ye wit when they are went.
SATAN: I bid you be not abashed,
But boldly make you boun
With tools that ye on traist,
And ding that dastard down.   180

JESUS: *Principes, portas tollite,*
Undo your gates, ye princes of pride,
Et introibit rex glorie,
The king of bliss comes in this tide.
SATAN: Out, harrow! What harlot is he   185
That says his kingdom shall be cried?
DAVID: That may thou in my Psalter see,
For that point I prophesied.
I said that he should break
Your bars and bands by name,   190
And on your works take wreak—
Now shall ye see the same.

JESUS: This stead shall stand no longer stocken:
Open up, and let my people pass.

164 *always* by all means   167 *hire* recompense   168 *still* all the time
170 *sam assent* together agreed   171 *wot* know   172 *ta'en* given   *tent* have
charge of   173–4 Do you believe you can destroy him, and display the [same
kind of] powers [as] he has?   176 *wit* inform   177 *abashed* perturbed
178 *boun* ready   179 *tools* weapons   *on traist* have confidence in   180 *ding*
beat   *dastard* wretch   181, 183 'Lift up your heads, O ye gates; . . . and the
King of glory shall come in' (Psalm 24: 7)   184 *tide* time   185 *Out, harrow*
diabolical cries   *harlot* scoundrel   186 *cried* proclaimed   190 *by name*
particularly   191 *wreak* vengeance   193 *stocken* shut in

RIBALD: Out! Behold, our bail is broken, 195
 And burst are all our bands of brass—
 Tell Lucifer all is unlocken.
BEELZEBUB: What then, is Limbo lorn? Alas,
 Gar Satan help that we were wroken;
 This work is worse than ever it was. 200
SATAN: I bad ye should be boun
 If he made masteries more.
 Do ding that dastard down
 And set him sad and sore.

BEELZEBUB: Yea, set him sore—that is soon said, 205
 But come thyself and serve him so.
 We may not bide his bitter braid,
 He will us mar and we were mo.
SATAN: What, faitours, wherefore are ye flayed?
 Have ye no force to flit him fro? 210
 Belive look that my gear be graithed,
 Myself shall to that gadling go.
 Ho, belamy, abide,
 With all thy boast and bere,
 And tell to me this tide 215
 What masteries makes thou here?

JESUS: I make no masteries but for mine,
 Them will I save, I tell thee now.
 Thou had no power them to pine,
 But as my prisons for their prow 220
 Here have they sojourned, not as thine,
 But in thy ward—thou wot well how.
SATAN: And what devil hast thou done ay syne,
 That never would nigh them near ere now?
JESUS: Now is the time certain 225
 My Father ordained before,

---

195 *bail* outer fortification 197 *unlocken* unlocked 198 *lorn* lost 199 Get
Satan to help us be avenged 204 *set him sad* give him grief 206 *serve*
deal with 207 *bide* endure *braid* assault 208 *and* even if *mo* more
numerous 209 *flayed* frightened 210 *flit him fro* expel him from [here]
211 *Belive* Quickly *graithed* made ready 212 *gadling* scoundrel 213 *belamy*
good friend 214 *bere* commotion 220 *prisons* prisoners *prow* benefit
222 *ward* (temporary) custody you are well aware of this 223 *ay syne* ever
since 224 *nigh* approach

That they should pass from pain
And won in mirth evermore.

. SATAN: Thy father knew I well by sight,
 He was a wright his meat to win,   230
 And Mary me means thy mother hight—
 The uttermost end of all thy kin.
 Who made thee be so mickle of might?
JESUS: Thou wicked fiend, let be thy din.
 My Father wons in heaven on height,   235
 With bliss that shall never blin.
 I am his own son,
 His foreward to fulfil,
 And sam ay shall we won
 And sunder when we will.   240

SATAN: God's son? Then should thou be full glad,
 After no chattels need thou crave!
 But thou has lived ay like a lad,
 And in sorrow as a simple knave.
JESUS: That was for heartly love I had   245
 Unto man's soul, it for to save;
 And for to make thee mazed and mad,
 And by that reason thus duly to have
 My Godhead here, I hid
 In Mary, mother mine,   250
 For it should not be kid
 To thee nor to none of thine.

SATAN: Ah, this would I were told in ilka town.
 So, since thou says God is thy sire,
 I shall thee prove by right reason   255
 Thou moots his men into the mire.
 To break his bidding were they boun,
 And, for they did at my desire,

---

228 *won in mirth* live in bliss   230–2 He earned his living as a carpenter, and I believe your mother was called Mary—that's all there is to your family   234 *let . . . din* be quiet   239 *sam ay* together always   240 *sunder* part   242 You need not want for anything   243 *ay* always   *lad* low-born person   244 *sorrow* humble circumstances   *simple* humble   247 *mazed* bewildered   248 *reason* means   251 *kid* known   254 *sire* father   256 You are arguing his people into a desperate plight   258 *for* because

From Paradise he put them down
In hell here to have their hire.   260
And thyself, day and night,
Has taught all men among
To do reason and right,
And here works thou all wrong.

JESUS: I work not wrong, that shall thou wit,   265
If I my men from woe will win.
My prophets plainly preached it,
All this note that I now begin.
They said that I should be obit,
To hell that I should enter in,   270
And save my servants from that pit
Where damned souls shall sit for sin.
And ilk true prophet's tale
Must be fulfilled in me;
I have them bought with bale,   275
And in bliss shall they be.

SATAN: Now since thee list allege the laws,
Thou shalt be attainted ere we twin,
For tho that thou to witness draws
Full even against thee will begin.   280
Solomon said in his saws
That whoso enters hell within
Shall never come out, thus clerks knows—
And therefore, fellow, leave thy din.
Job, thy servant, also   285
Thus in his time gan tell
That neither friend nor foe
Should find release in hell.

JESUS: He said full sooth, that shall thou see,
That in hell may be no release,   290
But of that place then preached he
Where sinful care shall ever increase.

263 *reason* [what is] reasonable   268 *note* business   269 *obit* dead
275 *bale* suffering   277 *thee list allege* you choose to cite   278 *attainted*
convicted   *twin* part   279–80 For those whom you cite as witnesses are equally
against you   281 *saws* sayings   283 *thus . . . knows* so wise men understand
289 *full sooth* very truly

And in that bail ay shall thou be
Where sorrows sere shall never cease,
And for my folk therefrom were free,   295
Now shall they pass to the place of peace.
They were here with my will,
And so shall they forth wend,
And thyself shall fulfil
Their woe without end.   300

SATAN: Oh, then see I how thou means among
   Some measure with malice to mell,
   Since thou says all shall not gang,
   But some shall alway with us dwell.
JESUS: Yea, wit thou well, else were it wrong,   305
   As cursed Cain that slew Abel,
   And all that haste themselves to hang,
   As Judas and Achitophel,
   Dathan and Abiram,
   And all of their assent,   310
   Als tyrants every one
   That me and mine torment.

And all that list not to lere my law
That I have left in land now new—
That is my coming for to know,   315
And to my sacrament pursue,
My death, my rising, read by row—
Who will not trow, they are not true.
Unto my doom I shall them draw,
And judge them worse than any Jew.   320
And all that likes to lere
My law, and leve thereby,
Shall never have harms here,
But wealth, as is worthy.

SATAN: Now here my hand, I hold me paid,   325
   This point is plainly for our prow.

294 *sere* manifold   301–2 Oh, then I see how you intend to mingle some modera-
tion with malice   303 *gang* go   310 *of their assent* of like mind   311 Also
all tyrants   313 *list . . . law* do not care to accept my law   314 *in . . . new* on
earth just recently   315 *know* acknowledge   316 *pursue* abide by   317 *read
by row* rightly understood   319 *doom* judgement   322 *leve thereby* believe
in it   324 *wealth* happiness   325 I am content

If this be sooth that thou hast said
We shall have mo than we have now.
This law that thou now late has laid
I shall lere men not to allow;   330
If they it take they are betrayed,
For I shall turn them tite, I trow.
I shall walk east and west,
And gar them work well war.
JESUS: Nay, fiend, thou shall be fast,   335
    That thou shalt flit not far.

SATAN: Fast? That were a foul reason—
    Nay, belamy, thou bus be smit.
JESUS: Michael, mine angel, make thee boun
    And fast yon fiend, that he not flit.   340
    And, Devil, I command thee go down
    Into thy cell where thou shalt sit.
SATAN: Out! Ay harrow! Help, Mahound!
    Now wax I wood out of my wit.
BEELZEBUB: Satan, this said we ere,   345
    Now shall thou feel thy fit.
SATAN: Alas for dole and care,
    I sink into hell's pit.

ADAM: Ah, Jesu, Lord, mickle is thy might,
    That meeks thyself in this manner,   350
    Us for to help as thou has hight,
    When both forfeit, I and my fere.
    Here have we lived without light
    Four thousand and six hundred year;
    Now see I by this solemn sight   355
    How thy mercy hath made us clear.
EVE: Ah, Lord, we were worthy
    Mo torments for to taste,

327 *sooth* the truth   328 *mo* more   329 *late* just   *laid* established
330 *lere . . . allow* teach men not to accept   331 *take* approve   332 *turn*
pervert   *tite* quickly   334 *well war* much worse   335 *fast* chained
336 *flit* go   337 *foul reason* wicked intention   338 *bus* must   *smit* struck
down   342 *cell* prison cell   343 *Mahound* Muhammad   344 *way . . .*
wood I go mad   346 *feel thy fit* undergo your appointed punishment   347 *dole*
misery   350 *meeks* humbles   351 *hight* promised   352 *forfeit* trans-
gressed   *fere* spouse   355 *solemn* awesome   356 *clear* free   358 *taste*
undergo

But mend us with mercy
As thou of might is most.   360

JOHN THE BAPTIST: Ah, Lord, I love thee inwardly,
That me would make thy messenger
Thy coming on earth for to cry,
And teach thy faith to folk in fere;
And sithen before thee for to die   365
And bring bodeword to them here,
How they should have thine help in hie.
Now see I all thy points appear
As David, prophet true,
Oft-times told unto us;   370
Of this coming he knew,
And said it should be thus.

DAVID: As I have said, yet say I so,
Ne derelinquas, domine,
Animam meam in inferno,   375
Leave not my soul, Lord, after thee
In deep hell where damned shall go;
Nor suffer never thy saints to see,
The sorrow of them that wons in woe
Ay full of filth, and may not flee.   380
ADAM: We thank his great goodness
He fetched us from this place.
Make joy now, more and less.
ALL: We laud God of his grace.

Then they shall sing.

JESUS: Adam, and my friends in fere,   385
From all your foes come forth with me.
Ye shall be set in solace sere
Where ye shall never of sorrows see.
And Michael, mine angel clear,
Receive these souls all unto thee   390
And lead them as I shall thee lere,
To Paradise with play and plenty.

361 *inwardly* deeply   364 *in fere* all together   366 *bodeword* tidings   367 *in hie* soon   370 *Oft-times* Frequently   374–5 'For thou wilt not leave my soul in hell' (Psalm 16: 10)   384 *laud* praise   389 *clear* bright   392 *play* joy

My grave I will go till,
Ready to rise upright,
And so I shall fulfil   395
That I before have hight.

MICHAEL: Lord, wend we shall after thy saw,
    To solace sere they shall be sent.
    But that these devils no draught us draw,
    Lord, bless us with thy holy hend.   400
JESUS: My blessing have ye all on row,
    I shall be with you where ye wend,
    And all that leally love my law,
    They shall be blessed without end.
ADAM: To thee, Lord, be lofing,   405
    That us has won from woe.
    For solace will we sing
    Laus tibi cum gloria.

393 *till* to   399 play no trick on us   401 *on row* in order   403 *leally*
loyally   405 *lofing* praising   408 'Praise to you with glory'

THE CARPENTERS

The Resurrection

By the time of the York plays there was already an anciently established tradition of presenting the Resurrection in quasi-dramatic or dramatic form as
part of the liturgy of Easter Sunday. The *Visitatio Sepulchri* of the medieval
church drama contained a sung Latin dialogue between clerics representing
the Angel and the three Marys at the empty tomb, the substance of which the
York dramatist carefully incorporated into lines 235 to 252 of his play. The
piece is also directly connected to the liturgy through the angelic singing of
the Easter anthem 'Christus resurgens' at the moment when Christ steps
wordlessly from the tomb and goes his way. The play presents the Resurrection
primarily in a ceremonial and numinous aspect, by drawing on the emotional
associations of Easter in the audience's mind, with the lyrical laments and
rejoicings of the three Marys acting as a powerful directive. Mrs M. Twycross
has given an illuminating account of this and other aspects of the play in
performance.

The presentation of Pilate, the High Priests, and the soldiers is quite different in style, and shows something of this dramatist's range. Like other
biblical episodes of major theological importance, the Resurrection became
the object of considerable apocryphal elaboration, and the play owes a good
deal to the *Northern Passion* and the *Gospel of Nicodemus*, contemporary northern
verse narratives, in the treatment of these characters. However, elements such
as the sinister conspiratorial atmosphere surrounding Pilate and the High
Priests, the Centurion's powerful description of the upheavals caused in nature
by the death of its Creator, and the human comedy of the soldiery were
evidently the playwright's own inventions. The dramatic function of the soldiers
in relation to the audience is particularly well handled. Their initial swagger-
ing suggests that they are little different from their villainous employers. But
by the end, their frank incredulity at the disappearance of Jesus and their
eventual decision to make a clean breast of their failure has elicited something
akin to sympathy. Like Joseph in *Joseph's Trouble*, they are, with the audience,
natural man in the presence of a divine mystery.

There is a substantially similar copy of this play in the Towneley manuscript, which probably means that it was also seen at Wakefield. The Towneley
copy helpfully identifies 1, 2, and 3 Mary as the Magdalene, Mary the
mother of James and Joses (Mark 16: 1), and Mary Salome, the sister of the
Virgin (John 19: 25). The verse-form employed is the same as that found in
the *Temptation* in this selection. Like several of the York craft-guilds, the
Carpenters' origins appear to lie in an early religious guild, in their case the

Holy Fraternity of the Resurrection, which doubtless explains their association with this episode in the cycle.

PILATE: Lordings, listen now unto me:
   I command you in ilk degree,
   As doomsman chief in this country
   For counsel kenned,
   At my bidding you owe to be,   5
   And bainly bend.

   And Sir Caiaphas, chief of clergy,
   Of your counsel let here in hie.
   By your assent since we did die
   Jesus this day,   10
   That ye maintain, and stand thereby
   That work alway.

CAIAPHAS: Yes sir, that deed shall we maintain,
   By law it was done all bedene,
   Ye wot yourself, without ween,   15
   As well as we.
   His saws are now upon him seen
   And ay shall be.

ANNAS: The people, sir, in this same stead,
   Before you said with a whole-head   20
   That he was worthy to be dead,
   And thereto swore.
   Since all was ruled by righteous rede,
   Neven it no more.

PILATE: To neven methinketh it needful thing.   25
   Since he was had to burying,
   Heard we neither of old ne young
   Tidings between.
CAIAPHAS: Centurion, sir, will bring tiding
   Of all bedene.   30

2 *in . . . degree* according to your status   3 *doomsman* judge   4 Known for
sagacity   5 *owe* ought   6 And readily obey   8 *let . . . hie* let us hear
quickly   9 *die* put to death   14 *bedene* indeed   15 You know yourself,
without doubt   17 *saws* words   *upon . . . seen* visited upon him   18 *ay*
for ever   19 *stead* place   20 *with a whole-head* unanimously   23–4 Since
this was circumspectly done, say no more about it   26 *had* taken   27 *ne*
nor   28 Any news   30 *bedene* soon

We left him there for man most wise,
If any rebels would aught rise
Our righteous doom for to despise
Or it offend,
To seize them till the next assize   35
And then make end.

CENTURION: Ah, blessed Lord, Adonai,
What may these marvels signify,
That here was showed so openly
Unto our sight   40
This day, when that the man gan die
That Jesus hight?

It is a misty thing to mean.
So selcouth a sight was never seen,
That our princes and priests bedene   45
Of this affray
I will go wit, without ween,
What they can say.

God save you, sirs, on ilka side,
Worship and wealth in worlds wide;   50
With mickle mirth might ye abide
Both day and night.
PILATE: Centurion, welcome this tide,
Our comely knight.

Ye have been missed us here among.   55
CENTURION: God give you grace gradely to gang.
PILATE: Centurion, our friend full long,
What is your will?
CENTURION: I dread me that ye have done wrong
And wonder ill.   60

31 *for* as a   32 *aught* at all   33 *doom* judgement   34 *offend* violate
36 *make end* determine their case   41 *gan* did   42 *hight* was called   43 *misty*
obscure   *mean* speak of   44 *selcouth* remarkable   46 *affray* disturbing
occurrence   47 *wit* inform   *ween* doubt   49 *ilka* every   50 [May
you have] reverence and prosperity throughout the world   51 *mickle mirth* great
well-being   53 *tide* time   56 *gradely . . . gang* to prosper   57 *full long* of
old   60 And very unfortunately

CAIAPHAS: Wonder ill? I pray thee, why?
    Declare it to this company.
CENTURION: So shall I, sirs, tell you truly,
    Without train.
    The righteous man then mean I by   65
    That ye have slain.

PILATE: Centurion, cease of such saw;
    Thou art a lered man in the law,
    And if we should any witness draw
    Us to excuse,   70
    To maintain us evermore ye owe,
    And not refuse.

CENTURION: To maintain truth is well worthy.
    I said you, when I saw him die,
    That he was God's son almighty   75
    That hangeth there;
    Yet say I so, and stand thereby
    For evermore.

CAIAPHAS: Yah, sir, such reasons may ye rue.
    Ye should not neven such note anew,   80
    But ye could any tokenings true
    Unto us tell.
CENTURION: Such wonderful case never yet ye knew
    As now befell.

ANNAS: We pray thee, tell us of what thing.   85
CENTURION: All elements, both old and young,
    In their manners they made mourning
    In ilka stead,
    And knew by countenance that their king
    Was done to dead.   90

    The sun for woe he waxed all wan,
    The moon and stars of shining blan,

64 *train* deception   65 *then . . . by* I mean by this   68 *lered* learned
69 *draw* call upon   71 You ought always to uphold us   79 *reasons* assertions
80 *neven* mention   *note* a matter   *anew* again   81 *But* Unless   *tokenings*
signs   83 *wonderful case* an extraordinary thing   87 *manners* various ways
89 *knew . . . countenance* showed in their appearance   90 *done* put   91 *waxed*
. . . wan became dark   92 *blan* ceased

The earth trembled and also man
Began to speak;
The stones that never was stirred ere then   95
Gan asunder break.

And dead men rose, both great and small.
PILATE: Centurion, beware withal,
Ye wot our clerks the eclipses they call
Such sudden sight.   100
Both sun and moon that season shall
Lack of their light.

CAIAPHAS: Yea, and if dead men rose bodily,
That might be done through sorcery,
Therefore we set nothing thereby   105
To be abashed.
CENTURION: All that I tell, for truth shall I
Evermore trast.

In this ilk work that ye did work
Not alone the sun was murk,   110
But how your veil rove in your kirk,
That wit I would.
PILATE: Swilk tales full soon will make us irk,
And they be told.

ANNAS: Centurion, such speech withdraw,   115
Of all these words we have none awe.
CENTURION: Now since ye set nought by my saw,
Sirs, have good day.
God grant you grace that ye may know
The sooth alway.   120

ANNAS: Withdraw thee fast, since thou thee dreads,
For we shall well maintain our deeds.
PILATE: Such wonder reasons as he redes
Was never before.

93 *also* like   95 *ere* before   101 *that season* at that time   105–6 Therefore we are insufficiently concerned by this to be worried about it   108 *trast*
believe   109 *ilk* same   110 *murk* dark   111 *rove* was torn   *kirk*
temple   112 I should like to know that   113 *Swilk* Such   *irk* bored
114 *And* If   116 *none* no   117 *set . . . by* disregard   120 *sooth* truth
121 you are afraid   123–4 Such extraordinary things as he relates never
happened before

CAIAPHAS: To neven this note no more us needs,   125
　　Neither even ne morn.

　　Therefore look no man make ill cheer;
　　All this doing may do no dere.
　　But to beware yet of more were
　　That folk may feel,   130
　　We pray you, sirs, of these saws sere
　　Advise you well.

　　And to this tale take heed in hie,
　　For Jesu said even openly
　　A thing that grieves all this Jewry,   135
　　And right so may:
　　That he should rise up bodily
　　Within the third day.

　　And be it so, as mote I speed,
　　His latter deed is more to dread   140
　　Than is the first, if we take heed
　　Or tent thereto.
　　To neven this note methink most need
　　And best to do.

ANNAS: Yea, sir, if all that he said so,   145
　　He has no might to rise and go,
　　But if his men steal him us fro
　　And bear away.
　　That were till us and other mo
　　A foul fray,   150

　　For then would they say everilkone,
　　That he rose by himself alone.
　　Therefore let him be kept anon
　　With knights hend,

125 We need not mention this matter again   127 *make . . . cheer* be gloomy
128 *dere* harm   129 *were* doubt   131 *saws sere* various reports   132 To
think carefully   133 *in hie* quickly   136 And surely should   139 *mote*
may   *speed* prosper   142 *tent* attend   143 *most need* very necessary   145 *if*
all even though   147 *But if* Unless   *fro* from   149 *other mo* many others
150 A gross breach of the peace   151 *everilkone* every one of them   153 *kept*
anon guarded immediately   154 *hend* trustworthy

Until three days be come and gone 155
And brought to end.

PILATE: In certain, sirs, right well ye say,
For this ilk point now to purvey
I shall ordain if I may.
He shall not rise, 160
Nor none shall win him thence away
On no-kins wise.

Sir knights, that are in deeds doughty,
Chosen for chief of chivalry,
As we ay in your force affy 165
Both day and night,
Wend and keep Jesu's body
With all your might.

And for thing that ever be may,
Keep him well to the third day, 170
And let no man take him away
Out of that stead—
For and they do, soothly I say
Ye shall be dead.

1 SOLDIER: Lordings, we say you for certain, 175
We shall keep him with mights and main.
There shall no traitors with no train
Steal him us fro.
Sir knights, take gear that most may gain,
And let us go. 180

2 SOLDIER: Yes, certes, we are all ready boun,
We shall him keep till our renown.
On ilka side let us sit down
Now all in fere,
And soon we shall crack his crown 185
Whoso comes here.

---

158 *purvey* provide   159 *ordain* issue orders   161 *win* remove   162 Under
any circumstances   163 *doughty* bold   165 *affy* place trust   167 *Wend*
Go   169 And whatever happens   173 *soothly* truly   179 *most . . .*
gain will be most useful   181 *certes* indeed   *boun* prepared   182 *till* for
the sake of   184 *in fere* together

Then the Angel sings 'Christ arising'.

1 MARY: Alas, to death I would be dight,
   So woe in work was never wight,
   My sorrow is all for that sight
   That I gan see,   190
   How Christ my master, most of might,
   Is dead from me.

   Alas, that I should see his pine,
   Or yet that I his life should tine,
   Of ilka mischief he was medecine   195
   And boot of all,
   Help and hold to ilka hine
   That on him would call.

2 MARY: Alas, who shall my bales beet,
   When I think on his wounds wet?   200
   Jesu, that was of love so sweet
   And never did ill,
   Is dead and graven under the grit,
   Without skill.

3 MARY: Without skill the Jews ilkone   205
   That lovely Lord have newly slain,
   And trespass did he never none
   In no-kin stead.
   To whom now shall I make my moan,
   Since he is dead?   210

1 MARY: Since he is dead, my sisters dear,
   Wend we will on mild manner
   With our anointments fair and clear
   That we have brought,
   To noint his wounds on sides sere   215
   That Jews him wrought.

187 *dight* put   188 No person was ever in so woeful a condition   192 *dead
from* dead [and gone] from   193 *pine* suffering   194 *tine* endure the loss
of   195 *mischief* misfortune   196 *boot of* remedy for   197 *hold* support
hine creature   199 *bales beet* grief assuage   203 *graven* buried   *grit* earth
204 *skill* reason   208 In any place   215 *noint* anoint   *on . . . sere*
variously

2 MARY: Go we sam, my sisters free,
    Full fair us longs his corse to see;
    But I wot not how best may be,
    Help have we none.   220
    And who shall now here of us three
    Remove the stone?

3 MARY: That do we not but we were mo,
    For it is huge and heavy also.
1 MARY: Sisters, a young child, as we go   225
    Making mourning,
    I see it sit where we wend to,
    In white clothing.

2 MARY: Sisters, certes, it is not to hide,
    The heavy stone is put beside.   230
3 MARY: Certes, for thing that may betide,
    Near will we wend,
    To lait that lovely and with him bide
    That was our friend.

ANGEL: Ye mourning women in your thought,   235
    Here in this place whom have ye sought?
1 MARY: Jesu, that to death is brought,
    Our Lord so free.
ANGEL: Women, certain here is he nought,
    Come near and see.   240

    He is not here, the sooth to say,
    The place is void that he in lay,
    The sudary here see ye may
    Was on him laid.
    He is risen and went his way,   245
    As he you said.

    Even as he said, so done has he,
    He is risen through great poustie,

---

217 *sam* together   *free* worthy   218 Anxiously we desire to see his body
219 *may be* it should be done   223 We could not do that unless there were
more of us   225 *young child* youth (i.e. the angel)   229 *is . . . hide* cannot
be concealed   230 *beside* aside   231 *for . . . betide* whatever should happen
233 *lait* seek   243 *sudary* shroud   248 *poustie* power

He shall be found in Galilee
In flesh and fell.   250
To his disciples now wend ye,
And thus them tell.

1 MARY: My sisters dear, since it is so,
That he is risen death thus fro,
As the angel told me and you two—   255
Our Lord so free—
Hence will I never go
Ere I him see.

2 MARY: Mary, us thar no longer lend,
To Galilee now let us wend.   260
1 MARY: Not till I see that faithful friend,
My Lord and leech.
Therefore all this, my sisters hend,
That ye forth preach.

3 MARY: As we have heard, so shall we say.   265
Mary, our sister, have good day.
1 MARY: Now very God, as well he may—
Man most of might—   267a
He wis you, sisters, well in your way,
And rule you right.

Alas, what shall now worth on me?   270
My caitiff heart will break in three
When I think on that body free,
How it was spilt.
Both feet and hands nailed to a tree,
Without guilt.   275

Without guilt the true was ta'en,
For trespass did he never none;
The wounds he suffered many one
Was for my miss.

250 In bodily form   259 *us thar* we need   *lend* remain   262 *leech* healer
263 *hend* worthy   264 Proclaim *this*   267 *very* true   267a *From
Towneley MS*   268 *wis* guide   270 *worth on* happen to   271 *caitiff*
wretched   272 *free* gracious   273 *spilt* destroyed   276 *true* true man
279 *miss* sin

It was my deed he was for slain, 280
And nothing his.

How might I, but I loved that sweet,
That for my love tholed wounds wet,
And sithen be graven under the grit,
Such kindness kithe? 285
There is nothing till that we meet
May make me blithe.

1 SOLDIER: What, out alas, what shall I say?
  Where is the corse that herein lay?
2 SOLDIER: What ails thee, man? Is he away 290
  That we should tent?
1 SOLDIER: Rise up and see.
2 SOLDIER: Harrow, for ay
  I tell us shent.

3 SOLDIER: What devil is this, what ails you two,
  Such noise and cry thus for to make too? 295
1 SOLDIER: Why is he gone?
3 SOLDIER: Alas, where is he that here lay?
4 SOLDIER: We, harrow! Devil, where is he away?

3 SOLDIER: What, is he thusgates from us went,
  That false traitor that here was lent, 300
  And we truly here for to tent
  Had underta'en?
  Sikerly, I tell us shent
  Wholly, ilkone.

1 SOLDIER: Alas, what shall we do this day, 305
  That thus this warlock is went his way?
  And safely, sirs, I dare well say
  He rose alone.
2 SOLDIER: Wit Sir Pilate of this affray,
  We mun be slain. 310

281 And none of his   282 *sweet* dear creature   283 *tholed* endured
284 *sithen be* then to be   285 *kithe* make known   288 *out* expr. of consternation   289 *corse* body   290 *away* gone   291 *tent* guard   292 *Harrow*
as 288   293 This will be the death of us   294 *What devil* What the devil
298 *We* as 288   299 *thusgates* in this way   300 *lent* placed   303 *Sikerly*
Truly   309–10 Should Sir Pilate discover this outrage, we are doomed

3 SOLDIER: Why, can none of us no better rede?
4 SOLDIER: There is not else but we be dead.
2 SOLDIER: When that he stirred out of this stead,
    None could it ken.
1 SOLDIER: Alas, hard hap was on my head   315
    Among all men.

    Fro Sir Pilate wit of this deed,
    That we were sleeping when he yode,
    He will forfeit, without dread,
    All that we have.   320
2 SOLDIER: Us must make lies, for that is need,
    Ourselves to save.

3 SOLDIER: Yea, that rede I well, also mote I go.
4 SOLDIER: And I assent thereto also.
2 SOLDIER: An hundred shall I say, and mo,   325
    Armed ilkone,
    Came and took his corse us fro
    And us near slain.

1 SOLDIER: Nay; certes, I hold there none so good
    As say the sooth even as it stood,   330
    How that he rose with main and mood
    And went his way.
    To Sir Pilate if he be wood
    This dare I say.

2 SOLDIER: Why, dare thou to Sir Pilate go   335
    With these tidings and say him so?
1 SOLDIER: So rede I. If he us slay
    We die but once.
3 SOLDIER: Now he that wrought us all this woe,
    Woe worth his bones!   340

4 SOLDIER: Go we then, sir knights hend,
    Since that we shall to Sir Pilate wend.

311 Why, has none of us any better advice to offer?   312 *not else* no alternative
314 *ken* perceive   315 *hap* luck   317 *Fro* When   318 *yode* went
319 *forfeit* confiscate   *dread* doubt   321 We must needs invent a story
323 Yes, so I advise, as I hope to prosper   325 *mo* more   329 I think
there is no alternative   331 *mood* boldness   333 *wood* enraged   337 *rede*
counsel   340 *Woe worth* A curse on

I trow that we shall part no friend
Ere that we pass.
1 SOLDIER: And I shall him say ilk word till end,   345
Even as it was.

Sir Pilate, prince without peer,
Sir Caiaphas and Annas in fere,
And all ye lordings that are here
To neven by name,   350
God save you all on sides sere
From sin and shame.

PILATE: Ye are welcome, our knights keen,
Of mickle mirth now may ye mean,
Therefore some tales tell us between   355
How ye have wrought.
1 SOLDIER: Our waking, lord, without ween,
Is worthed to nought.

CAIAPHAS: To nought? Alas, cease of such saw.
2 SOLDIER: The prophet Jesu, that ye well know,   360
Is risen and gone for all our awe,
With main and might.
PILATE: Therefore the devil himself thee draw,
False recrayed knight.

Cumbered cowards I you call,   365
Have ye let him go from you all?
3 SOLDIER: Sir, there was none that did but small
When that he yode.
4 SOLDIER: We were so feared, down gan we fall
And dared for dread.   370

ANNAS: Had ye no strengh him to gainstand?
Traitors, ye might have bound in band

343–4 I believe that we shall not be parting on friendly terms by the time we go
346 *Even* Just   354 *mean* speak   355 *between* in the meantime   357 *waking*
watch   *ween* doubt   358 Has come to nothing   361 *for . . . awe* in spite
of any fear [he may have had of us]   363 *draw* punish   364 *recrayed* cowardly
365 *Cumbered* Miserable   367 *small* little   369 *feared* afraid   370 *dared*
cowered   371 *strengh* power   *gainstand* withstand   372 *band* rope

Both him and them that ye there found,
And ceased them soon.
1 SOLDIER: That deed all earthly men livand   375
Might not have done.

2 SOLDIER: We were so rad everilkone,
When that he put beside the stone,
We were so stonied we durst stir none,
And so abashed.   380
PILATE: What, rose he by himself alone?
1 SOLDIER: Yea, sir, that be ye trast.

4 SOLDIER: We heard never since we were born,
Nor all our fathers us before,
Such melody, midday ne morn,   385
As was made there.
CAIAPHAS: Alas, then are our laws lorn
For evermore.

2 SOLDIER: What time he rose good tent I took,
The earth that time trembled and quook,   390
All kindly force then me forsook
Till he was gone.
3 SOLDIER: I was afeared, I durst not look,
Ne might had none;

I might not stand, so was I stark.   395
PILATE: Sir Caiaphas, ye are a cunning clerk:
If we amiss have ta'en our mark,
I trow sam fail—
Therefore, what shall worth now of this work?
Say your counsel.   400

CAIAPHAS: To say the best forsooth I shall,
That shall be profit to us all.

374 And quickly stopped them   375 *livand* alive   377 *rad* frightened
379 We were so stunned, none of us dared move   380 *abashed* discountenanced
382 *trast* sure   387 *lorn* overthrown   389 *tent* heed   390 *quook*
quaked   391 *kindly force* natural strength   393 *durst* dared   394 Nor
had any strength   395 *stark* rigid   396 *cunning* wise   397 *amiss* off-
target   *ta'en . . . mark* taken our aim   398 I believe we both shall miss
399 *worth* come   *work* business   401 *forsooth* truly

Yon knights behoves their words again-call,
How he is missed.
We nold, for thing that might befall,   405
That no man wist.

ANNAS: Now, Sir Pilate, since that it is so
That he is risen dead us fro,
Command your knights to say, where they go,
That he was ta'en   410
With twenty thousand men and mo,
And them near slain;

And thereto, of our treasury
Give to them a reward forthy.
PILATE: Now of this purpose well pleased am I,   415
And further, thus:
Sir knights, that are in deeds doughty,
Take tent to us,

And harken what that ye shall say
To ilka man both night and day: 420
That ten thousand men in good array
Came you until,
With force of arms bore him away
Against your will.

Thus shall ye say in ilka land,   425
And thereto on that same covenant
A thousand pound have in your hand
To your reward—
And friendship, sirs, ye understand,
Shall not be spared.   430

CAIAPHAS: Ilkone, your state we shall amend,
And look ye say as we you kenned.
1 SOLDIER: In what country so ye us send,
By night or day,

---

403 Those knights must withdraw what they have said   405–6 We would not
wish, on any account, that this should be known   409 *where* wherever   414 *forthy*
therefore   415 *purpose* plan   422 *you until* to you [and]   426 *on . . .
covenant* as part of the same undertaking   431 *state* status   *amend* improve
432 *kenned* instructed   433 *what* whatever

Whereso we come, whereso we wend,   435
So shall we say.

PILATE: Yea, and whereso ye tarry in ilk country,
    Of our doing in no degree
    Do that no man the wiser be
    Ne frain before,   440
    Ne of the sight that ye gan see
    Neven it neither even ne morn.

For we shall maintain you alway,
And to the people shall we say
It is greatly against our lay   445
To trow such thing.
So shall they deem, both night and day,
All is leasing.

Thus shall the sooth be bought and sold,
And treason shall for truth be told,   450
Therefore ay in your hearts ye hold
This counsel clean.
And fare now well both young and old,
Wholly bedene.

438 *in . . . degree* on no account   439 *Do that* Let   440 Nor [let anybody]
ask questions   445 *lay* law   446 *trow* believe   448 *leasing* lies
452 *clean* entirely   454 All of you

THE MERCERS

The Last Judgement

Much of the York *Last Judgement* is derived directly from Christ's revelation of the final eschatological mysteries in the twenty-fifth chapter of St Matthew's gospel. It successfully preserves the solemn grandeur of the gospel's language in its dialogue, and reflects the stark symmetry of the narrative in its staging and arrangement of speeches. The general judgement of mankind has been adumbrated repeatedly throughout the cycle, and the play itself draws together the threads of the entire story of salvation. There are marked verbal echoes of the plays associated with the Fall, and the earlier universal destruction of the Flood, particularly in God's recapitulation at the beginning. After the dead have risen, Christ's speeches from the judgement seat begin by dwelling on his act of redemption in the Passion. Their tenor is identical to that of his appeals to mankind from the cross in the plays of the *Crucifixion* and *Death of Christ*, and his words are accompanied by a display of his wounded body, together with the instruments with which he was tormented, held up by angels. Below, to his right, the souls of the saved await their waftage to join him in heaven, whilst on his left the devils sally forth from a gaping hell-mouth to herd in the damned. The iconography of the scene is familiar from innumerable paintings and sculptures of the period, and (as the researches of Professor Johnstone and Dr Dorrell have revealed) the York Mercers aimed to produce very much the same visual effect, with their ample provision for casting and properties, and elaborate pageant-wagons.

It has been remarked that in one sense the inclusion of the Last Judgement in the cycles is not strictly necessary, as Christ's work of redemption has been completed with the Resurrection and the Ascension, and the cycle's spiritual message fully stated. On the other hand, the Judgement is the only event of the future dramatized in the cycle, and this has the effect of placing the audience within a temporal continuum stretching beyond the end of Christ's earthly life. It shows them that the time of mercy, in which they live, is not of infinite duration, and it thereby calls upon them to search their consciences and choose whether they will be among the saved or the damned. In the York version this disturbing penitential theme is balanced by the triumphal ending, a tableau showing God reconciled with the saved, to the accompaniment of angelic singing.

The Mercers were amongst the wealthiest guildsmen in York, and occupied the area in the neighbourhood of the Pavement, the commercial centre of the city, and the location of the final station of the Corpus Christi play.

GOD: First when I this world had wrought—
    Wood and wind and waters wan,
    And all-kin thing that now is aught—
    Full well methought that I did then.
    When they were made, good me them thought;   5
    Sithen to my likeness made I man,
    And man to grieve me gave he nought,
    Therefore me rues that I the world began.

    When I had made man at my will,
    I gave him wits himself to wis,   10
    And Paradise I put him till,
    And bade him hold it all as his.
    But of the tree of good and ill
    I said, 'What time thou eats of this,
    Man, thou speeds thyself to spill—   15
    Thou art brought out of all thy bliss'.

    Belive broke man my bidding.
    He weened have been a god thereby;
    He weened have witten of all-kin thing,
    In world to have been as wise as I.   20
    He ate the apple I bade should hang,
    Thus was he beguiled through gluttony;
    Sithen both him and his offspring
    To pine I put them all forthy.

    Too long and late methought it good   25
    To catch those caitiffs out of care.
    I sent my Son with full blithe mood
    To earth, to salve them of their sore.
    For ruth of them he rest on rood
    And bought them with his body bare;   30
    For them he shed his heart-blood—
    What kindness might I do them more?

2 *wan* dark   3 *all-kin* every kind of   *is aught* exists   6 *Sithen* Then
7 And man thought nothing of offending me   8 *me rues* I regret   10 *wis*
guide   11 *till* into   12 *hold* govern   13 *ill* evil   14 *What time*
Whenever   15 *thou . . . spill* you hasten your own destruction   17 *Belive*
Quickly   18 *weened* thought to   19 *witten* known   24 *pine* affliction
forthy therefore   25 Eventually I thought it good   26 *catch* take   *caitiffs*
wretches   *care* misery   27 *mood* disposition   28 *salve* heal   *sore* pain
29 For pity of them he was on the cross   30 *bought* ransomed

Sithen afterwards he harrowed hell,
And took out those wretches that were therein;
There fought that free with fiends fele,   35
For them that were sunken for sin.
Sithen in earth then gan he dwell,
Ensample he gave them heaven to win,
In temple himself to teach and tell,
To buy them bliss that never may blin.   40

Sithen have they found me full of mercy,
Full of grace and forgiveness,
And they as wretches, witterly,
Have led their life in litherness.
Oft have they grieved me grievously,   45
Thus have they quit me my kindness;
Therefore no longer, sikerly,
Thole will I their wickedness.

Men see the world but vanity,
Yet will no man beware thereby;   50
Ilka day their mirror may they see,
Yet think they not that they shall die.
All that ever I said should be
Is now fulfilled through prophecy,
Therefore now is it time to me   55
To make ending of man's folly.

I have tholed mankind many a year
In lust and liking for to lend,
And uneaths find I far or near
A man that will his miss amend.   60
In earth I see but sins sere,
Therefore mine angels will I send
To blow their bemes, that all may hear
The time is come I will make end.

---

35 *free* worthy one   *fele* numerous   36 *sunken* gone down [to hell]   37 *gan*
did   38 *Ensample* Example   *win* reach   40 *buy* obtain   *blin* end
43 *witterly* indeed   44 *litherness* wickedness   46 *quit* repaid   47 *sikerly*
truly   48 *Thole* Suffer   51 *Ilka* Every   55 *to* for   57 *tholed*
permitted   58 *lust . . . liking* pleasure and delight   *lend* remain   59 *uneaths*
scarcely   60 *miss* error   61 *but . . . sere* nothing but sinfulness everywhere
63 *bemes* trumpets

Angels, blow your bemes belive,   65
Ilka creature for to call.
Lered and lewd, both man and wife,
Receive their doom this day they shall,
Ilka lede that ever had life—
Be none forgotten, great ne small.   70
There shall they see the wounds five
That my Son suffered for them all.

And sunder them before my sight,
All sam in bliss shall they not be.
My blessed children, as I have hight,   75
On my right hand I shall them see;
Sithen shall ilka waried wight
On my left side for fearedness flee.
This day these dooms thus have I dight
To ilka man as he hath served me.   80

1 ANGEL: Lofed be thou, Lord of mights most,
That angel made to messenger.
Thy will shall be fulfilled in haste,
That heaven and earth and hell shall hear.
Good and ill, every-ilka ghost,   85
Rise and fetch your flesh that was your fere,
For all this world is brought to waste.
Draw to your doom, it nighs near.

2 ANGEL: Ilka creature, both old and young,
Belive I bid you that ye rise;   90
Body and soul with you ye bring,
And come before the high justice.
For I am sent from heaven king
To call you to this great assize,
Therefore rise up and give reckoning   95
How ye him served upon sere wise.

67 *Lered . . . lewd* Learned and unlearned   69 *lede* person   70 *ne* nor
73 *sunder* part   74 *sam* together   75 *hight* promised   77 *waried wight*
wicked person   78 *fearedness* terror   79 *dight* ordained   81 *Lofed* Praised
of . . . most greatest of power   82 *to* as   85 *every-ilka ghost* each and every
soul   86 *fere* companion   88 Assemble for your judgement, it approaches
96 *upon . . . wise* in various ways

1 GOOD SOUL: Lofed be thou, Lord, that is so sheen,
   That on this manner made us to rise,
   Body and soul together, clean,
   To come before the high justice.   100
   Of our ill deeds, Lord, thou not mean,
   That we have wrought upon sere wise,
   But grant us for thy grace bedene
   That we may won in Paradise.

2 GOOD SOUL: Ah, lofed be thou, Lord of all,   105
   That heaven and earth and all has wrought,
   That with thine angels would us call
   Out of our graves hither to be brought.
   Oft have we grieved thee, great and small;
   Thereafter, Lord, thou deem us nought,   110
   Ne suffer us never to fiends to be thrall,
   That oft in earth with sin us sought.

1 BAD SOUL: Alas, alas, that we were born,
   So may we sinful caitiffs say;
   I hear well by this hideous horn   115
   It draws full near to doomsday.
   Alas, we wretches that are forlorn,
   That never yet served God to pay,
   But oft we have his flesh forsworn—
   Alas, alas, and welaway.   120

   What shall we wretches do for dread,
   Or whither for fearedness may we flee,
   When we may bring forth no good deed
   Before him that our judge shall be?
   To ask mercy us is no need,   125
   For well I wot damned be we,
   Alas, that we swilk life should lead
   That dight us has this destiny.

---

97 *sheen* radiant   99 *clean* completely   101 *thou . . . mean* do not speak
103 *bedene* forthwith   104 *won* dwell   110 Do not judge us, Lord, accordingly   111 *thrall* enslaved   112 *sought* persecuted   117 *forlorn* lost
118 *to pay* so as to please [him]   119 *forsworn* abjured   120 *welaway* cry
of lamentation; 'woe'   125 *us is* we have   126 *wot* know   127 *swilk*
such   128 *dight* prepared for

Our wicked works they will us wry,
That we weened never should have been witten;   130
That we did oft full privily,
Apertly may we see them written.
Alas, wretches, dear mun we buy—
Full smart with hell-fire be we smitten.
Now mun never soul ne body die,   135
But with wicked pains evermore be bitten.

Alas, for dread sore may we quake,
Our deeds are our damnation.
For our miss, meaning mun we make,
Help may none excusation.   140
We mun be set for our sins' sake
Forever from our salvation,
In hell to dwell with fiends black,
Where never shall be redemption.

2 BAD SOUL: As careful caitiffs may we rise,   145
Sore may we wring our hands and weep.
For cursedness and for covetise
Damned be we to hell full deep.
Recked we never of God's service,
His commandments would we not keep,   150
But oft then made we sacrifice
To Satanas when others sleep.

Alas, now wakens all our were,
Our wicked works may we not hide,
But on our backs us must them bear—   155
They will us wray on ilka side.
I see foul fiends that will us fear,
And all for pomp of wicked pride.
Weep we may with many a tear,
Alas, that we this day should bide.   160

---

129 *wry* betray   130 *weened* believed   *witten* known   131 Those that
we often did most surreptitiously   132 *Apertly* Openly   133 *dear . . . buy*
we must pay dearly   134 *smart* sharply   135 *mun* may   137 *sore*
fearfully   139 *meaning* lamentation   140 *excusation* attempt at explanation
141 *set* removed   145 *careful* sorrowful   147 *cursedness* wickedness
covetise covetousness   149 *Recked* Thought   152 *sleep* slept   153 *were*
fear   156 *wray* betray   157 *fear* appal   160 *bide* experience

Before us plainly are forth brought
The deeds that us shall damn bedene;
That ears have heard, or heart has thought,
Since any time that we may mean;
That foot has gone or hand has wrought,   165
That mouth hath spoken or eye has seen—
This day full dear then be it bought;
Alas, unborn and we had been.

3 ANGEL: Stand not together, part you in two!
   All sam shall ye not be in bliss;   170
   Our Lord of heaven will it be so,
   For many of you have wrought amiss.
   The good, on his right hand ye go,
   The way till heaven he will you wis.
   Ye waried wights, ye flee him fro   175
   On his left hand, as none of his.

JESUS: This woeful world is brought to end,
   My Father of heaven he will it be;
   Therefore to earth now will I wend
   Myself to sit in majesty.   180
   To deem my dooms I will descend;
   This body will I bear with me—
   How it was dight, man's miss to mend,
   All mankind there shall it see.

My apostles and my darlings dear,   185
   The dreadful doom this day is dight.
   Both heaven and earth and hell shall hear
   How I shall hold that I have hight:
   That ye shall sit on seats sere
   Beside myself to see that sight,   190
   And for to deem folk far and near
   After their working, wrong or right.

I said also when I you sent
   To suffer sorrow for my sake,

164 *mean* speak of   167–8 Today it shall be paid for most dearly; alas, would
that we had never been born   171 *will* wishes   174 *wis* show   175 *ye
. . . fro* flee from him   179 *wend* go   181 *deem . . . dooms* deliver my
judgements   183 How it was afflicted, to atone for man's sin   188 *hold* fulfil
189 *sere* various   191 *deem* judge   192 *After* According to   *working*
behaviour

All tho that would them right repent   195
Should with you wend and winly wake;
And to your tales who took no tent
Should fare to fire with fiends black.
Of mercy now may nought be meant,
But, after working, wealth or wrake.   200

My highting wholly shall I fulfil,
Therefore come forth and sit me by
To hear the doom of good and ill.
1 APOSTLE: I lof thee, Lord God almighty;
Late and early, loud and still,   205
To do thy bidding bain am I.
I oblige me to do thy will
With all my might, as is worthy.

2 APOSTLE: Ah, mightful God, here is it seen
Thou will fulfil thy foreward right,   210
And all thy saws thou will maintain.
I lof thee, Lord, with all my might,
That for us that have earthly been
Swilk dignities has dressed and dight.
JESUS: Come forth, I shall sit you between,   215
And all fulfil that I have hight.

Here he goes to the judgement seat, with song of angels.

1 DEVIL: Fellows, array us for to fight,
And go we fast our fee to fang.
The dreadful doom this day is dight—
I dread me that we dwell full long.   220
2 DEVIL: We shall be seen ever in their sight
And warely wait, else work we wrong,
For if the doomsman do us right,
Full great party with us shall gang.

195 *right* properly   196 *winly* with joy   197 *tales* words   *tent* heed
198 *fare* go   199 *meant* spoken   200 But, according to [their] deeds, [they
shall have] bliss or punishment   201 *highting* promises   205 i.e. In all
circumstances   206 *bain* willing   207 *oblige me* pledge myself   209 *mightful*
mighty   210 *foreward* promise   *right* justly   211 *saws* words   *maintain*
uphold   213 *earthly* on earth   214 Such honours has ordained and prepared
218 *fee* property   *fang* seize   220 I fear we delay too long   222 *warely*
wait carefully watch   224 *Full . . . party* A large proportion   *gang* go

3 DEVIL: He shall do right to foe and friend,   225
 For now shall all the sooth be sought.
 All waried wights with us shall wend,
 To pain endless they shall be brought.

JESUS: Ilka creature, take intent
 What bodeword I to you bring: 230
 This woeful world away is went,
 And I am come as crowned king.
 My Father of heaven, he has me sent
 To deem your deeds and make ending.
 Come is the day of judgement;   235
 Of sorrow may ilka sinful sing.

 The day is come of caitifness,
 All them to care that are unclean,
 The day of bale and bitterness—
 Full long abiden has it been;   240
 The day of dread to more and less,
 Of ire, of trembling, and of teen,
 That ilka wight that waried is
 May say, 'Alas, this day is seen'.

 Here may ye see my wounds wide,   245
 The which I tholed for your misdeed.
 Through heart and head, foot, hand and hide,
 Not for my guilt, but for your need.
 Behold both body, back, and side,
 How dear I bought your brotherhead.   250
 These bitter pains I would abide—
 To buy you bliss thus would I bleed.

 My body was scourged without skill,
 As thief full throly was I threat;

---

226 *sooth* truth   228+ *Some lines probably missing in MS*   229 *take intent* pay
attention   230 *bodeword* message   231 *went* gone   234 *make ending*
bring things to a conclusion   236 *sinful* sinful person   237 *caitifness*
wretchedness   238 *care* afflict   239 *bale* sorrow   240 *abiden* awaited
242 *ire* wrath   *teen* trouble   246 *tholed* endured   247 *hide* skin
250 *bought . . . brotherhead* ransomed all believers   251 *would abide* was willing
to suffer   253 *skill* reason   254 *throly* roughly   *threat* threatened

On cross they hanged me, on a hill,   255
Bloody and blo, as I was beat,
With crown of thorn thrusten full ill.
This spear unto my side was set—
Mine heart-blood spared they not for to spill;
Man, for thy love would I not let.   260

The Jews spat on me spitously,
They spared me no more than a thief.
When they me struck I stood full stilly,
Against them did I nothing grieve.
Behold, mankind this ilk is I,   265
That for thee suffered swilk mischief.
Thus was I dight for thy folly—
Man, look, thy life was to me full lief.

Thus was I dight thy sorrow to slake;
Man, thus behoved thee to borrowed be.   270
In all my woe took I no wrake,
My will it was for the love of thee.
Man, sore ought thee for to quake,
This dreadful day this sight to see.
All this I suffered for thy sake—   275
Say, man, what suffered thou for me?

My blessed children on my right hand,
Your doom this day ye thar not dread,
For all your comfort is comand—
Your life in liking shall ye lead.   280
Come to the kingdom ay-lastand
That you is dight for your good deed;
Full blithe may ye be where ye stand,
For mickle in heaven shall be your meed.

---

256 *blo* livid   *beat* beaten   257 *thrusten* pierced   *ill* severely   260 *let*
prevent [these things]   261 *spitously* with contempt   263 *stilly* meekly
264 I never became angry with them   265 *ilk* same   266 *mischief* indignity
267 *dight* treated   268 *lief* dear   269 *slake* end   270 Thus, man, it
was necessary for you to be saved   271 *wrake* retribution   278 *thar* need
279 *comand* coming   281 *ay-lastand* eternal   282 *you . . . dight* is prepared
for you   284 *mickle* great   *meed* reward

When I was hungry, ye me fed; 285
To slake my thirst your heart was free;
When I was clotheless, ye me clad,
Ye would no sorrow upon me see.
In hard press when I was stead,
Of my pains ye had pity; 290
Full sick when I was brought in bed,
Kindly ye came to comfort me.

When I was will and weariest
Ye harboured me full heartfully;
Full glad then were ye of your guest, 295
And plained my poverty piteously.
Belive ye brought me of the best
And made my bed full easily,
Therefore in heaven shall be your rest,
In joy and bliss to be me by. 300

1 GOOD SOUL: When had we, Lord that all has wrought,
Meat and drink thee with to feed,
Since we in earth had never nought
But through the grace of thy Godhead?
2 GOOD SOUL: When was't that we thee clothes brought, 305
Or visited thee in any need,
Or in thy sickness we thee sought?
Lord, when did we thee this deed?

JESUS: My blessed children, I shall you say
What time this deed was to me done: 310
When any that need had, night or day,
Asked you help and had it soon.
Your free hearts said them never nay,
Early ne late, midday ne noon,
But as oft-sithes as they would pray, 315
Them thurt but bid, and have their boon.

Ye cursed caitiffs of Cain's kin,
That never me comforted in my care,

286 *free* willing 289 When I was placed in difficult circumstances 291 *in* to 293 When I was distraught and most weary 294 *harboured* sheltered *heartfully* generously 296 *plained* lamented 298 *easily* comfortably 312 *soon* readily 315 *oft-sithes* often *pray* ask 316 They only needed to ask, and their request was granted

I and ye forever will twin,
In dole to dwell for evermore.   320
Your bitter bales shall never blin,
That ye shall have when ye come there;
Thus have ye served for your sin,
For derf deeds ye have done ere.

When I had mister of meat and drink,   325
Caitiffs, ye catched me from your gate.
When ye were set as sirs on bink,
I stood thereout, weary and wet;
Was none of you would on me think,
Pity to have of my poor state,   330
Therefore till hell I shall you sink—
Well are ye worthy to go that gate.

When I was sick and sorriest
Ye visited me not, for I was poor;
In prison fast when I was fest   335
Was none of you looked how I fore.
When I wist never where for to rest,
With dints ye drove me from your door;
But ever to pride then were ye prest,
My flesh, my blood, oft ye forswore.   340

Clotheless when I was oft, and cold,
At need of you, yode I full naked;
House ne harbour, help ne hold
Had I none of you, though I quaked.
My mischief saw ye manifold,   345
Was none of you my sorrow slaked,
But ever forsook me, young and old,
Therefore shall ye now be forsaked.

1 BAD SOUL: When had thou, Lord that all thing has,
    Hunger or thirst, since thou God is?   350

319 *twin* part   320 *dole* woe   321 *bales* torments   323 *served* deserved
324 *derf* wicked   *ere* before [now]   325 *mister* need   326 *catched* drove
327 *bink* bench   328 *thereout* outside   332 *gate* way   333 *sorriest*
most wretched   335 When I was held fast in prison   336 *fore* fared
337 *wist* knew   338 *dints* blows   339 *prest* inclined   342 *At* In
yode went   343 *harbour* shelter   *hold* assistance   344 *quaked* shivered
345 You saw my misfortune in many forms   346 *slaked* assuaged

When was that thou in prison was?
When was thou naked or harbourless?
2 BAD SOUL: When was it we saw thee sick, alas?
When kid we thee this unkindness?
Weary or wet to let thee pass,   355
When did we thee this wickedness?

JESUS: Caitiffs, as oft as it betid
That needful aught asked in my name,
Ye heard them not, your ears ye hid,
Your help to them was not at home.   360
To me was that unkindness kid,
Therefore ye bear this bitter blame;
To least or most when ye it did,
To me ye did the self and the same.

My chosen children, come unto me,   365
With me to won now shall ye wend
There joy and bliss shall ever be,
Your life in liking shall ye lend.
Ye cursed caitiffs, from me ye flee,
In hell to dwell without end;   370
There ye shall never but sorrow see
And sit by Satanas the fiend.

Now is fulfilled all my forethought,
For ended is all earthly thing.
All worldly wights that I have wrought,   375
After their works have now woning.
They that would sin, and ceased nought,
Of sorrows sere now shall they sing;
And they that mended them whilst they might
Shall bield and bide in my blessing.   380

And thus he makes an end, with melody of angels crossing from place
to place.

---

352 *harbourless* without shelter   354 *kid* showed   355 *pass* go   357 *betid*
happened   358 *needful* the needy   *aught* anything   367 *There* Where
368 *lend* pass   371 *but* anything but   373 *forethought* plan   376 *woning*
dwelling-place   378 *sere* manifold   380 *bield* dwell

The Oxford World's Classics Website

www.worldsclassics.co.uk

- Information about new titles
- Explore the full range of Oxford World's Classics
- Links to other literary sites and the main OUP webpage
- Imaginative competitions, with bookish prizes
- Peruse the Oxford World's Classics Magazine
- Articles by editors
- Extracts from Introductions
- A forum for discussion and feedback on the series
- Special information for teachers and lecturers

www.worldsclassics.co.uk

American Literature

British and Irish Literature

Children's Literature

Classics and Ancient Literature

Colonial Literature

Eastern Literature

European Literature

History

Medieval Literature

Oxford English Drama

Poetry

Philosophy

Politics

Religion

The Oxford Shakespeare

A complete list of Oxford Paperbacks, including Oxford World's Classics, Oxford Shakespeare, Oxford Drama, and Oxford Paperback Reference, is available in the UK from the Academic Division Publicity Department, Oxford University Press, Great Clarendon Street, Oxford OX2 6DP.

In the USA, complete lists are available from the Paperbacks Marketing Manager, Oxford University Press, 198 Madison Avenue, New York, NY 10016.

Oxford Paperbacks are available from all good bookshops. In case of difficulty, customers in the UK can order direct from Oxford University Press Bookshop, Freepost, 116 High Street, Oxford OX1 4BR, enclosing full payment. Please add 10 per cent of published price for postage and packing.